THIRD EDITION
DATA ENTRY

Concepts and Applications

Beth Moorer Buzby

Jefferson State Junior College
Birmingham, Alabama

Kathy Locke

Spartanburg Technical College
Spartanburg, South Carolina

EMCParadigm

Developmental Editor: Cynthia Miller
Copyeditor: Marjorie Lisovskis
Text/Cover Design: Joan Silver
Desktop Publishing and Illustrations: PJ Komar

Acknowledgments: We wish to thank the following instructors and technical experts who contributed to this book:

Ms. Mary E. Williams
Herzing Institute
Birmingham, Alabama

Ms. JoAnn McMasters
PSI Institute
Indianapolis, Indiana

Mr. Jack H. Mossburg
PMI Mortgage Insurance Company
San Francisco, California

Library of Congress Cataloging in Publication Data
Buzby, Beth Moorer
  Data entry : concepts and applications / Beth Moorer Buzby, Kathy Locke. -- 3rd ed.
      p.   cm.
     Includes index.
     ISBN 1-56118-590-6
     1. Electronic data processing--Data entry.   I. Locke, Kathy.
  II. Title.
  QA76.9.A96B89   1996
  005.7'2--dc20   94-25812
                                             CIP

Contents

Chapter 1
INTRODUCTION TO DATA ENTRY

Today you are living along the "Information Highway." Facts, figures, and images concerning all of us flow in the electronic stream that rushes into and around our homes and organizations as traffic flows on a freeway at rush hour. Every day new techniques and new equipment increase the size of this highway or smooth the surface so speed and efficiency can increase. Voice, data, and image transmissions are done at rates that make the transmission rates we considered amazingly fast 5 years ago seem like the Pony Express today.

Among the factors that have transformed the electronics and computer industries are the rise of graphics and imaging, technical advances in transmission media, and increasingly sophisticated programming. At the base of all the technology, changing with the times but retaining the same fundamental operational characteristics, is the computer. It is the single most powerful and most helpful tool in our world.

Computers free us from many noncreative and time-consuming tasks, such as the addition and subtraction of the masses of figures required in accounting. Computers allow us to spend our time on tasks that are more interesting or demand creative thought. As long as a process does not require creative thinking or involve the handling of unexpected situations, a computer can almost always handle it faster and more accurately than people can. This can be done, of course, only if we give the machine an explicit and detailed set of instructions (called a **program**) on how the process should be carried out.

But giving such instructions to the computer and feeding it the facts and figures it needs to carry them out can present a problem. In order to communicate, two entities must speak the same language, and human beings and the computer do not. We record our data in the form of certain symbols—numbers, letters, and special characters. Computers record their data in the form of electricity and magnetism. When two people who do not speak the same language wish to exchange information, some type of interpretation is required.

When we do not need to transmit a great deal of information to another person, we may use a language-to-language dictionary, such as an English-to-Spanish or Spanish-to-English dictionary, and translate for ourselves. When we need to communicate much information, however, this approach is not satisfactory, and we must find someone to interpret for us. The same two

1

situations exist when we transmit data to computers, and various types of data entry devices have been developed to handle different situations.

When speed of translation and transmission is not essential, we use devices such as the scanners at the supermarket check-out counter that (1) read the Universal Product Code (UPC) on grocery items, (2) translate the lines of the code to electrical impulses, and (3) send the data along a cable to a computer.

When bulk data is to be translated, this is most often done by a group of skilled technicians called **data entry operators** who use a family of key-driven devices called **data entry equipment**. These devices accept our symbols, which the operator indicates to them by striking keys on a keyboard similar to that of a typewriter. The devices then translate these physical symbols into an electronic or magnetic form that the computer can accept.

As a data entry operator, you will have the responsibility of translating data and instructions needed by the computer. Timely, accurate data and instructions are the base on which all data processing rests—and without which it cannot function. Although many other people with many different responsibilities contribute to the overall function of data processing, the work of the data processing department cannot be performed without the assistance of skilled and reliable data entry operators.

THE DATA PROCESSING DEPARTMENT

An organization's data processing department is responsible for managing one of its most important resources: its information. This management involves a series of steps that convert unorganized facts, or **raw data**, into useful information. The collection, storage, and processing of data must be done with speed and precision in order to produce the reports a company needs to conduct its daily business. Facts and figures concerning everything that is done in the business are placed in computer storage files. These files must be organized in a logical manner so that data can be quickly added to or retrieved from them. It is vital that the contents of the files be accurate and up-to-date.

The masses of data in these files are used by computer programs in preparing printed or displayed reports. Many reports are created each day, and they take many forms, including current figures on the amount of merchandise in the warehouse, sales totals for the current month, paychecks for employees, or a screen displaying the count of items in inventory. A business can require hundreds of different types of reports. Each report is produced by a computer program, so hundreds of computer programs must be written or purchased and then kept up-to-date. A program must be run on the computer whenever the report that the program produces is needed.

All these activities and many others related to the collection and management of data are the responsibility of the Data Processing Department. The organization of a typical data processing department is shown in Figure 1-1.

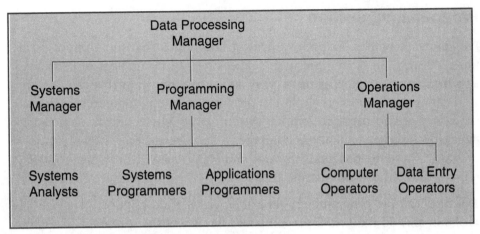

Figure 1-1. Data processing organizational chart.

Systems section

In general, a **system** is a way of doing something or accomplishing some purpose. Your body supplies its cells with oxygen using the heart, lungs, arteries, and veins. Together these organs make up the cardiovascular system. A city uses a collection of stop lights, traffic signs, street markings, and police to control the flow of vehicles through its streets. This, of course, is its traffic system. You may have a system, or organized procedure, for taking notes in class or a system for picking the winner of the Super Bowl.

In data processing, the term *system* also refers to a way of accomplishing a purpose. It refers to all the forms, procedures, and programs needed to collect and process data in order to produce useful information for a business. (The term *system* as defined here applies to the systems section of a data processing department and its functions. The term is sometimes also used to describe the computer and computer-related equipment in an organization. We will use the term in the previous sense, not including hardware.)

The **systems analysts** plan the entire system for collecting data, storing it, and producing reports. They study the information needs of the business and produce detailed plans of the best ways to meet those needs. An analyst's plan, or **system design**, includes a great number of details such as the following:

1. Layout, or design, of the forms on which data and information are to be recorded
2. Description of the way this data is to be entered by data entry operators
3. Plans for the computer files needed
4. Descriptions of programs needed
5. Procedures to be followed by employees in each step along the path that the data takes from original form to printed report

Programming section

Programs are written in **programming languages** that the computer can translate into its own language. The Programming Section employs **applications programmers** and **systems programmers**. Briefly, applications programmers write the programs that the computer follows to process data and produce reports; systems programmers write or maintain the systems programs that the computer follows to process the applications programs. Systems programs are not immediately involved with producing reports, and we will not discuss them.

The applications programmers take the analyst's description of a needed program and do the actual planning and writing of that program. They first study the data to be given to the program (**input**) and the information or results desired (**output**) and draw up a logical plan for producing the output from the input. They then follow this plan as they write, in a programming language, the list of instructions that is called an **applications program**. Writing instructions in a programming language is called **coding**. Applications programmers also tailor programs that are purchased rather than written in the department, making them fit the local applications more closely.

The Programming Section is responsible for coding and **maintaining** all programs. Maintaining a program means keeping it up-to-date. For example, when the federal government increases the amount of money withheld from an employee's pay for income tax, all the programs that involve processing payroll data must be changed to reflect the increase.

Operations section

The Operations Section is divided into two areas: **Computer Operations** and **Data Entry**. Computer Operations personnel run the computer; Data Entry personnel prepare input for the computer.

COMPUTER OPERATIONS AREA. Computer operators feed programs and data into the computer, monitor the computer **run**, and collect the results. While the program runs, the computer and the operator can communicate using an input device that looks like a typewriter and an output device that resembles a television tube. The computer lets the operator know how the work is going and signals if there is a problem. The computer can give many different kinds of messages to the operator, such as asking whether the data for this program is on disk or tape, or even issuing a message to indicate that the printer is out of paper. The operator can issue many commands to the computer, such as telling it to cancel a program that is not running properly or to print out data put into temporary storage by programs that have already run. When a program has finished its run, the operator collects the report it has produced and/or makes a note of the actions it took.

DATA ENTRY AREA. Data entry operators take the data that comes to the Data Processing Department and convert it into a form that a computer can accept.

Because this data comes from all departments of the business, it is in many forms. The Customer Relations Department may send electronic images on disk or by electronic transmission, perhaps digitized pictures of coupons filled in by customers asking for a rebate or requesting a free sample. The Payroll Department may send the weekly time cards showing the number of hours that each employee worked. The Accounts Receivable Department may transmit figures showing the amounts of money received from customers.

The data entry operator must enter all of this data accurately and in the proper form, or **format**. The systems analyst who planned data collection for each program sets up rules to be followed in entering the data for each individual program.

These rules are called a **procedure**. They explain when, where, how, and with what device the data is to be recorded. They are made available to the data entry operator in several forms. (See Chapter 2, "Documentation for Data Entry," for examples of **procedure documentation**.) Data to be used by a particular program must be recorded precisely as the procedure directs, with all characters in their designated places.

STUDY QUESTIONS

1   We have stated that a system is a way of doing something and that in data processing a system includes forms, procedures, and programs (instructions). When you take a quiz, you process data. List the forms, procedures, and instructions that are usually involved when you take a multiple-choice quiz.
2   In the Data Processing Department, who would perform the following tasks?
    • Feeding a program and data into a computer and collecting the output from the run
    • Coding a program that will produce employee paychecks
    • Planning the format or layout of the blank checks for employees
    • Taking handwritten time cards and converting the data written on them into machine-acceptable form
3   Explain the difference between input and output.

DATA ENTRY DEVICES

Data entry operators key data into a data entry device through a keyboard similar to that of a typewriter. The device translates the keyed symbols and produces data in a form that is acceptable to the computer as input. There are many different types of data entry devices, ranging from the early keypunch to the newest microcomputer.

Batch applications and interactive applications

There are two types of data entry applications: **batch** and **interactive**. In a **batch application**, forms containing data are gathered until several are present, forming a group, or batch. When the batch is complete, the data from the forms is converted by the data entry operator into a form the computer can accept. A payroll situation in which employees fill out time cards each day is an example of a batch application. At the end of the pay period, these cards are gathered into a batch, and the data they contain is converted to a computer-acceptable format by a data entry operator.

In an **interactive application** (sometimes called an **online application**), the data is entered as it is received by an operator using an online data entry device. An example of an online, or interactive, application is an order entry application in which a sales clerk takes orders from customers over the telephone and uses an online device to key the data they give directly into the computer. The computer checks the correctness of the data and immediately uses the data to process the order.

Some applications are best served by batch processing, whereas others are best handled interactively. For example, directly entering and processing sales orders can result in a faster delivery of goods, but there is no rush with a payroll. Because it makes no sense to enter the number of hours worked by an employee at the end of each hour of the day, why not wait until the end of the week and enter all hours worked in one batch?

Types of data entry devices

Although people often refer to "the computer" as if all computers were identical, there are various sizes of computer systems with various capabilities. When computers were first used commercially in the 1950s, they were all very large, extremely expensive machines. Only a few organizations could afford them. As time passed and electronic technology became more sophisticated, computers became more compact, faster, and much cheaper. For example, the typical computer of the 1950s required an entire room and cost approximately half a million dollars. Today, an equally powerful machine can be bought for less than a thousand dollars and can sit conveniently on a desktop. Now, computers come made to order in almost any size. Generally, they are divided into three size groups: (1) full size, or **mainframe**; (2) medium size, or **minicomputer**; and (3) small size, or **microcomputer** (also called a **personal computer** or **PC**). Today, microcomputers are the most widely used data entry device.

Data entry equipment was actually developed before computers. The first device, the **keypunch**, was invented in the late 1800s. It represented characters in the form of holes in cards. These cards were processed by machines that sorted them, counted them, and calculated totals from numbers represented by the holes in the card. When the first computers were developed, they adopted the punched cards as a medium for their input data. Since the late 1970s, keypunches have generally been replaced by other data entry devices.

In the 1970s **keydisk machines** were developed. These took the data keyed in by the operator and recorded it as magnetic spots on the surface of a

diskette, or **floppy disk**. The diskette was about the size and shape of a 45-RPM phonograph record. It was made of a thin sheet of plastic with a metallic coating that could be magnetized. (The flexibility of the sheet of plastic is the origin of the second name for the diskette, the floppy disk.)

The diskettes, with the data recorded on them, were fed into an online diskette reader. The computer could read diskettes very rapidly because the data recorded on them was more compact and already in magnetic form.

The data diskettes produced by key diskette units were fed into a reading device for input into a computer. Key disk units, the next step in data entry devices, were online and fed data directly from the keyboard into the computer. Keydisk units were directly attached to the monitoring computer by a cable. The data entered by the operator flowed through the cable in the form of electric current to the computer, which was programmed to write the data on a storage device called a **disk**. The disk was similar to a diskette but was much larger and more rigid. Because a computer was involved in the data entry process, it could check the data being entered for accuracy and other characteristics. (As we will see when we discuss accuracy and verifying, this online checking is very desirable.)

Another advance in data entry devices was the computer terminal. There is much variety among terminals, and they can be bought with many different functional characteristics. For now, we will discuss the **CRT** (**cathode-ray tube**) terminal, which has a keyboard for input and a screen similar to that of a television set for output. The tube also has some limited input functions. A special electronic device called a **light pen** can be used to touch the surface of the tube and thus input data. The light pen looks like a fat ballpoint pen and is connected to the terminal with a cable. The electric impulse it emits as it touches the tube is sensed by the computer. Other terminal screens are **touch-sensitive** and can detect the touch of a human finger.

With the CRT terminal, as the data is keyed in, it appears on the television-like screen mounted above the keyboard. Data stays on the screen until the operator signals that it is complete; thus the operator has an opportunity to read it again and to make any needed changes or corrections.

If the terminal is near the computer, the terminal sends the data to the computer along a cable when the operator gives the signal. If the terminal is far away, or **remote**, it may send the data to the computer along a telephone line or by microwave transmission. Terminals are the only type of data entry devices that can be remote. A remote terminal can be miles away from the computer. You may have seen a remote terminal used by an airplane ticket agent to tell a computer on the other side of the United States that you have reserved a seat on the 10:14 flight to Columbus.

With terminals, as with keydisk units, the computer is directly involved with the data entry process. It can, among other things, perform many checking procedures and send error messages to the operator (in case of keying errors).

As we have said, microcomputers are the most widely used data entry devices. They can be connected to another computer and programmed to function just as a terminal does, sending the data to the other system. Or they can work independently, following a data entry program to write data on a diskette; that diskette may then be read by another program, such as a payroll program.

There are many other types of data entry devices, and there are many different varieties of the devices discussed above. Some types require skilled operators; others do not. In this text, we will study several widely used data entry devices that require skilled operators.

Data entry devices allow us to speak to the computer by translating our letters and figures into a form it can accept. The data entry operator has the responsibility of ensuring that we speak correctly to the computer by accurately preparing data for input. (There is a popular saying in the computer industry: "Garbage in, garbage out.") Bad (incorrect) data can be costly and, in some situations, even dangerous. For example, incorrect data used as input for a program that controls flight patterns at an airport could cause a tragic accident. The lessons in this text are designed to teach you to operate various devices and to help you build the speed and accuracy required to operate them successfully.

Scanners and their future in data entry

Until recently, career data entry operators performed "heads down" data entry, keeping their eyes on the document from which they keyed. Now scanners and imaging have introduced "heads up" data entry. In this approach, documents, such as coupons sent in by customers requesting a rebate, are read by a device called a scanner. Because operators now read from a screen before their face rather than from a document beside the keyboard, this is called "heads up" data entry.

A scanner is an input device that can capture the image of, say, the coupon clearly enough for that image to be displayed on a computer screen and read by a person. A centrally located scanner can capture images and then direct them to individual work stations or user departments. This feature makes it easier to decentralize data entry duties, since it is easier to control the electronic workflow than to control the physical paper. The image of the coupon captured by the scanner is displayed on the top of one side of the display screen of the data entry computer. A blank form is displayed beside the image. A data entry operator reads the image and keys the data into the blank form on the screen.

Although scanners are helpful tools in data entry, they do have some functional problems in selecting the desired data from the document being scanned (customer name and address), and older scanners could not transmit the information with the accuracy required for some applications. People can interpret many handwritten characters that computers cannot decipher. Technological improvements, however, have made it possible for many scanners today to read handwriting clearly.

The technology behind the scanner is a device that takes an image on paper and changes it into an electronic image in your computer. The scanner shines a high-intensity light beam on the paper, causing the paper to reflect a charged coupled device. The sensors cause the intensity of the characters or pictures to be translated into corresponding areas of black, white, or gray. The PC imports the data as a bit-mapped image, which is a series of dots. Scanners act like photocopiers in that they are taking a picture of the handwritten data. To interpret printed characters and convert them electronically for the computer, scanners use a process called **OCR (optical character recognition)**. This scanned data cannot be sorted (sorting is a necessary feature of data processing). A scanner captures handwritten information that has to be later edited for sorting.

There are several different types of scanners. **Handheld**, **sheetfed**, **flatbed**, and **overhead** are the major categories. Each has advantages to be considered when applying the job size. A **handheld scanner** is best suited for short documents since the device is held and moved by hand. It is the least expensive scanning device. A high-volume application would best be met by a **sheetfed scanner** with automatic document feed. Also appropriate for high volume is the **flatbed scanner.** It is like a copy machine, and can be monitored for paper jams. The **overhead scanner** is another type used for high volume. The scanner head and paper are stationary; the head comes over the document and scans it. Each scanner has advantages and disadvantages. The compatibility of the computer, printer, and scanner are critical. An operator would have to determine the best type of scanner for the job application.

The scanner technology is being perfected for handwritten forms so that these forms can be sorted into **fields**, such as customer names and product names. Scanners are used and will be more widely used in the office. As more companies become aware of the scanner devices, more actual usage in business will be seen. The office worker today needs to learn about the new scanners and about how they can become a helpful tool in computer technology.

STUDY QUESTIONS

1   Why are data entry operators frequently called key station operators?
2   Were the first data entry devices online or offline?
3   What is meant by "heads up" data entry?
4   What factors should be considered when purchasing a scanner?

JOBS IN DATA ENTRY

Within the Data Entry Area, there are various types and classifications of jobs. Let us look at an installation that has the following:

1.   Data Entry Operator Trainees

2.   Class C Data Entry Operators

3.   Class B Data Entry Operators

4. Class A Data Entry Operators

5. Lead Data Entry Operators

6. Data Entry Supervisors

Such an installation would exist only in a large company. Small companies may have one or two operators who cover all six categories (and also answer the phone).

Beginning operators start as **Data Entry Operator Trainees**. Trainees work under the close supervision of not only operators at higher levels but also the Data Entry Supervisor. They perform simple jobs and are assigned to enter data for only one application program. This means that they work on one type of device and key fairly simple data that has one format. The term **format** refers to how and where data is placed in one record. An inventory application, for example, might require a great many records, each of which contains the item number of a piece of merchandise in stock and the count of those items sold. A trainee entering this data keys a number, followed by a count, followed by another number, followed by another count, and so on. This training period gives the operator a chance to become familiar with the policies and procedures of the department. It also gives the supervisor a chance to evaluate the dependability, accuracy, and speed of the operator.

The **Class C Data Entry Operators** have successfully completed the training period. They also work under the direct supervision of the Data Entry Supervisor and operators at higher levels but are assigned more varied work. A Class C Operator still uses only one type of data entry device but enters data using several different formats.

The **Class B Data Entry Operators** use all the data entry devices in the section. In addition to recording data, they also check work done by other operators to ensure that it is accurate. They work under the supervision of both the Data Entry Supervisor and operators at higher levels.

The **Class A Data Entry Operators** can perform all data entry and data-verification jobs in the department under the general supervision of the Data Entry Supervisor and/or the Lead Data Entry Operator. Class A Operators are competent, experienced operators who can work independently. They also assist in training new operators and help other operators to learn procedures and jobs with which they are not familiar.

Lead Data Entry Operators are responsible only to the Data Entry Supervisor. They can perform any task in the section and help in supervising other operators. In addition, the lead operators train new employees and teach other operators the procedures needed for doing various jobs. They also assist the supervisor in scheduling the work to be done. A lead operator is, in effect, an assistant supervisor.

The **Data Entry Supervisor** is responsible to the Operations Manager. The supervisor plans and schedules the work assignments in the Data Entry Section, supervises all data entry activities, and keeps any necessary records on the work done in the section.

The jobs discussed here are by no means all the jobs to be found in the data entry field. There are many others. For instance, some businesses have **Data Entry Programmers** who write the programs that are used to operate data entry devices. Others are adding a **Data Entry Analyst** who studies the way things are done in the Data Entry Section and suggests improvements. The analyst also interacts with the other departments of the business that use computer services (**user departments**) to ensure that their data entry requirements are being satisfied. Many companies have **Data Control Clerks**; they perform duties such as collecting the forms that are to be sent to Data Entry and checking them for accuracy, taking the completed records to the Computer Operations Area, checking the computer reports for errors, and carrying each report to the section or sections that requested it.

The data entry field continually grows and changes. New job titles and job descriptions are created frequently.

Data processing is an exciting and rewarding field in which to work. If you want to succeed in the field, there are several characteristics and skills you should acquire. All employees in the Data Processing Department must be able to follow instructions, both written and spoken. Computer-related jobs require painstaking accuracy. People who work around computers must understand the directions they are given about their work and follow those directions to the letter. If they do not, the output will be "garbage" instead of useful information.

As you work through jobs in this text, form the habit of studying the instructions you are given so that you understand them fully before you begin work on an assignment. When an instructor or another student tells you about work to be done, use the opportunity to practice taking oral instructions. Now and then, another student will ask you about work to be done. Use this opportunity to practice giving clear instructions and information to others. The ability to communicate with others is a valuable asset.

An employee in any business who makes an effort to get along with others and to help make the office a cheerful place in which to work is a desirable employee. Employees who constantly complain about the work, the supervisor, the schedule, and so on are less desirable employees, regardless of their job skills. Of course, employees who want to succeed in any field must have dependable work habits. They must be at work promptly and regularly and conscientiously perform the tasks they are assigned.

We know that data must be accurate and current if it is to be useful. To create useful data, data entry operators must key rapidly and accurately. Although both are important, accuracy is more important than speed. No matter how quickly work on a job is completed, the output is of no use if it requires extensive corrections.

To summarize, a valuable data entry operator is one who can do all of the following:

1. Work carefully and follow instructions exactly

2. Communicate well with others

3. Make every effort to be tolerant and pleasant toward others

4. Regularly report for work and perform work conscientiously

5. Key information rapidly and accurately

STUDY QUESTIONS

1 Indicate which data entry operator or operators perform the following tasks:
   • Checking records previously created by another operator
   • Making out a work schedule for the Data Entry Section
   • Training new operators
2 If you were a data entry supervisor, whom would you hire? An operator who can complete
   • 200 records per hour with an average of one error in every 5 records
   • 175 records per hour with an average of one error in every 25 records
   • 250 records per hour with an average of one error in every 30 records, but who has a job history of frequent absences from work

Chapter 2
THE DATA CYCLE

We have examined the general function of data processing and the people involved in it. Now let us follow the data itself along the path it takes through a business. We will see that the data goes through three major steps:

1   It is created within the business or comes into the business.

2   It is converted into a machine-readable form.

3   It is processed by the computer and used to produce reports.

Figures 2-1 and 2-2 illustrate the flow of data through two types of systems.

A BATCH SYSTEM

Traditionally, data is created when forms are filled in by various departments or when completed forms come to the business from other sources. In addition, data is now created by operators who speak with customers or employees and key the information they receive into a microcomputer or terminal. For example, when customers place telephone orders, the operator taking the order may key it directly into the system rather than first writing it on paper and then entering it. This step of recording data, either on paper or electronically, is called **data capture** or **data collection**. Figure 2-1 illustrates the traditional data capture process; Figure 2-2 illustrates data capture in an environment in which online terminals or microcomputers are used for data entry.

In Figure 2-1, people are capturing data on paper for data entry. A programmer writes on coding forms, listing the instructions that make up a program. Order forms from customers come into the Sales Department. In the Payroll Department, a time sheet containing the number of hours worked this week is filled in for each employee (1). All these forms are sent to the Data Entry Area (2). The supervisor assigns the jobs to various operators. The keydisk is the data entry device used here. The facts, figures, and instructions from the forms are keyed by data entry operators into the keydisk data entry device, which records them on the large disk that is housed inside the machine (3). To do this, the operator puts the keydisk under the control of a data entry program (4). Because the entry devices are communicating with the central keydisk device, which is actually a type of computer, the data processing power of the computer can be used to aid in validating the data as it is entered. The data entry program can perform checks, such as determining whether items that should contain only digits do contain only digits. However, some data items cannot be checked by the computer. For example, how would the computer determine whether a name that was entered as Smith is correct or should be spelled Smyth? Items such as these must be checked by having an operator key the items again. Records that contain such fields are then checked for accuracy by another operator, who runs a **verification**, or data validation, program (5).

From this point on, in order to simplify the process we will follow only the data from the Payroll Department. The data is copied from the disk onto a tape, which is taken to the Computer Operations Department (6). The time sheets are filed temporarily in the Data Entry Area (7). In the Computer Operations Area, a computer operator mounts the tape onto a device that will allow the computer to read it and instructs the system to bring in a program from its Program Library to edit the data from the tape (8). The Program Library is a collection of programs and is kept on a disk similar to the one used by the keydisk data entry device. This disk is online. The programs in the library are recorded in magnetic form and can be brought into the computer very quickly. The edit program remains on disk, but a copy of it is brought into the computer (9). The computer then edits the data, checking it for accuracy. If the data from a record is correct, it is written on another magnetic tape (10). If the computer finds an error, it prints a line that contains the data read from the original tape and an explanation of the error, thus producing an edit report. (Figure 2-6 on page 28 illustrates an edit report.) If errors are found, the original tape and the edit report are returned to the Data Entry Area, where the errors are corrected (11).

After editing is complete and all errors have been corrected, the original tape is filed, and the tape with the edited data is used for input by the next program to be run. Next, the data is sorted. The computer operator instructs the computer to copy a sort program from the Program Library into the computer (12). The sort program arranges the data on tape in sequence by employee number. This sorted data is now ready for use by the next program.

A payroll program is now copied into the computer from the library (13). This program uses the data from the tape along with data from a disk file called the EMPLOYEE PAY RECORD master file (14). The tape contains the number of hours worked by each employee this week. The master file contains information about each employee, such as the pay rate, the authorized deductions, the amount of income tax that has been paid so far this year, the total amount earned so far this year, and the total number of hours worked this year.

Using data from the tape and the disk file, the program performs four functions:

1. Calculates the payroll
2. Prints checks for employees
3. Updates the master file
4. Prints two copies of a report called a Payroll Register

The master file is updated by adding the new data from the tape to the disk file so that the information on the disk is current and complete. The Payroll Register is a report with one line of print for each employee processed (15). The line contains the employee's name, identification number, Social Security number, and the general information from the disk file, including the new data just placed there.

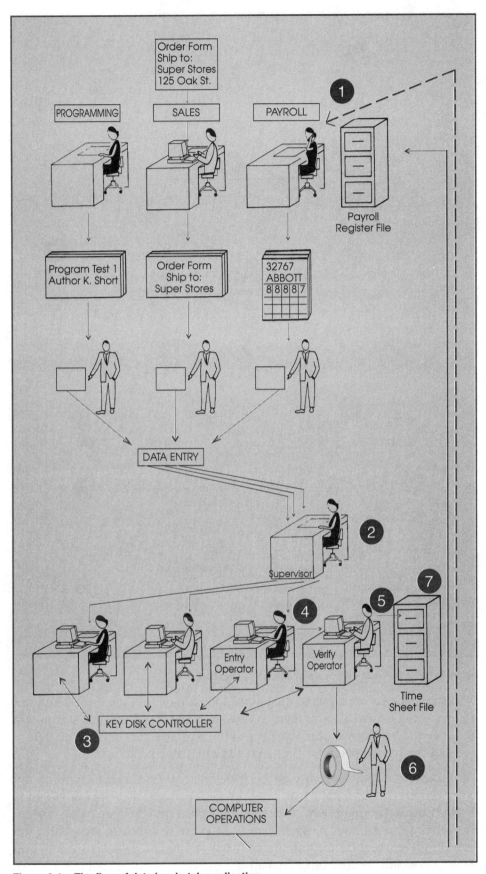

Figure 2-1a. The flow of data in a batch application.

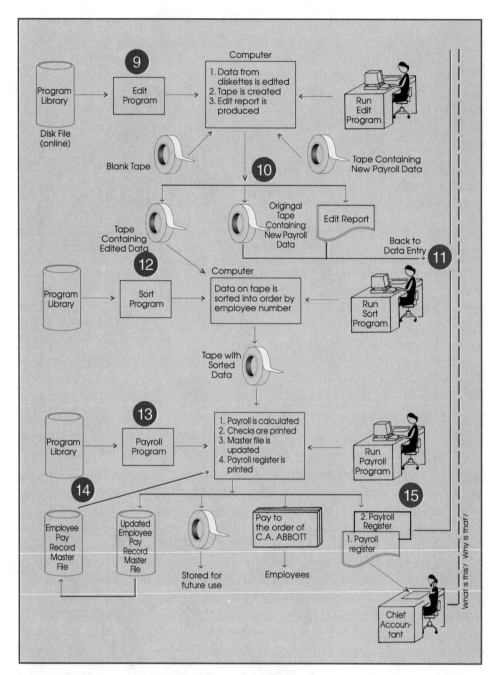

Figure 2-1b. Continued flow of data in a batch application.

Both the Chief Accountant and the Payroll Department use the Payroll Register as a source of information for their records. In Figure 2-1, the Chief Accountant has checked her copy of the register and found some puzzling entries. She is questioning the person who prepared the time sheets about them.

The updated master file can now be used to provide information for many other reports. For example, one program can examine the number of hours worked in each department to determine how often workers were absent from their jobs. Another program can use the file to produce reports for the federal government on the amount of funds withheld for Social Security and income tax. Still another program can use the data from the EMPLOYEE PAY

RECORD master file, along with data from other files, to produce a report on the **production rate**, which compares the total hours worked to the total amount of goods produced.

As the data moves from the time sheets in the Payroll Department to the EMPLOYEE PAY RECORD master file, it passes through many hands. At least seven people work with the payroll data, and, because people are human, there is a high probability that data will be lost or incorrectly recorded. Each time it is carried from one place to another, there is a possibility that a form will be lost or misplaced. Each time an employee records or checks the data, either on the time sheet or on the punched card, there is a possibility that an error will be made. Errors, however, cannot be tolerated. The data from the time sheets is used in creating many reports, and if the data is not accurate, all of these reports will give incorrect and misleading information to those who read them.

The system is designed to attack errors in two ways: (1) by preventing as many errors as possible and (2) by finding and correcting errors that are made before the data is used to update files or produce reports. In order to prevent errors, each person who works with the data is given a detailed description of how it is to be handled, and checking procedures are followed as the data moves from point to point. In order to find and correct existing errors, the recorded data itself is checked. In the system just examined, the data was checked twice after being entered: once by a data entry operator using a verify program and again by the computer edit program. (For more information on preventing and correcting errors, see "Data Validation: The Verification of Data" later in this chapter.)

AN INTERACTIVE SYSTEM

When online terminals are used for data capture and data entry, the step of writing the data on paper is skipped. In Figure 2-2a, data entry operators key data into the keyboard of a terminal. Although it is possible for each operator to be entering data for a different type of application, as in the previous example, we will examine an application in which a single application is used.

The operators in Figure 2-2a are taking telephone orders through the headsets they are wearing and are entering the data through the keyboards of online terminals. Each terminal is under the control of a data entry program that is currently running in the computer and that can accept data from many terminals concurrently.

Because the computer is involved in this step, many data items can be verified as they are entered. When an item does not seem correct, the computer asks the operator to enter it again. When data such as the name must be verified by the operator, the program asks the operator to enter it again and compares the new name to the old name to see if they match. The data is recorded in computer storage after it passes all checks. It can then be processed.

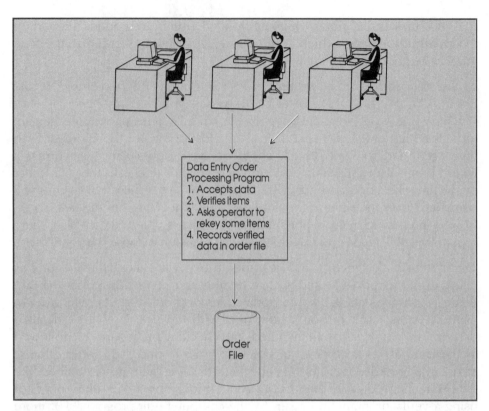

Figure 2-2a. The flow of data in an online or interactive application.

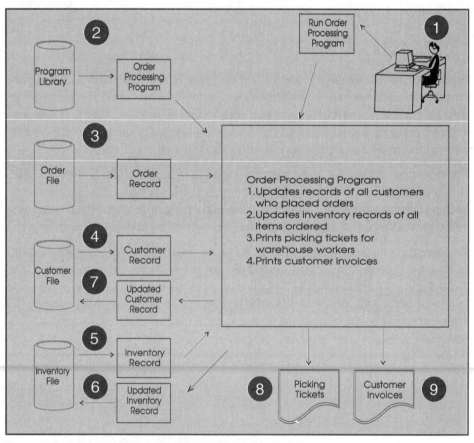

Figure 2-2b. Continued flow of data in an online or interactive application.

In Figure 2-2a, the program that ran the terminal and accepted the data uses it to update the ORDER file. In Figure 2-2b, a computer operator instructs the system to run the Order Processing Program (1). A copy of the Order Processing Program is brought into the computer from the disk where the Program Library, which contains copies of all programs, is kept (2). This program will access data in three files: the ORDER file, the CUSTOMER file, and the INVENTORY file.

Of course, the ORDER file is where the orders entered by the data entry operators have been recorded. The records in the CUSTOMER file contain general information about the customer and about the merchandise he or she has ordered. The INVENTORY file contains a record for each item the business sells and gives information such as how many items are on hand, item prices, and so on.

As the Order Processing Program runs, it takes a record from the ORDER file (3) and brings it into memory, looks up the record of the customer who placed the order and brings it into memory (4), and looks up the record of the item in the INVENTORY file, which it also brings into memory (5). It now has the data it needs to calculate the charge for the item (number ordered multiplied by the price). It also subtracts the number of items sold from the total in the inventory record that indicated the number available.

Next, the new number of items on hand is placed in the inventory record, and this updated inventory record is written back to the INVENTORY file (6). When every item the customer ordered has been processed in this way, the Order Processing Program can add the data about this order to the customer's record and write the updated customer record back to the CUSTOMER file (7). It can also print out a picking ticket (8) that tells the warehouse workers what items to pick for this order and a customer invoice (9) that is sent to the customer to request payment for the items ordered.

Of course, the data remains in the files after the Order Processing Program has run. The company will use it to produce many other reports, such as sales analysis reports, which identify slow-moving and fast-selling items, or dormant account reports, which identify customers who are not ordering as much as they once did.

In addition, this system reduces errors because the data is not recorded by hand and then recopied into the machine. As you can see, it also saves a great deal of time and effort in recording, rerecording, and transporting data.

When you are working as a data entry operator, you will be responsible for the accuracy of data. In order to meet this responsibility, you must study and follow all instructions you are given. You must also work to develop the ability to key data accurately and then practice to maintain your skill. Remember that although data entry requires many skills, the ability to do your work *accurately* is the single most important attribute you can have.

1. Data goes through a cycle made up of three steps. In which step are data entry operations performed?
2. Suppose an operator keying a payroll record mistakenly enters the hours worked for one day as 88 instead of 8 and does not realize that an error has been made. Where and by whom can the error be detected?
3. Is it correct to say that each piece of data is designed for one program and is processed only by that program? Why?
4. Is it correct to say that after data is placed in a master file it is never changed? Why?
5. Name the reports produced by the payroll program discussed in this chapter and explain the use of each report.

CENTRALIZED DATA ENTRY AND DISTRIBUTED DATA ENTRY

We have discussed organizations in which all the data entry operations are done in one location: the Data Entry Area. This gathering of all data entry devices and operators into one area is called **centralized data entry**. There is another approach, called **decentralized data entry** or **distributed data entry**, that places data entry operators and equipment throughout the company or business. The Sales Department has its own data entry operator and data entry device, the Payroll Department has its own operator and device, and so on. Rather than forms being sent to the Data Entry Area for conversion into computer-acceptable records, in distributed data entry the data is converted in the department in which it originates, and the results are sent on to the Data Processing Department.

Although we are speaking of distributed data entry as the placement of devices in different departments of a company or business, it should be noted that some distributed systems place devices at remote locations throughout a network of branch stores or offices.

There are, of course, advantages and disadvantages to both approaches. An important advantage of distributed data entry is that it creates the computer input near the people who originate the data. If the data entry operator has any questions about the data on the form (perhaps a blank isn't filled in or a number is unreadable), these questions can be answered quickly by consulting the person who filled in the form. One or two operators handle all the work for the department and become very familiar with the data that they handle. An alert, truly knowledgeable operator is an asset in catching and correcting errors before they are passed on to the computer.

On the other hand, some users of distributed data entry find that the data entry devices placed in different departments frequently sit idle for lack of work when they could be used to do other jobs from other departments if they were in a central location. If operators do not have enough work to keep them busy full-time, they are usually assigned other duties in the user department. Generally, however, when operators begin doing different types of work in addition to data entry, their data entry skills decline.

Some data processing situations lend themselves to distributed data entry. Others are best handled with centralized data entry. Systems that combine some centralized data entry with some distributed data entry are best for some businesses. Each business must make its own decision based on its own requirements and experience.

STUDY QUESTIONS

> **1** You are a data entry supervisor in charge of a department employing four operators. One department of the business asks that an operator be placed within it. It suggests that the three other operators remain in a centralized data entry area. What factors must you consider in deciding whether to grant the request?

TERMS USED IN DESCRIBING DATA AND DATA STORAGE

In order to discuss any specialized subject, we must know the vocabulary used to describe the physical parts of the subject and the ways in which these parts are related. People who work with data use many terms to refer to the bits and pieces of data, the ways in which these individual pieces are organized, the ways in which they are stored, and the ways in which they are processed. This section presents standard terms used to describe (1) the organization of data, (2) ways in which data is stored, and (3) miscellaneous terms relating to data entry.

Terminology of data organization

When we describe data, four terms are always used: character, item, record, and file. A **character** is a single symbol that may be **numeric** (8), **alphabetic** (Q), or **special** (%). In the terminology of data processing, all characters that are not letters or numbers are called **special characters**. Your name is a fact made up of alphabetic characters. Your weight is a fact made up of numeric characters. Because it contains both letters and numbers, your street address is an **alphanumeric** (or **alphameric**) fact.

In data processing, a fact is called an **item**. Your height and weight are two items about you. Other items about you are your Social Security number, the color of your hair, your age, and your favorite dessert. A collection of items relating to the same subject is called a **record**. All the information that a department store has concerning a customer is that person's customer record. A student's record is made up of all the items a school has that relate to that student.

The next grouping of data is a collection of related records. This is usually called a **file**. Another term sometimes used for a group of related records is **data set**. All the data on an individual employee kept by a payroll department is that employee's payroll record. The payroll records of all employees together form the PAYROLL file.

The most recent development in grouping data is to go one step beyond the file concept to a **database**. Creating a database for a company means combining data in company files into one large, cross-referenced file that is put into computer storage. This huge file, or database, is then used by many departments.

Before the use of databases began, each department within a large organization kept its own files. For example, the Accounts Receivable Department had on hand all data concerning money owed to the business. The Accounts Payable Department kept all data about money that the business owed to others. The Inventory Control Section maintained current figures about the amount of merchandise in the warehouse. All other departments also kept their own files. Keeping all these separate files meant that many of the same items were stored in many separate files throughout the business, or that they were stored in many separate files in computer storage.

For example, when the business bought a case of canned corn from one organization and then sold it to another, the information about that case of corn had to be put into several files. Because the company from which the purchase was made had to be paid, the information about the purchase had to be put into the ACCOUNTS PAYABLE file. Because the company that bought the corn had to be billed, the information about the corn had to be put into the ACCOUNTS RECEIVABLE file. Because the corn was stored in the warehouse until it was sold, information about its storage had to be put into the INVENTORY file, both when it was brought into the warehouse and again when it left the warehouse. Data was also added to other files.

When files are combined into a single database, the data is recorded in only one place, but it can still be used by all departments. This system results in a saving of storage space and in a reduction of the time required to prepare the data for storage (in Data Entry). It also reduces the time required to actually put the data into computer storage.

Databases are made possible by sophisticated computer systems with storage areas that can hold thousands or millions of characters. They operate at incredibly fast speeds, ranging from microseconds (1/1,000,000 of a second) to nanoseconds (1/1,000,000,000) down to picoseconds (1/1,000,000,000,000). The great speed with which great masses of data can be stored and then searched to find a record makes databases practical.

Let us look at the organization of data again, step by step:

1.   **Characters** are combined to form **items**.

2.   Related **items** are combined to form **records**.

3.   Related **records** are combined to form **files**.

4.   **Files** may be combined into a **database**.

Note that each time the data in Figure 2-3 is combined, only *related* data is combined. Your student record must contain data that relates only to you if it is to be a useful source of information. Imagine the confusion that would arise if your student record contained your Social Security number, someone else's name, and still another person's home address! In a business, the items for one employee are combined to form that employee's record. The records for all employees are combined to form an EMPLOYEE file.

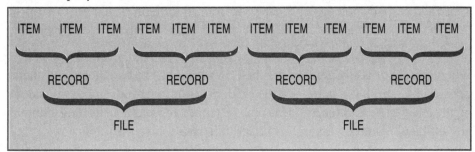

Figure 2-3. Item-record-file relationship.

Terminology of data storage

The terms character, item, record, file, and database describe the symbols that make up data (character, item) and the ways in which this data is grouped (record, file, database). There are other terms used to describe the areas in which data is stored. When data storage is designed, space is planned for each record within a file and for each item within a record. For example, Positions 1 through 5 in a record might be reserved to hold a product number. (Each product a company handles is assigned an individual number that identifies it, just as your Social Security number identifies you.) When the product number is recorded, it is placed in Positions 1 through 5. No other item will ever be placed in Positions 1 through 5, and the product number will never be placed in another area of the record. This space—allowed to hold one item—is called a **field**. Fields, like items, may be referred to as numeric, alphabetic, or alphanumeric. The way that they are named depends on the nature of the item to be stored there.

No matter what medium is used for data storage, the use of the terms item, record, file, and field is constant. *Record* refers to a collection of related items, and *file* refers to a collection of related records, regardless of whether the items and records are on cards, tapes, disks, or diskettes. Space for fields may be set aside on a disk record, a tape record, or a diskette record.

On disk and diskette, sizes of files are calculated, and areas are reserved for each file before data entry begins. (This planning is not necessary on other storage media.) The area set aside for an entire file is sometimes called an **extent**. (We will note here that on some storage media in some situations the storage allowed for a single character is called a **byte**. This definition can vary, and we will define the term *byte* as we use it.)

Miscellaneous terminology

The documents from which operators read as they enter data are called **source documents**. A source document may be a sheet of paper, an adding-machine tape, a card, etc. Anything from which the operator reads while working is called a source document.

When the field for an item is planned, enough space is allowed for the largest item that will be put there. If student numbers begin at 1 and run up to 999999, six positions are allowed for the Student Number field. Obviously, student numbers under 100000 will not fill up the field.

When a number is smaller than the field in which it is to be entered, it is lined up with the right-hand margin of the field, or **right justified**. Unused positions on the left are filled with zeros. (In some instances, these empty leading columns are left blank. Unless you are instructed otherwise, insert leading zeros.)

Alphabetic data, on the other hand, is **left justified**, or begun at the left margin of the field. Unneeded positions on the right of the items are left blank. These rules for justification simply follow the standard practice of always lining up numbers so that the tens' position of one number is under the tens' position of the one above, or of writing a list of names so that all begin at the left margin of the field. Figure 2-4 illustrates the correct method of entry.

Type of Field	Item to Be Entered	Proper Method of Entry
Numeric Field		
_ _ _ _ _	93	0 0 0 9 3
Alphabetic Field		
_ _ _ _ _	HAT	H A T _ _

Figure 2-4. Right and left justification.

Two other terms used in data processing are **input** and **output**. **Input** refers to something that is put into a machine; **output** refers to the results or data put out by the machine when a job or procedure is finished. A data entry operator reads items from a source document and keys them into a machine (input). The machine gathers these items into records (output). These terms can be used as nouns or verbs. We say that operators prepare *input* or that they *input* data; we say that the computer produces *output* or that it *outputs* data.

1 A student makes a grade of 94 on the first quiz of the year. Positions 21 through 23 in the student records for this class are reserved to hold the first quiz grade.
  • Is the grade an item or a field?
  • Are Positions 21 through 23 an item or a field?
2 If you gather all the information a store has on the employees who work in the Data Processing Department, what is the proper term for the group of data you have collected?
3 Name one advantage of a database over a system of multiple files.
4 What do the terms *field* and *extent* have in common?
5 If you record your name in a field, do you right justify it or left justify it? Do you right justify or left justify your weight?
6 In Figure 2-1, what is the input for the sort program?
7 In Figure 2-1, what is the output from the sort program?

DATA VALIDATION: THE VERIFICATION OF DATA

Bad data is costly. Accurate data is so important that many organizations pay special premiums to operators who keep their error levels low. Once recorded, data must be checked for accuracy before it is stored in computer files or used in any calculations. This checking may be done in one of two ways: (1) by data entry machines that can be switched to **VERIFY mode** to check the records they produce or (2) by **computer verification**.

Key verifying

Checking records using either verifiers or other data entry equipment put into VERIFY mode is called **key verifying**. The operator is given a group of records and the source document from which they were created. She or he puts the records or selected fields from each record into the data entry device and keys the data in again, just as though it were being entered for the first time. Instead of recording the data, the machine compares the characters keyed in with the characters in the original record. If a character keyed into a position does not match the character at the same position in the record, the machine notifies the operator. The operator may then correct the error or make a note that it is to be corrected later. As we have seen, in online environments the computer may perform some checks and may notify operators to perform others. Compared to computer verification, key verification is slow and costly. It is, however, the best method of checking some types of data, such as names.

Computer editing

Computer **edit programs** are used to check records before they are processed by other computer programs. Records are fed into the computer, which has already been given the edit program describing the general layout of the records. The edit program also contains a great deal of information about the data that the records should contain. It can make checks and output error messages to indicate (1) what type of error it has found and (2) where the error is within the record.

The output from an edit program is an **edit report**. The edit report contains a line of print for each error found. The erroneous record is printed, along with a message calling attention to the error. If a record contains several errors, a message is printed pointing out each error. Edit checks include the following:

1. **Format checks.** In a format check, the computer checks to ensure that each field that should contain data actually contains data. It also checks the type of data so that if a field is alphabetic and has a number in it, or vice versa, the computer will output an error message.

2. **Limit, reasonableness, or magnitude checks.** Some numeric fields contain data items that have predictable limits. The salaries in a department, for instance, might run from $175.00 per week to $250.00 per week. For this department, $250.00 is the limit of the salary. When fields have predictable limits, these figures are given to the computer. As it reads the record including the field, the computer compares the value recorded in the field to the largest value that should be recorded there. If the item exceeds the limit, the computer outputs an error message. (Instances of people receiving checks for $10,000.00 instead of $100.00 occur because a programmer did not include a limit check on the amount field.)

3. **Range checks.** On items such as the number of an automobile part in which all the values are known, the computer is told what the smallest and largest numbers are. The computer then examines each number. If any number fails to fall within the specified range, it is noted as being incorrect on the edit report.

4. **Modular checks, or check digits.** A self-checking number contains an extra digit that is used to determine the accuracy of the other digits. Many data entry devices are equipped to examine this **check digit** and thus determine whether the other digits are correct. If the device that prepared the records does not have the self-check feature, the computer may be used to examine numeric fields that have a check digit. This checking is done by a computer in the same way that it is done by a data entry device.

5. **Ascendancy checks.** Some numbers are always in ascending order from one record to the next. Forms such as invoices, for example, may be preprinted with numbers so that the first is numbered 00001, the next 00002, and so on. When these numbers are placed in records, the computer can compare them to see that the form number in the current record is larger than the form number in the previous record.

6. **Extension checks.** Occasionally, there are two or more fields on a record that, when put through an arithmetic formula, can yield another field on the record. For instance, if a record contains fields for number of items sold, unit price, and amount of sale, the computer can multiply the number of items sold (6 yo-yos) by the price of each ($1.50) to find the amount of sale ($9.00). If the amount of sale on the record does not match the amount of sale calculated by the computer, one of the fields on the record is wrong.

7. **Validity checks.** For some fields in a record, it is possible to give the computer a list of all the items that should be recorded there. Suppose, for instance, that one field is to contain a salesperson number and that there are 50 salespeople in the firm with numbers ranging from 16 to 1930. All 50 valid sales numbers can be given to the computer so that it can check the salesperson number it reads against all current salesperson numbers.

8. **Batch totals.** Records within data entry jobs are usually divided into groups called batches. (See "Data Control" later in this chapter.) When a batch is given to an operator for recording, it frequently has an adding-machine tape attached. This tape contains a total of some field in the records. If each record has a field in which the price of an item is entered, all these prices for all the records can be added together to give a **batch total**. The batch total is entered into a special record called a **total record**, which is read into the computer along with the batch of data records. The computer then calculates its own batch total and issues an error message if the two totals do not match. Batch total calculation is also available on some data entry devices.

9. **Hash totals.** Hash totals are similar to batch totals except that a hash total does not represent a reasonable arithmetic sum. A hash total for a document might be the sum of all the numbers on the document, including a form number, a salesperson number, a part number, a price, and a date. Adding such items together makes no sense arithmetically, but if the hash total calculated by the computer does not match the hash total from the adding-machine tape (on the total record), there is an error in some field.

In online environments, batch and hash totals are often calculated by the computer program. For example, if sales amounts are being entered, the program adds each amount to a running batch total until a predetermined number of records, say 50, has been input. Then it will display a message asking the operator to enter again the sales amounts (but not the other data) for the last 50 records. The program will total these amounts as they are entered, and when the second round of entry is complete it will compare the first total with the second total. If they do not match, an error exists.

10. **Cross-footing checks.** Cross-footing checks verify the totals of fields within a number of records. The procedure is similar to that in which extension checks were done within a single record. Consider the records in Figure 2-5. The Total of New Balance (22750) should equal the Total of Previous Balance (35573) minus the Total of Amounts Paid (20573) plus the Total of Amounts Charged (07750):

35573 - 20573 + 7750 = 22750

The computer can sum each of the fields and see if the totals balance. If they do not, it has found an error.

	Amount Paid on Account	Amount Charged to Account	Previous Balance	New Balance
Record 1	10000	02500	25000	17500
Record 2	09573	00000	09573	00000
Record 3	01000	05250	01000	05250
Total of Amounts Paid	20573	Total of Amounts Charged 07750	Total of Previous Balance 35573	Total of New Balance 22750

Figure 2-5. Cross-footing check.

We have discussed some of the checks that an edit program can make on prerecorded data. The full range of checks that can be made is limited only by the available computer equipment and the ingenuity of the programmer who writes the edit program. Output from a typical edit program is illustrated in Figure 2-6.

EMP NO	RECORD TYPE	RECORD CODE	LAST NAME	FIRST NAME	SOC SEC NO	SALARY CODE	PAY PD CODE	ERROR
59274	750	A	SHORT,	KATHERINE	514 23 2746	1	2	LAST NAME NOT ALPHABETIC
99274	750	A	BAKER	CHERYL	423 12 3649	1	1	INVALID EMPLOYEE NUMBER
27364	700	C	JUETTNER	WILLIAM	382 63 2893	2	U	ILLEGAL PAY PERIOD CODE
42847	750	9	FRITZ	FRANCIS	514 87 2736	1	1	CARD CODE NOT ALPHABETIC
32740	700	A	PEAK	ELLEN	J12 23 7325	1	9	SOC SEC NO NOT NUMERIC
35375	750	C	MAYNARD	G6ENN	414 34 2137	5	3	ILLEGAL SALARY CODE
								FIRST NAME NOT ALPHABETIC

Figure 2-6. Edit program output.

Online verification

From the operator's viewpoint, **online verification** is much easier and more efficient than an edit run. When data is entered through an online device, such as a CRT terminal, all the computer edit checks just discussed can be made by the computer while the data is being entered. In an online situation, the computer signals you when it finds an error in the input. You can then correct the error while you still have the source document before you. On the other hand, correcting records using the output from an edit run involves searching through source documents to find the item that should have been keyed and then searching for the erroneous record to be corrected.

Online entry also permits the computer to help you with other error-preventing and error-catching routines. **Boundary checks**, for example, alert you if you overrun a field and try to continue the data item in the next field. Some fields may be left blank now and then, but others should always have data entered into them. The computer can signal if you mistakenly leave empty one of the fields that should always have data entered into it. Some fields should not only have data in them but should also have a character in each position. These can be checked by the computer to ensure that no position is blank.

Computer edit runs, then, can check for more types of errors than key verification. Online entry with computer editing provides the same types of checks as computer edit runs (on previously completed records) *and* allows the use of other keying aids to help you avoid making mistakes. Online entry provides checks at a time when you can correct the errors quickly and easily. In both edit runs and online entry, the computer can assist you with other details. Usually, numeric fields are filled with leading zeros when the item is not as large as the field. A computer program can put these zeros in for you. Material can be either right justified or left justified automatically, and unwanted characters, such as periods following initials in name fields, can be automatically removed.

Despite the advantages of computer verification, some types of items are best key verified. Alphabetic fields, for example, that cannot be fully checked by any of the methods described except key verification can be verified online by having the computer instruct the data entry device to operate as an **offline** verifier for the length of the field to be key verified. You can then enter an item in the field. After the item is complete, the computer returns to the first position of the field, and you can key verify the item you just entered.

STUDY QUESTIONS

1 An installation pays its five data entry operators an average of $7.50 per hour for a total cost of $37.50 per hour. Although computer time costs many times as much per hour, the company performs its data verification with computer edit runs because it has found computer editing to be cheaper than key verifying. Why is this true?

2 As a data entry operator, how would you use an edit report?

3 Define the following terms: key verify, computer editing, format check, limit check, range check, modular check, ascendancy check, extension check, validity check, batch total, hash total, cross-footing check, online verification, batch application, interactive application.

▋ DATA CONTROL

A business must protect its data. We have already seen how important correct data is. Many different machines and techniques are used to validate and verify recorded data. The step of verification fits into a larger system of data controls, which is designed to ensure that no document or data item can be lost. Another purpose of data controls is to provide an **audit trail**, that is, a pathway whereby any item can be traced back step-by-step to the source from which it came. Let us look at an example of a data control system. You will see that it includes a number of procedures and forms for keeping a record of the flow of data through the business to ensure that no data is lost.

Jobs, job steps, and batches

To discuss data control, we must use three terms: **job**, **batch**, and **job step**. A **job** is a large unit of work. All of the work received for the Sales Department or for the Purchasing Department can constitute a job. A **batch** is a subdivision of a job. Large jobs are broken into batches for several reasons. A large job that will take one operator five days can be done by five operators in one day if it is broken into five equal units. If an error is made in a batch so that the batch total does not check, the operator may have to look through 200 records to find the error. If such totals were taken only by job instead of by batch, one might have to check through 2,000 records in the job to find the error. The division of work into smaller batches makes a job easier to do, easier to correct, and easier to control. An intermediate division called a **job step** is sometimes inserted between the job and the batch in very large jobs. Then, a job step becomes a subdivision of a job, and a batch becomes a subdivision of a job step.

Transmittal forms and transmittal logs

Let us look at a data control system in a batch environment. In our system, orders come into the Sales Department, where a sales clerk writes them on an order form like the one in Figure 2-7. These forms come in pads. Each form in the pad is printed with its own number. The forms in one pad might begin with the number 200 and run to 299. The forms in the next pad would then begin with 300 and run to 399, and so on. No two forms have the same number.

```
#17639
                      TELEPHONE ORDERS
                                    Date  12/01

Bill to:
     Account No. 26149C
     Name        MRS. LAURA HICKS
     Street      2800 WEST GARY
     City        LAWTON              State  OK    Zip 73501
Ship to:
     Name        MR. AND MRS. MARK HICKS
     Street      P.O. BOX 1007
     City        CASPER              State  WY    Zip 82601
```

Item Number	Description	Color	No.	Unit	Unit Price	Total Price
216A	SALTED NUT MIX	—	5	LB.	3.00	15.00
409R	TILE CHEESE TRAY	RED	1	EA.	14.25	14.25
						29.25

```
                           Taken by  #16
```

Figure 2-7. Telephone order form.

When the order is written up, the date is included. After a number of orders have accumulated in the Sales Department, the order forms are sent to the Data Entry Section. Before the forms leave the Sales Department, a **document transmittal form** (Figure 2-8) is attached to the group of forms sent out. The transmittal form contains (1) an identification of the type of forms in the group, (2) the date, (3) the job number, (4) a count of the forms in the group, (5) the number of the first form in the group, (6) the number of the last form in the group, and (7) the numbers of any forms that are missing (forms that have been voided). A total of the amount of sales is calculated, and the adding-machine tape is attached.

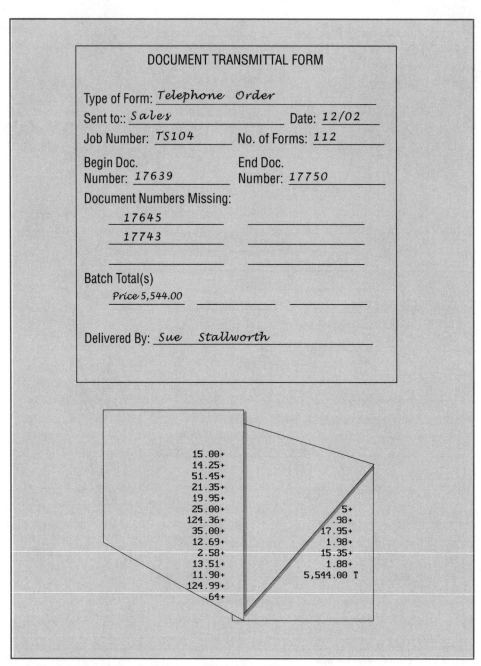

Figure 2-8. Document transmittal form with adding-machine tape.

Before the order forms leave the Sales Department, an entry is made for each group in a **forms transmittal log** in the Sales Department (Figure 2-9). This entry includes (1) the date and time when they were sent, (2) where they were sent, (3) the job number, (4) the beginning and ending form numbers in the group, (5) the count of forms in the group, (6) the operations to be performed using the forms, and (7) the name or initials of the person who actually carried the forms. Because the forms are to be returned for filing in the Sales Department, the log also contains entries for the date and time the forms are returned from the Data Entry Section and for the name or initials of the person returning them.

FORMS TRANSMITTAL LOG

Department _Sales_

Job Number	Number of Forms	Begin Form Number	End Form Number	Service Requested	Delivered				Returned		
					Date	Time	To	By	Date	Time	By
TS104	112	17639	17750	Enter & Verify	12/02	8:05	Data Entry	S. Stallworth	12/02	1:10	J. Morstall

Figure 2-9. Forms transmittal log.

When the forms arrive in the Data Entry Area, the Data Entry Supervisor checks the form numbers, the batch total, and the count of forms in the group. If anything does not check out, the Sales Department is called to resolve the difference. Receipt of the forms is recorded on a **Data Entry Area work log** similar to the forms transmittal log in the Sales Department (Figure 2-10). The Data Entry Supervisor divides the forms into working batches and creates a batch slip for each batch (Figure 2-11). The slip is fastened to the forms.

DATA ENTRY AREA WORK LOG

Date: _12/02_

RECEIVED			JOB NO.	BATCH NO.	ENTRY OPERATOR				VERIFY OPERATOR				FORWARDED				Records to Operations		
From	Date	Time			No.	Time Out	In	Total Records	No.	Time Out	In	Total Records	To	Date	Time	By	Date	Time	By
Sales	12/02	8:15	TS104	1	16	8:30	10:00	225	23	10:15	12:10	225	Sales	12/02	1:00	JM	12/02	1:00	JM

Figure 2-10. Data entry area work log.

JOB NUMBER: _TS104_		DATE: _12/02_
BATCH NUMBER: _1_		NUMBER OF DOCUMENTS: _112_
ENTRY OPERATOR: _____		VERIFY OPERATOR: _____

Figure 2-11. A batch slip.

When a batch is assigned to an operator to enter, the operator's number and the time are recorded on the work log. When the batch is complete, it is logged back in with the time at which it was completed and the count of records created. If it is to be verified, another operator then logs the batch out with operator number and time, verifies it, and logs it back in with the time and the count of records verified.

The supervisor rechecks the batch total, the form numbers, and the form counts when the batch has been completed. The records created are sent on to the Computer Operations Area. The work log is updated to show where the records are sent, when they are sent, and by whom they are sent. The order forms go back to the Sales Department for filing. They are sent with the original document transmittal form and total tape. Their departure is noted on the work log with entries for their destination, courier, and date of transmittal.

By examining the work log, the supervisor can tell how much work has been received, how much has been completed and sent on, and the status of the work still remaining in the section. The log also provides a detailed record of work done and of the movement of data through the section for future reference.

The logs kept in the different departments of the business and the checking that is done each time documents are moved make it highly unlikely that any form will be lost. Batch totals and record counts also make it highly unlikely that any record will be lost.

Audit trails

In addition to protecting data, a control system should establish a clear **audit trail**. With such a trail, any record in any file can be quickly and easily traced back to the document from which it was created. A common way of establishing a tracing technique is to put in each record the number of the form from which it is created. In the application just discussed, for instance, the number of the sales order form would be recorded on all records created from that form. Some applications require each record to contain job number, batch number, form number, and record number.

The amount of control needed varies a great deal. A small business whose work does not include a variety of jobs can use minimum controls. A large business with both a larger variety of jobs and a larger quantity of work requires more control. Special jobs, such as the conversion of a records system from typed or written records to a computer system, may require extensive controls. In such a conversion, all the information of a company is involved, and it must be rigidly protected.

Controls in interactive environments

The controls we have discussed apply to batch applications, but interactive applications must also control and protect data. In interactive environments, the system plays a larger role in creating data controls. We have already seen how batch and hash totals are managed by interactive data entry programs. Other data control is also required by the system. Let us consider a system in which a data entry operator is using a terminal that is online to a mainframe, or large computer.

Like the batch application we just examined, operators using this interactive application accept telephone orders. Rather than write them on paper forms, however, they enter them through a keyboard, filling in a form that is displayed on a screen (see Figure 2-12).

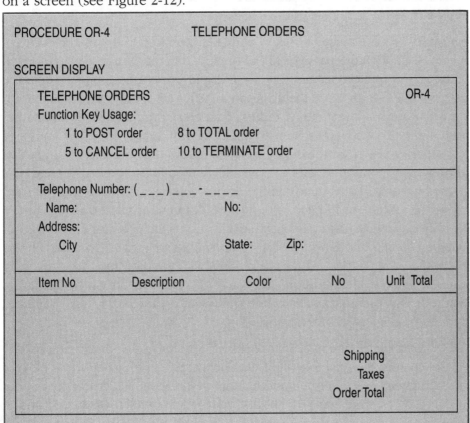

Figure 2-12. Data entry screen for telephone orders.

A paper order is never created; the data is sent directly to the main computer, so the data controls required and the records kept on transmitted forms are thus quite different.

When an operator turns on a terminal to begin work, the system asks for a **password**, or **user identification**, as shown in Figure 2-13. Each person who will use the system has been issued a confidential password that identifies him or her to the system. When the operator keys in the password, the system checks to determine (1) if it is a legal password and (2) which applications the owner of this password is authorized to use. If the password is not legitimate, the operator is asked to enter it again. If another illegal entry is made, the system may deactivate the terminal.

Name: _

Password:

Figure 2-13. Sign-on screen with password request.

An operator who wishes to use a particular application enters the name of the application. If the password is not included in the list of those authorized to access the application, the system will display a message telling the operator that he or she cannot use the application. After all, it may be acceptable for new operators to use a name/address data entry program to add the names and addresses of new customers to the CUSTOMER master file, but until they are more experienced they should not be allowed to use the program that allows the operator to modify the balances of customer accounts. The password, then, is the first control. It prevents unauthorized people from using the system and limits access to the different applications. Because it identifies its owner, the system can tag all records the operator enters with an operator identification. Because the computer has an internal clock and always knows the date, it can also tag the records with the date and time they were entered and the identification number of the terminal on which they were entered. This provides a clear audit trail whereby the record can be traced back to its origin within the business.

Other control information can be kept by the system rather than being written on documents. For example, the Data Entry Area work log can easily be kept by the system. Because the system controls the terminals, it has data about which records were entered (and/or verified), by which operators, and at what times during the day. The operators or the Data Entry Supervisor can display the log information whenever it is needed.

Did you notice that the displayed form (Figure 2-13) begins with a telephone number? This is another control technique that also reduces the amount of keying necessary. When customers call, the operators first ask for their home telephone number. The data entry program accepts the number and uses it to search the computer's files for the customer's name and address. If these are not found, the person may not be a legitimate charge customer, and the operator checks further before accepting the order. If the customer's name and address are found, they display on the screen. When the customer gives a name and address, the operator can check the information against the display.

This data need not be entered again unless a change must be made. Thus the **lookup technique** of the data entry program both provides a control to prevent unauthorized orders and reduces the amount of keying required.

We can almost say that the types of checks and helps that can be provided by the system in an interactive application are limited only by the imagination of the person who designed the system. Here we have examined a few that are frequently encountered, but do not be surprised to find others.

STUDY QUESTIONS

1 How can you find out whether a batch of records you entered has been verified?
2 If a data entry operator misplaces a form and does not enter the data it contains, when will the error be caught?
3 Which forms or techniques detect the loss of a form?
4 Which forms or techniques detect the loss of a record?

Assume you are using an interactive system and answer the following questions:

* In what two ways does a password protect the system?
* What happens if someone does not have a password and tries to enter words at random?
* How can an audit trail be kept when there is no document number to put into the records?
* What are two advantages of the lookup technique in data entry?

DOCUMENTATION FOR DATA ENTRY

The documentation of a procedure is the description of how that procedure is to be performed. Good, complete documentation is very important in data processing because ideas and instructions must often pass through the hands and minds of several people as they travel from the person who designed a procedure (in this case, the systems analyst) to the person who will actually perform the procedure (in this case, the data entry operator).

Some interesting experiments in documentation have been done in schools that teach classes in systems analysis, programming, and data entry. At Modesto Junior College in Modesto, California, for example, Kathleen Short assigns a problem to her systems analysis class. She then gives her programming class the specifications that the systems class writes up for the programs and the data needed to solve the problem. The programming class writes the programs described and sends the specifications for the records the programs need to the data entry class, along with the data to be put into the records. The data entry class then creates the records. The first assignment of the year usually makes an important point: Good documentation is essential. The point is forcefully made, because the records produced by the data entry class frequently have no resemblance to the analysts' original design.

Working in data processing without adequate documentation is like playing the old party game of "Gossip." After the rumor started by one player has been whispered in turn from person to person in the circle, the factual content has changed so much that the difference between the beginning and ending rumors is laughable. Unusable records created because of erroneous or misunderstood instructions can also be considered humorous, but it is wry humor indeed if you are the operator who created them and who must now correct them!

Tools for documentation

Data entry installations have job descriptions and job instructions on file for every task to be performed. **Narrative procedures, job instruction sheets,** and **record layout forms** are three types of documentation for data entry. These are created by a systems analyst. In planning data collection for a computer application, the analyst designs the format of each data record to be input by each program. This plan, or **record layout**, is then passed on to data entry operators to guide them as they create the record. The layout may be given to operators in the form of a narrative, on a job instruction sheet, or on a record layout form.

INLINE DOCUMENTATION. In an interactive environment, the computer can provide a great deal of information and assistance for the operator. In such an environment, we find traditional written explanations of how things are to be done, but we also find **inline documentation**. Inline documentation is included within the computer program itself and causes the program to display messages and other helps on the screen to assist the operator.

Two techniques frequently used in inline documentation are **menus** and **prompting messages**. A menu is simply a list of choices from which the operator can pick. When an operator begins a job, a menu similar to the following appears on the screen:

JOB: CUSTOMER RECORDS

        DO YOU WISH TO

        1. ADD A RECORD

        2. CHANGE THE CONTENTS OF A RECORD

        3. DELETE A RECORD

        4. EXIT

        YOUR CHOICE:_

At this point, the menu may seem less than clear to you, but if you are told to key in the number beside the function you wish to perform, it becomes clearer. To our menu, let us add a prompting message:

JOB: CUSTOMER RECORDS

      DO YOU WISH TO

      1. ADD A RECORD

      2. CHANGE THE CONTENTS OF A RECORD

      3. DELETE A RECORD

      4. EXIT

      YOUR CHOICE:_

(ENTER THE DIGIT OF THE FUNCTION YOU WISH TO USE. THEN PRESS THE ENTER KEY.)

The combination of menu and prompting message provides clearer documentation. Although prompting messages are frequently used along with menus, they also appear at various points in the data entry process to explain just what the proper procedure is at a given point.

WRITTEN PROCEDURE DOCUMENTATION FOR ONLINE SYSTEMS: STRUCTURED ENGLISH NARRATIVES. Even after the addition of the prompts, you may still have questions about menu choice 4: EXIT. We could add another prompt to the screen, and it might be appropriate here, but it is not practical to cover all possibilities with menus and prompts. They increase the size of the data entry program itself, which can cause a problem in small systems. For this and other reasons, it is best to have more complete descriptions of procedures in the **procedure log**. One type of notation used in describing procedures is the **structured English narrative**.

Figures 2-12 and 2-14 illustrate how a combination of inline documentation and written instructions is used to document an interactive system. An application that involves taking customer orders over the telephone, named PROCEDURE OR-4, is described. In Figure 2-14 (the first page of the printed documentation), the procedure is identified. The screen display that will appear when it is used is illustrated in Figure 2-12; this illustration would accompany the documentation of the procedure in the procedure log. Notice that the screen contains prompting messages that tell the operator which keys to use to (1) post an order, (2) cancel an order, (3) total an order, and (4) terminate entry. Other prompts indicate where individual items, such as the phone number, should be entered.

Figure 2-14 contains the narrative description of this procedure written in structured English. The directions are stated in standard English words, but the layout uses indentations and key words such as IF and ELSE to lead the user's eye down the page. Let us follow its steps.

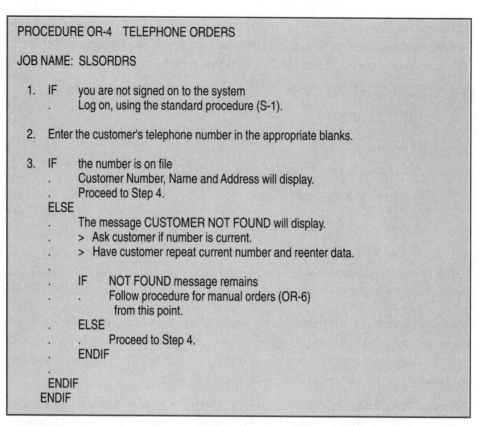

```
PROCEDURE OR-4   TELEPHONE ORDERS

JOB NAME:  SLSORDRS

  1.  IF      you are not signed on to the system
      .       Log on, using the standard procedure (S-1).

  2.  Enter the customer's telephone number in the appropriate blanks.

  3.  IF      the number is on file
      .       Customer Number, Name and Address will display.
      .       Proceed to Step 4.
      ELSE
      .       The message CUSTOMER NOT FOUND will display.
      .       > Ask customer if number is current.
      .       > Have customer repeat current number and reenter data.
      .
      .       IF    NOT FOUND message remains
      .       .     Follow procedure for manual orders (OR-6)
      .               from this point.
      .       ELSE
      .       .       Proceed to Step 4.
      .       ENDIF
      .
      ENDIF
      ENDIF
```

Figure 2-14a. Structured English documentation for telephone order procedure.

Step 1 uses the IF to ask if you are logged onto the system and tells you what procedure to follow (S-1) if you are not. All the procedures are named and are indexed by these names in the procedure log. In this system, procedures that are used frequently or used by many applications are classified as standard procedures and given some identification number that begins with S. Procedures related to taking customer orders have the prefix OR.

Step 2 instructs you to enter the telephone number provided by the customer. The Order Entry Program that is controlling this application will use the telephone number to look up the customer's record in the CUSTOMER file.

Step 3 uses the IF...ELSE structure to tell you how to handle different results. If the customer number is found by the Order Entry Program, the customer information will display, and you can skip to Step 4 in the procedure.

If the customer telephone number is not found (the condition indicated by the ELSE phrase), the screen displays the message CUSTOMER NOT FOUND, and you are told to inquire whether the number is the customer's current telephone number. You rekey the number. If the NOT FOUND message does not clear, you are told to leave this procedure and follow the one called OR-6. OR-6 will tell you how to take the order on a paper form.

The order produced following Procedure OR-6 will be double-checked by a supervisor before it is filled to determine if it is a legitimate order from a legitimate customer. This procedure does not indicate that the order will be checked, but Procedure OR-6 will contain details on how and by whom the checking is done.

4. Ask the customer for his account number and compare it to the one displayed on the screen.

5. IF   the account numbers match
   · Proceed to Step 6.
   ·
   ·
   ELSE
   · > Ask the customer for the number again and recheck.
   · > IF   the numbers still do not match
   ·
   ·   · - Tell the customer you are having trouble finding the record and transfer the call to your supervisor.
   ·
   ·   · - Cancel the order by pressing Function Key 5.
   ENDIF

6. Read displayed customer data to customer.

7. IF   any customer data field is in error
   · > Correct by placing cursor under item and rekeying.
   ELSE
   · > Proceed to Step 8.
   ENDIF

8. FOR EACH item ordered
   A. Enter item number.

   B. IF   the item is not on file
      · > The message NOT STANDARD ITEM will display.
      · > Follow procedure for non-standard items (OR-8) from this point.
      ELSE
      · > The Item Description, Color, and Unit Price will display.
      ENDIF

   C. Enter the number of items wanted.

   D. System will calculate and insert price.

9. WHEN customer has no more items to order

   A. Signal that the order is complete (Function Key 8).

   B. System will calculate and insert shipping, taxes, and order total.

   C. Read order to customer.

   D. IF   changes are necessary
      · > Place cursor under erroneous field and rekey data. (Enter item number
      ·   of 00000 to cancel order of item.)
      · > Return to Step 9A.
      ENDIF

   E. WHEN order is correct
      · > Post the order (Function Key 1).

Figure 2-14b. Structured English documentation for telephone order procedure.

Step 4 tells you to ask the customer for his or her account number. Of course, this number is on the screen, but having the customer give it to you further ensures that this order is being placed by a legitimate customer, not merely someone who happens to know the customer's phone number.

Step 5 tells you to go on to Step 6 if the customer number is correct. If it is not, the ELSE condition tells you to ask for the number a second time. If the number still does not match the one on the screen, you are to transfer the call to your supervisor and cancel your entry with Function Key 5.

Step 6 has you read the name and address to the customer.

Step 7 tells you how to correct any errors. Now you are ready to take information about the items the customer wants to order.

Step 8 outlines the procedure to be followed for each item the customer orders. Notice that the words FOR EACH are used to indicate that the procedure is to be repeated as long as necessary.

First, you enter the item number, which the system uses to locate the item in the file. If the item cannot be found, a message will display (NOT STANDARD ITEM). In this case, you are told to leave this procedure for another procedure called OR-8. If the item is found (the ELSE condition), the description, color, and unit price will display on the screen.

In Step 8C, you ask the customer the quantity to be ordered and enter the number wanted on the screen. The system calculates and inserts the price (8D).

Step 9 outlines the steps to be taken when the customer has completed the order. You are told to signal the computer program that the order is finished by pressing Function Key 8 (9A). The system will calculate the shipping charges, taxes, and the order total and display these on the screen (9B).

The order totals are read to the customer (9C), and any changes are made. Simple changes are made by rekeying the new data over the old data. If the customer changes his or her mind about ordering a particular item, the line that references that item is removed from the order by entering an item number of 00000 on the line to replace the item number previously there. Steps 9A, 9B, and 9C are repeated until the customer approves the order.

When the order is correct, you post it by pressing Function Key 1, and it is written on the customer order file.

After you have used this procedure for a while, you do not need all the details included here, and the prompting messages on the screen are sufficient documentation. However, this detailed documentation is valuable when new employees are being trained and when experienced employees must use an application with which they are not familiar.

Notice how much keying the online application saves. If the telephone and item numbers the customer provides are correct, the operator enters only the telephone number, the item number, and the count of each item the customer wants. All the other information is either brought from the files and displayed on the screen by the system or calculated and displayed on the screen by the system. In these applications, people and computers each do what they do best: The computers calculate and fetch data from files; the people use their judgment and tact to handle the customer and the order.

Job instruction sheets

Job instruction sheets are another widely used type of documentation for data entry. Figure 2-15 illustrates a job instruction sheet for a keydisk data entry device.

3740 JOB INSTRUCTION SHEET

JOB NO: DS010	JOB NAME: DAILY SALES		ENTER ✓ VERIFY
REC. PRODUCED: DETAIL SALES REC.	REC. LENGTH: 80		DISPOSAL: File By Job No. in Verify File

SWITCHES	SETTINGS		SOURCE DOCUMENT USED:
AUTO SKIP/DUP	ON	OFF	Daily Sales Slips
AUTO REC ADV	ON	OFF	DISPOSAL:
PROG NUM SHIFT	ALL CHAR	NUMBERS ONLY	File with Diskette in Verify File

FIELD	POSITIONS FROM	THRU	TYPE OR FUNCTION	TYPE OR FUNCTION SYMBOLS
1. STORE NUMBER	1	3	N & D	A - Alphabetic
2. DEPARTMENT NUMBER	4	5	N & D	N - Numeric D - Duplicate
3. SALESMAN NUMBER	6	7	N	S - Skip
4. SALES SLIP NUMBER	8	14	N	RA - Right Adjust LA - Left Adjust
5. ITEM NUMBER	15	22	N & SC	BF - Blank Fill
6. ITEM DESCRIPTION	23	40	A	ZF - Zero Fill B - Bypass
7. PRICE	41	45	N	SC - Self Check
8. NUMBER SOLD	46	48	N	FT - Field Totals TR - Field Totals with
9. SALE TYPE	49	49	N	Read Out
10. RECORD TYPE	80	80	A & D	TRR - Field Totals with Read Out & Reset
11.				
12.				KEYSTROKES PER RECORD:
13.				AVG = 45
14.				
15.				

REMARKS:

SALE TYPE: PROGRAM NUMBER = 36
    CASH SALE   = 1   TURN OFF AUTO SKIP/DUP
    CREDIT SALE = 2   FOR FIRST RECORD.
RECORD TYPE = S

Figure 2-15. Job instruction sheet.

The job instruction sheet in Figure 2-15 is for use with the IBM 3741, a keydisk data station. The job for which the record is to be entered is described at the top of the form. The job number is DS010. It may seem strange that DS010 is called a job number when it contains letters as well as numbers, but this is often the case. The name of the job is DAILY SALES. Of course, many different types of records will be entered in order to keep up with the daily sales of this company, but the one produced using this job instruction sheet is called the DETAIL SALES RECORD. These records are to be entered with a program that has already been created and given the number 36 for identification.

On the left side of the form is a list of the switches on the IBM 3741. Marked beside each switch is the way it should be set for this particular job. The operator is told that the source documents to be used are the store's copies of the DAILY SALES SLIP that are filled out when a purchase is made. When the records have been entered, the diskette and the source documents are to be placed in the VERIFY file.

The remainder of the job instruction sheet describes the contents of the record. You can see that the STORE NUMBER is to be entered into Positions 1 through 3. It is a numeric field and can be duplicated. (Items that are the same on all records can be copied from record to record, or duplicated.) The DEPARTMENT NUMBER goes into Positions 4 and 5. It is also numeric and can also be duplicated. The SALESPERSON NUMBER, a numeric item, is placed in Positions 6 and 7. The SALES SLIP NUMBER is entered in Positions 8 through 14, another numeric field. The ITEM NUMBER is entered into Positions 15 through 22. It is a self-checking number like those covered in the discussion of verification. The ITEM DESCRIPTION, the only alphabetic field in the record, goes into Positions 23 through 40. The PRICE is put into Positions 41 through 45, and the NUMBER SOLD goes into Positions 46 through 48. A code describing the SALE TYPE is put into Position 49. The remarks at the bottom of the sheet say that if the sale is for cash, the digit 1 is to be put into Position 49; if the sale is for credit, the digit 2 is to be put into Position 49. A RECORD TYPE code to indicate that this is a sales record is entered in Position 80. This code is always the letter S. A note reminds the operator to turn off the AUTO SKIP/DUP switch for the first record. The number of KEYSTROKES PER RECORD is indicated at the bottom of the sheet. In this example, the figure given must be an average because the data in the Item Description field will vary in length from item to item. The digits entered into the Store Number and Department Number fields are not included in the keystroke count because these two fields are duplicated rather than manually keyed.

You may wonder why the instructions do not specify right justification, left justification, zero fill, blank fill, and so on. The company has certain standard practices, which are explained to all new operators. These are followed unless the instruction sheet specifies otherwise. All numeric fields, for instance, will always be right justified and zero-filled unless the job instruction sheet directs otherwise.

To summarize, a job instruction sheet gives a data entry operator the following information:

1. The number and name of the job

2. The name of the record produced using these job instructions

3. The switch settings for the job

4. The source documents to use

5. Where the documents and diskettes are sent when the job is finished

6. Where each field is located

7. The type of each field

8. Any special function to be programmed for the fields

9. The number of keystrokes per record

10. Other general information, such as the codes for the record just described

Job instruction forms vary from business to business, but all of them are designed to give the data entry operator the information needed in order to prepare a program for the job and to key the job.

STUDY QUESTIONS

1 Is documentation necessary in a small shop with only two or three employees?

2 Is documentation necessary in a large shop in which operators specialize, each doing one or two applications, so that each operator is thoroughly familiar with the work he or she performs?

Chapter 3
MICROCOMPUTER DATA ENTRY

As we have noted, the most powerful data entry device is the computer itself, and microcomputers are frequently used for data entry. They may either be *networked* or *stand alone*. A *computer network* is formed by several individual computers that are connected so that they may work independently or share programs and data. *Stand-alone computers* are not connected and work independently. In either case, the micro can assist in data entry by editing data as it is entered and by pointing out items to be corrected, displaying messages for the operator, and so on.

HARDWARE, SOFTWARE, AND PROCEDURES

The microcomputer can do many things. What it will do is determined by two factors: (1) the program that controls it and (2) the functions the operator requests. People using computers work not only with machines but with a complete system made up of several components. When using microcomputers, we must consider three main factors: the **hardware**, the **software**, and the **procedures**. Let us first briefly examine the hardware, software, and procedures we will be using and then study them more closely.

An overview of hardware

The **hardware** is the machinery. Figure 3-1 shows the microcomputer called the IBM Personal Computer, or PC, along with its support equipment.

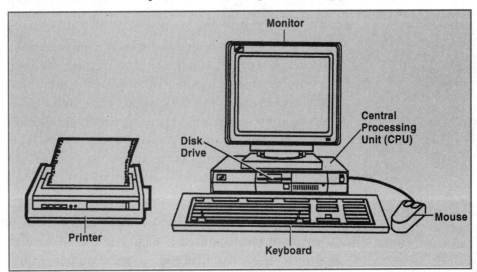

Figure 3-1. The IBM Personal Computer and its support equipment.

THE CENTRAL PROCESSING UNIT. The **central processing unit (CPU)** is the part of the computer that performs the processing tasks. It is housed in the large box, or system unit, on which the display screen sits; thus it is invisible to the casual observer. The CPU contains (1) circuitry that interprets the instructions of the controlling program and sees that they are executed and (2) an electronic storage area called the **memory** that holds the controlling program and any data it is currently processing. The program to be used must be loaded into the memory before the control circuitry can execute its instructions.

When we hear the term *computer*, we often picture collections of equipment. However, this small processing unit is actually the computer. Other devices are support equipment that provide services for the computer.

INPUT AND OUTPUT DEVICES. Because the computer requires instructions and data to be in electronic or magnetic form, we use **input devices** to accept the data we enter and translate it into electronic impulses for the computer. We also use **output devices** to take the electronic data inside the computer and change it to a form that humans can understand. The system in Figure 3-1 uses a keyboard for input. It has two output devices: a display screen and a printer. Output displayed on the screen is called **softcopy** output; output printed on paper is called **hardcopy** output. You will also hear hardcopy output referred to as a **listing** or **printout**.

STORAGE DEVICES. Programs and data are held in the memory of the CPU while they are in use. The contents of the memory are in electronic format, however, and therefore they are lost when the current is turned off. Anything that is to be kept must be stored on the medium called the **disk** before the system is turned off. Material that is written on the disk can be read back into memory very quickly. The disk **drive** writes data onto the disk and reads it back into the memory when it is needed. The disk drives can be seen on the front of the box that houses the CPU. The disks are somewhat similar to CDs, and their functions are similar in many ways. A disk stores instructions and data in much the same way that a CD stores music, and the disk drive plays back the instructions and data from the disk to the CPU much as a CD player plays back the music from the CD to the CD player.

There are other similarities between a computer system and a CD system. The functions of a computer screen and the speakers of a CD player are basically the same: to produce output. A computer's disk drive and its reading and recording mechanism, the **read/write head**, are like the drive and the scanner on the CD player. There is, however, a crucial difference: The CD can only produce music, whereas the computer can do many things (including producing music). The ability to store a program in its memory, to follow the instructions of that program, and then to store and follow another program with different instructions makes the computer very versatile and powerful.

Another type of storage device besides the disk is the **hard disk**. Hard disks are made of metal and each platter is coated with an oxide material that allows data to be magnetically recorded on the platter's surface. Hard disks have a greater storage capacity than disks. Hard disks are used in microcomputers and main frame computers. The hard disk can be sealed into a disk cartridge or a number of platters can be stacked vertically into a disk pack. These disk cartridges and disk packs can be installed in the computer or can be removable. Because the hard disk can store so much more data than a disk, it is a very popular means of storage.

COMMUNICATION DEVICES. A **network system** is a device to allow computers to communicate and share information. The network system can be simple or complex. A network links various parts of a computer system together. A simple network could be the linkage between the keyboard, disk drives, and screen. When you think of a network system, it usually involves linking one computer to another computer. The distance could be a few feet across the room or thousands of miles across the country or world. A network system needs a sender, receiver, communication equipment, and communication channels. The sender and receiver can be a personal computer. The communication equipment is a modem, and the communication channel is a telephone line. Telephone lines can be twisted pair wire, coaxial cable, or fiber optics. The transmission can be microwaves, satellite, or wireless. Another term for networks is LAN (local area network).

When signing onto a network, an operator usually must type in his or her name and password. Next a menu comes up on the screen so the operator can select what software application to use. Once the program is selected, the operator selects the records to run in the program. For example, in a database program you would select the database software. Once it is running, you select what set of data files you want to check. If you have clearance, you can edit the files. If you have **read only access**, you can only view the files and cannot make changes to the files.

Software

Software is the program or collection of programs that provides instructions for the computer. The way the computer system functions depends on the program it is following. When you finish entering data for one application, such as payroll, and wish to enter data for another, such as inventory, you signal the computer to read from the disk a program that accepts inventory data. The computer will then take the payroll program out of memory and replace it with the inventory program. (Of course, copies of both programs remain on disk, just as music remains on a CD after it has been played.) To exchange programs, you follow specific procedures, that is, techniques that have been adopted for your installation.

Procedures

Just as programs are instructions for the machines to follow when they process data, procedures are instructions for people to follow when they process data. Most computers are programmed to assist operators by displaying instructions on the screen. You will remember that we examined two types of displayed instructions (menus and prompting messages) in Chapter 1.

Of course, many tasks to be performed do not involve the computer, such as storing disks, labeling disks containing data, and so on. Procedures must be established for each installation, and each installation should maintain a **procedure log** that contains written descriptions of all procedures currently in use. You will remember the discussion of procedures for online data entry in "Documentation for Data Entry" in Chapter 2. For other examples of data entry procedures, see Appendix C for the procedures to be followed when using the data entry program available with this text for the jobs in Chapter 4.

STUDY QUESTIONS

1 How is a computer network different from a group of stand-alone computers?
2 Define the terms *hardware*, *software*, and *procedures*.
3 What piece of hardware actually performs the processing tasks?
4 What is the general purpose of input devices?
5 What is the general purpose of output devices?
6 If there is a storage area (the memory) inside the system unit, why is there a need for external storage devices such as disks?
7 What is the function of a program?
8 Why would an office need more than one data entry program?
9 Give an example of two types of procedures:
   • A procedure that is displayed by the program
   • A procedure that does not involve operating the computer

MICROCOMPUTER JOB 1:
GENERAL SYSTEM FUNCTIONS

This exercise requires the performance of simple tasks to acquaint the inexperienced user with the switches, adjustments, and keys on the personal computer and its support equipment. There will be three other similar exercises throughout this chapter.

As a beginner, you may accidentally call for some function that produces effects you do not understand and do not want. If you reach a point where the system does not work the way you want it to work and all else fails, there is a way to recover. You can **reboot** the system and begin again by holding down the CTRL and ALT keys and pressing the DEL key. This will have the same effect as turning the system off and on again except that the internal checking will not be done; therefore, it will not take as much time.

Reboot only when you are at your wit's end. Rebooting erases the computer memory, and you will lose any work you have done since the last **boot**.

Experienced users may not need to practice this exercise. If in doubt, ask your instructor if you should complete this Job.

PURPOSE

The purpose of this exercise is to let you use the system and become familiar with its general layout. You will input data into the memory of the system, observe it on the screen, and produce a hardcopy. To do this, you will use DOS Edit. If you do not have DOS Edit, these (and subsequent) exercise(s) can be completed in QBASIC, BASIC, or a word processing program. Ask your instuctor how to access these programs. For the Data Entry Jobs in Chapter 4, you will need a more powerful program.

PREPARATION

For this job you will need the following equipment:

1. For Steps 1-8, a computer with a display screen
2. For Steps 9-11, a computer with a screen and a printer

PROCEDURE

To avoid errors, first read through all the steps listed below. Then go to the computer and work through the steps to complete Microcomputer Job 1. Caution: During the exercise, do not experiment with keys other than those specified. If you use keys that are not specified, you may get unexpected results that will spoil your printout.

1. For this exercise you will use DOS Edit, a very simple text editor that is provided with your operating system.

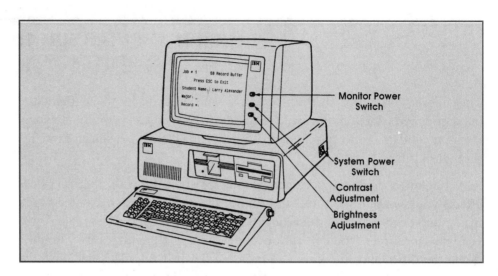

Figure 3-2. Data entry screen for Job 1 indicating monitor switches.

2. If your system has a printer, locate the Power switch and turn it on.
3. If your screen has its own Power switch, turn it on.
4. Turn on the central processing unit (CPU).
5. Be patient. The system does some internal checking of its equipment. When the check is complete, the system will attempt to read from the disk (you will see the light on the drive glow), and it will then boot up using the DOS operating system. When this has been completed, type EDIT. The screen will look like the following:

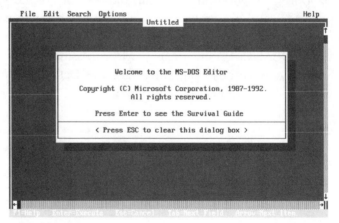

6. Press ESC to clear the dialog box.
7. Locate the blinking cursor on the screen and observe its shape.
8. Locate the cursor positioning keys that contain small arrows. These keys will move the cursor in the direction they point. Try them and observe the action of the cursor. Note: If you have not hit the Enter key, only the left and right arrow keys will move the cursor.
9. Press the CAPS LOCK key to place the keyboard in upper shift. Then key in this sentence:
    MICROCOMPUTER JOB 1 HAS BEEN COMPLETED BY = KEY IN YOUR NAME

The material you have keyed automatically displays on the screen. If you have a printer, you can create a hardcopy.

9. Check your printer status lights. They will tell you whether or not
   A. the power is on,
   B. the printer is ready,
   C. there is paper in the printer, and
   D. the printer is online.
10. You are going to print, so the printer must be online. If it is not, press the Online switch to place the printer online.
11. Locate the Print Screen (PrtSc) key. Press it (while holding down the Shift key). The printer will print the entire screen contents, including the material you did not enter. This is acceptable for now. In future exercises, you will use programs that produce cleaner, faster output.
12. Take the printer offline by again pressing the Online switch and press the Form Feed button. On dot matrix printers, advance the paper so that you can tear off the sheet.
13. Turn off the equipment.

Figure 3-3.Windows Program Manager screen with icons for various software.

WINDOWS ENVIRONMENT

Another way of operating your computer is to use Windows. When you turn on your computer, instead of viewing a screen with a C prompt or a menu with different software listed, a screen called a Program Manager appears with various icon application groups. Windows is a popular graphical user interface that allows you to use various application software such as WordPerfect, Lotus 1-2-3, dBase, and other programs.

The Program Manager screen as shown has the following common icons: Main, Accessories, Games, and other icons depending on your system. Other icons might be WordPerfect, Lotus 1-2-3, and dBase IV. Within the Main and Accessories icons are other icons. In Main there may be: File Manager, Control Panel, Print Manager, Clipboard, MS-DOS Prompt, PIF Editor, and Windows Set-up. Likewise, in the Accessories icon the following icons may appear: Write, Paintbrush, Terminal, Notepad, Recorder, Cardfile, Calendar, Calculator, Clock, Object Packages, Character Map, Media Player, and Sound Recorder. When you use the Windows interface, you do not have to worry about memorizing codes as you do in the DOS environment. You click on an icon such as File Manager and you are able to manage your files by reading the various operations available to you. If you want to format your new disk, you would place the disk in Drive A and click on File Manager from the Main icon. You would then see a screen with the words File, Disk, Tree, View, Options, Window, and Help across the top of the screen in a line called a bar. You would click on Disk and the following options would come up for you to select: Copy Disk..., Label Disk..., Format Disk..., Make System Disk..., and Select Drive.... You would then click on Format Disk and check to see that the A drive was specified (if not, you would select the A drive by clicking on the down arrow to arrive at the A drive). You would then click on OK and then one more dialog box would come up to ask you if you want to format this disk and you would click on Yes. In DOS, you would have to have a C prompt and type in Format A:. You would have to remember exactly what to type and where to type the format command.

The following are some common terms you need to know when you use Windows:

I-beam appears on the screen showing where the mouse pointer is located.

The **arrow** is the mouse cursor when you point at an icon or at the top of the screen.

Double-headed arrow is the mouse cursor that allows you to change the size of a graphic box or, depending on which program you are in, has other features.

Four-headed arrow is the mouse cursor that, for example, allows you to move a graphic box in WordPerfect.

Drop-down menu appears when you click on an option like File from the Menu Bar.

Dialog box appears from the drop-down menu when your selection has ellipses after the word. The dialog box is used quite extensively in WordPerfect and Lotus. The dialog box gives you many choices to select from when you are defining information to the computer.

Radio button is a round circle before a selection in a dialog box. If you select a radio button, a dark circle appears inside the round circle meaning you have selected this option.

Terms such as Cut, Copy, Paste, Open, Close, Exit, Save, and Save As are common Windows terms used in both WordPerfect and Lotus. **Cut** means to take something out of the text. **Copy** means to select a word or body of words and copy to your short term buffer memory to recall again. **Paste** means to take whatever you have copied and place it somewhere else in the text. **Open** is used to indicate a way to retrieve an old document you have saved on your disk or hard drive. **Close** means to clear the screen of the present document. **Exit** means to leave the software program you are presently using. **Save** and **Save As** are two different ways to keep a copy of a document on your disk or hard drive. Save As will always ask you what file name to call the document to be saved. Save will not ask you to name the document if you have already named it. Save is a quicker way to save, but must be used with an already named document.

THE MONITOR, THE SCREEN, AND THE CURSOR

The data on the disk cannot be read by people, but the microcomputer can be programmed to read it, translate the magnetic spots into characters humans can understand, and either print it on paper or display it on the screen. A standard screen can display 25 lines, each of which can hold 80 characters. Screens of other sizes are also available.

Monitor controls

The output device most frequently used by the operator is the screen of the system monitor. Figure 3-2 shows a monitor with a screen, a System Power switch, a Monitor Power switch, and two control knobs: a **brightness adjustment** and a **contrast adjustment**. Some monitors do not have a separate power switch; they are turned on when the overall system is turned on.

All display units have one or more controls that allow you to adjust the brightness and contrast of the screen display to a comfortable level. These controls are operated like the brightness and contrast knobs of a television set; varying brightness and contrast of the display helps to avoid eye fatigue. Monitors come with many other options: white characters displayed on a black background, black and green display, black and amber display, full color display with selection of a range of colors, the capability to display pictorial (**graphic**) output in addition to letters, and so on. In data entry, these options can be attractive but are not of primary importance.

Formatted screens and the cursor

As you use data entry programs, menus and prompts appear on the screen. The data you enter also appears on the screen. In Figure 3-2, the screen is **formatted**; that is, it displays prompts to indicate where data items are to be entered.

A blinking square or line of light called the cursor appears in the first position on the screen where data can be entered and moves along as you key in data. The cursor indicates where the next character will appear if you press a key. The shape of the cursor (line or square) indicates whether or not you are in the INSERT mode. This is a useful feature that we will discuss when we examine the keyboard.

1   What is the size of a standard screen?
2   What is the purpose of the brightness and contrast controls for everyday data entry?
3   What is the purpose of the cursor?
4   What does the cursor look like?
5   Identify some of the options available in screen displays.
6   What is a formatted screen?

STUDY QUESTIONS

PRINTERS AND HARDCOPY OUTPUT

Computer output comes in many forms, such as digits, letters or graphic symbols on a screen, lines printed on paper, microfilm, spoken (or audio) output, and many others. Most users, however, are concerned with only two types: (1) output that is displayed on a screen, or **softcopy** output, and (2) output that appears on paper, or **hardcopy** output. The most widely used hardcopy device is the printer.

The need for hardcopy output

Printers are available in a wide range of prices and with a wide variety of features. They are often used when a printed copy of output (**hardcopy**) is needed. In data entry, a hardcopy of the data on disk is occasionally required, and a printed summary or edit information is often useful. For example, after a job has been entered, a count of the records entered can be printed and compared against the number of records in the batch to determine if any records were skipped. Similarly, when data is verified, the number of errors found and the contents or other identification of the erroneous records can be printed. Some data entry installations reward workers' increased productivity with increased pay, and the computer can be programmed to calculate the total number of error-free keystrokes and to print this information for the supervisor at the end of the work day. Hardcopy output is useful for all these applications.

Printer controls

Although printers have varying features, most of them have at least the three following features: (1) They can be placed online or offline by the setting of the **Online switch**. (2) They can advance the paper one line when the **Line Feed button** is pressed. (3) They can advance the paper one form (page) when the **Form Feed button** is pressed. The operator requests these functions by pressing control switches on the printer's control panel.

In addition to control switches, the control panel contains a series of control lights that provide information about the status of the printer. In Figure 3-4, the close-up illustration of the control panel shows the control lights and control switches. The lights give general information, such as whether the printer is turned on and whether it has paper in it. The control switches allow the operator to place the printer online or offline and to advance the paper.

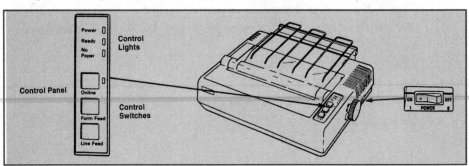

Figure 3-4. The printer and its control switches.

You will remember from Chapter 1 that *online* means that the data entry device is directly connected to and communicating with the CPU. When printing is to occur, the printer must be online so that the computer can transfer the data to be printed. The offline setting is used when the paper is to be adjusted. The small light beside the Online switch in Figure 3-4 is lit when the printer is online and is dark when the printer is offline. The Online switch is a **toggle**: When online, pressing the switch changes the system to offline, and when offline, pressing the switch changes the system to online.

As printing occurs, the printer automatically advances the paper. In order to advance the paper when the machine is not printing, the operator must first take the machine offline and then use either the Line Feed button or the Form Feed button. Pressing the Line Feed button once causes the paper to advance one line. Holding it down causes the paper to advance until the button is released. The Form Feed button works the same way but advances the paper by sheets instead of lines. Before requesting a printout, you will use these buttons to adjust the paper so that the top of a sheet is positioned under the printing mechanism.

The **Power switch** turns the printer itself off and on. In Figure 3-4, it is located on the right side of the printer in the rear.

STUDY QUESTIONS

1   List two situations in which hardcopy output is needed.
2   List two things that can be determined by looking at the printer control lights.
3   When must a printer be online?
4   When must a printer be offline?
5   Explain the function of the Online switch.
6   Explain the function of the Line Feed button.
7   Explain the function of the Form Feed button.
8   How can you tell when the printer is online?

MICROCOMPUTER JOB 2:

MONITOR AND PRINTER CONTROLS

This exercise requires the performance of simple tasks to acquaint the inexperienced user with the switches, adjustments, and keys on the personal computer and its support equipment. There will be two other similar exercises throughout this chapter.

Experienced users may not need to practice this exercise. If in doubt, ask your instructor if you should complete this Job.

PURPOSE

The purpose of Microcomputer Job 2 is to allow you to use the control buttons and switches of the printer and monitor to (1) position the paper for hardcopy output, (2) adjust the screen display for softcopy output, and (3) produce a printed hardcopy of the softcopy output displayed on the screen.

PREPARATION

For this Job you will need the following equipment:

1. A computer with a display screen and printer

As in Microcomputer Job 1, in Job 2 you should not use keys other than those specified in your instructions until you have completed the Job and obtained the required printouts. In particular, do not use any arrow keys other than the small cursor positioning keys.

PROCEDURE

1. Turn on the equipment and wait for the screen display that appears when the system checking is complete.
2. On the monitor, adjust each control knob first to its maximum setting and then to its minimum setting. Note how the displayed material changes. Find the settings that are most comfortable for you. Note: If the screen is blank at any time that you think it should contain a display, perhaps the brightness control is set too low. Try turning it up.
3. Type EDIT, then press ESC to clear the dialog box.
4. Fill the screen with the characters specified below. Do not be concerned if there are characters already on the screen; simply write on top of them. Use the Delete key to erase any characters that you do not replace by overwriting.

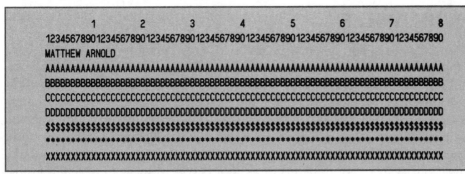

Figure 3-5. Data entry screen for Job 2.

       A. Use the small arrow keys to position your cursor at the beginning of the second line and enter these characters over and over again until you have filled the entire line: 1234567890. You may use the digit keys of the keypad, those on the top line of the keyboard, or a combination of both.

       B. Use the cursor positioning keys to place the cursor on Line 1 and add consecutive digits over each zero on the line of numbers you just entered (see Figure 3-5).

       C. On the third line, enter your name.

       D. Fill the other lines with any other data. To fill the remaining lines, you may want to use the **typematic** feature of the keyboard. Typematic keys repeat as long as they are held down. Try using this feature with a letter or digit. When you are finished, the screen should look something like the screen in Figure 3-5.

5. Check the printer controls. Take the printer offline by pressing the Online switch. Then follow these steps for dot matrix printers. (These steps are not possible with laser printers.)

       A. Press the Line Feed button three times. The paper will advance for three lines.

       B. Hold the Line Feed button down for a moment or two and observe the effect.

       C. Press the Form Feed button once. The paper will advance to the same line on the next page.

6. Prepare for hardcopy output.

       A. Use the Line Feed button to position the first line of a fresh sheet under the printing mechanism.

       B. Put the printer online.

7. Print the screen by pressing Alt-F, highlighting Print, and pressing Enter twice.

8. Take the printer offline and use the control buttons to advance the paper so that you can cleanly remove the entire sheet from the printer.

9. Count the characters per line (the 1234567890 scale will help). Count the lines per page, including any displayed by the controlling program. Write these figures on the printout of the screen.

Note: You will find number lines, such as the one you just created at the top of your screen, to be very helpful when you must key data into precise positions on a blank screen.

THE MOUSE

A special piece of equipment used in the Windows environment is the mouse. A mouse is a device that sits on a pad for easier mobility. It can have two or three buttons. The left button is usually used for the primary button to click or double click to select your program choices. Buttons can be programmed to various functions that are on the keyboard. For example, you could program the center button to act like a cursor return key. Clicking means you push down and release the left mouse button quickly. Before you click, you would have your pointer positioned on the choice you would like to make in the program. Double clicking is pushing the left button down two times rapidly. This action is required for some selections. Clicking and double clicking are required in various Windows-type application programs. Another mouse operation is dragging. This is when you push down on the left button and hold it down as you drag the mouse across the pad (the mouse pointer will move across the screen). When you drag you are literally moving something you have selected to another area on the screen. The various buttons on your mouse will be programmed for different actions depending on the software you are running at the time. Some programs only require the left button, whereas some require both a right and a left button to execute actions in the program.

THE KEYBOARD

At first glance, the keyboards of the microcomputer shown in Figure 3-6 look much like the keyboard of a typewriter. The alphabetic keys are in the same location as on a typewriter. Unlike on a typewriter, however, on these keyboards the numeric keys appear in two locations: along the top row and again in an adding-machine configuration on the right of the keyboard. (The plus and minus signs and the asterisk also appear with the numbers at both locations for user convenience.) When entering primarily alphabetic data, the operator may find it more convenient to use the digit and sign keys on the central keyboard, whereas the numeric keypad on the right is more convenient for entering primarily numeric data.

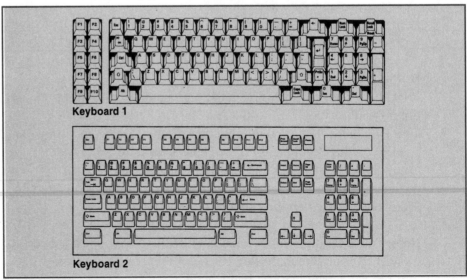

Figure 3-6. Two keyboards available for the IBM personal computer.

Keyboard 1 has ten function keys on the left side of the keyboard. It is an older model keyboard. Keyboard 2 has twelve function keys on the top of the keyboard. Keyboard 1 combines the cursor positioning (or arrow) keys, numeric keypad keys, and special purpose keys into one keypad.

Other keys contain equally familiar symbols: the dollar sign, period, asterisk, and so on. At second glance, however, we see that the computer keyboard contains keys that are marked with arrows or abbreviated names, such as CTRL. The IBM PC keyboard contains four types of keys: (1) **data keys**, (2) **cursor positioning** (or **arrow**) **keys**, (3) **function keys**, and (4) **special purpose keys**. The **data keys** are those that contain letters, numbers, and special characters. They, of course, are used to enter data into the memory. In Figure 3-7, the data keys are shaded.

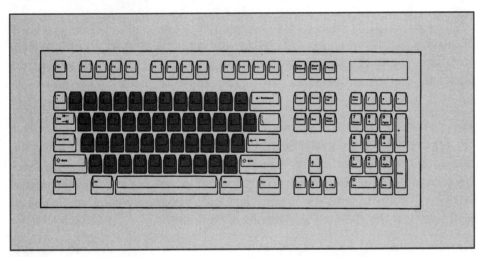

Figure 3-7. The data keys.

Keys that move the cursor

Different keys can be used to move the cursor in different ways. The **cursor positioning** (or **arrow**) **keys** shown in Figure 3-8 allow you to move the cursor around the screen. If you make a keying error, you can put the cursor at the beginning of the incorrect data and enter the correct data. The four cursor positioning keys on the numeric keypad were used in Jobs 1 and 2 and are marked with small arrows. The direction of the arrow on the key indicates the direction the cursor will move if that key is pressed. Moving the cursor does not change the data over which it passes. Pressing an arrow key causes the cursor to move one position; holding it down causes it to repeat the movement. Keys that repeat their function when they are held down are called **typematic**; most keys on the micro keyboard are typematic.

Figure 3-7. Numeric keypad and Cursor Positioning, Backspace, Enter (Cursor Return), and Tab keys.

Two other arrow keys appear between the numeric keypad and the central keyboard. The **Backspace key** will also move the cursor to the left, but it differs from the other left arrow key in that it erases the data over which it passes.

The oversize key with the arrow that points both down and left is the **Enter key**, or **cursor return**. The Enter key is a special key that has two functions: (1) It moves the cursor to the beginning of the next line, and (2) it signals the computer that the data on the screen is complete and should be processed. We should note that data entry programs may override the entry function of this key. The documentation for the data entry program will tell the operator how to signal the CPU when a record is complete.

The key to the left of the Q key that contains two arrows is the **Tab key**. It is used to move the cursor to the left or right margin of the screen or the field in which the cursor appears. Its exact function, like that of the cursor return key, is determined by programming.

Four other keys move the cursor or allow you to skip around within the data you have keyed into the memory. These are the **Home**, **End**, **Page Up (PgUp)**, and **Page Down (PgDn) keys** shown in Figure 3-9. Many programs deactivate these keys, and most data entry programs do not use them. When these keys are active, however, they allow you to skip around in the data or text stored in memory.

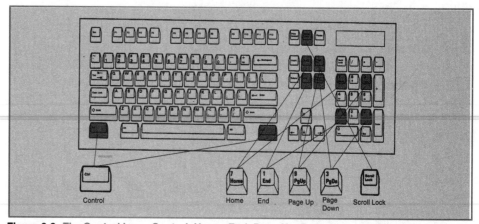

Figure 3-9. The Control keys: Control, Home, End, Page Up, Page Down, and Scroll Lock.

For example, let's assume that you are performing a word-processing application and are entering a research paper that is 15 pages long. As you key in data, the screen will fill, and when you have filled the last line on the screen each line on the screen will move up one line, out of sight. The line that was previously at the top of the screen will disappear, and a fresh blank line will appear at the bottom. As you continue to key, this process is repeated. Thus when you have finished entering your paper, 14 pages will have scrolled up and disappeared. They will remain in memory, but you will be able to see only the last screen of the data you entered. Picture the text as an ancient scroll—one long roll of paper on which the writing appears. Now picture your screen as a magnifying glass that enables you to read the tiny, ancient writing. The Page Up, Page Down, Home, and End keys allow you to move this magnifying glass over the portion of the text you want to read. The PgUp key moves the magnifying glass up ten lines of the text; the PgDn key moves it down ten lines. The Home and End keys allow you to jump from wherever you are reading to the beginning or end of the text. On Keyboard 1, however, the **Control key** (CTRL) must be held down while the Home and End keys are pressed in order to activate their function. (This prevents you from accidentally jumping to the beginning or end of the text when you did not intend to do so.) Again, these keys are not normally used in data entry applications.

In applications other than data entry, you sometimes give commands to cause your text to scroll, or automatically advance line by line. The **Scroll Lock key** (see Figure 3-9) will stop the scrolling action.

STUDY QUESTIONS

1   What is meant by clicking, double clicking, and dragging?
2   How is the mouse used in the Windows environment?
3   What are the four types of keys?
4   What is the general function of the data keys?
5   Why do the digits, the plus sign, and the minus sign appear in two locations on a micro keyboard?
6   What is a typematic key?
7   What is the difference between the right arrow on the 4 key of the numeric keypad and the right arrow on the key to the left of the NumLock key?
8   What are the two names of the key that contains the down-left arrow? What are its two functions?

Function keys

The **function keys** (see Figure 3-10) cause the computer to take some action. They are also called **soft keys** because their function is determined by the software.

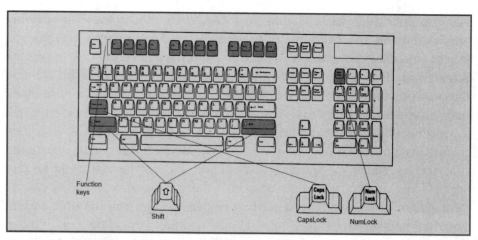

Figure 3-10. Function keys and Shift, CapsLock, NumLock keys.

The keys that are marked F1, F2, and so on are the function keys. Because their function is determined by the software, when one program is running, the F1 key may replace the layout of the record that appears on the screen with the layout of another record. When another program is running, the F1 key may cause the program to terminate. The documentation for the procedure you are using will explain how the keys work. You should always review the documentation before you use the program.

Special purpose keys

The micro keyboard also contains several **special purpose keys**. The most familiar special purpose keys are the **Shift keys** (see Figure 3-10). The Shift keys are the two large arrows at either end of the bottom row of data keys. They work much like the Shift keys on a typewriter: They give either a capital letter or, on a key that contains two characters, the upper character or function. Thus pressing the key that contains a colon and a semicolon without pressing the Shift key at the same time causes the semicolon to appear, whereas pressing that key and the Shift key at the same time gives a colon. As you discovered in Job 2, the Shift key must also be held down if you want to activate the function that is indicated on the upper part of a key. On Keyboard 1, for example, you must hold down the Shift key to activate the print screen function of the PrtSc key. Of course, the **Print Screen key** (PrtSc) is another function key.

The **CapsLock** key shown in Figure 3-10 will lock the shift and give all capital letters, but it works only for the alphabetic keys. For numeric keys, you must hold down the Shift key, or you can press the NumLock key to lock in the shift.

Caution: Don't forget to release the NumLock key when you are finished with the numeric keys. For example, on Keyboard 1, when you press the right arrow and get the digit 6 rather than a cursor movement, you know that the NumLock is engaged. To release either the CapsLock or the NumLock, press the CapsLock or NumLock key again.

The **Escape key** (ESC) (see Figure 3-11) is also set by the program and allows the user to escape from the current program or layout to another. Again, if the Escape key is enabled by a program, specific information on its function in the application should appear in the prompting messages or in the procedure documentation. Watch for a brief note on the screen that says "ESC to terminate" or perhaps "ESC to previous menu." This message explains how the ESC key will work in that particular application.

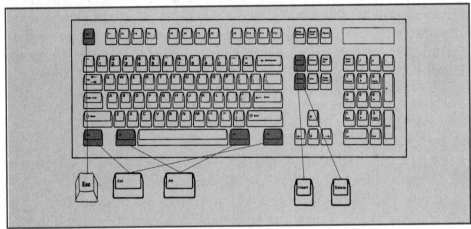

Figure 3-11. Escape, Control, Alt, Insert, Delete keys.

The two special purpose keys you will find most useful are the **Insert** (INS) and **Delete** (DEL) keys. These keys are shown in Figure 3-11 and allow you to insert characters into or delete characters from data that has already been entered. They also realign the remainder of the text. For example, suppose you omitted the *u* in *Saturday*, entering *Satrday*. To correct this, you place the cursor under the *r* in *Satrday* and press the Insert key. The cursor will change from a slender line to a square to indicate that you are now in the INSERT mode. Now you press the *U* key. The *u* appears between the *t* and the *r*, and all the text to the right of the *u* moves right one position. To leave the INSERT mode, press the INS key again.

The Delete key is also helpful in correcting errors. If you have keyed *diay* for *day*, put the cursor under the *i* and press the DEL key. The *i* will disappear, and the rest of the line will move one position to the left for correct alignment. We should note thatin data entry applications, operators are striving for speed and accuracy, and sight checking material on the screen works against both these goals. Sight check and use the INS and DEL keys only when you are instructed to do so.

The two remaining special purpose keys are the **Control** (CTRL) and **Alt** keys, which are also shown in Figure 3-11. These keys are used to modify the function of other keys. We have discussed the function of the Scroll Lock key. Note that the word Break appears on the shaft of the Scroll Lock key on Keyboard 1. If you hold down the CTRL key and press the Scroll Lock key, you activate the **Break function**. (On Keyboard 2, simply press Break.) This cancels operation of the current program.

Caution: Do not use this key inadvisedly, or all the current work will be lost. The CTRL/Break key is used when a program is out of control or has locked the system. Of course, the CTRL key can be used to modify the function of many keys. Check your documentation for details.

The ALT key also modifies the function of other keys and also can be set by the controlling program. The user's response to total disaster (that is, when the current program fails and renders the system unusable and CTRL/Break will not resolve the problem) is to hold down CTRL and ALT and press the DEL key. This combination gives the same result as turning off the computer and turning it on again except that it works much faster. This reboot skips the normal step in which all the internal checking is done. You will remember from Job 1 that the internal checking process is time consuming.

STUDY QUESTIONS

1   What is meant by a general reference to the function keys?
2   What does the F3 key do?
3   For which set of numeric keys (central keyboard or keypad) does the NumLock key work? How is NumLock turned off?
4   For which keys does CapsLock work? How is it turned off?
5   If you press the down arrow key and get the digit 2, what is the problem?
6   Explain how the Insert and Delete keys work. When should you not use them?

MICROCOMPUTER JOB 3:

THE KEYBOARD KEYS

This exercise requires the performance of simple tasks to acquaint the inexperienced user with the switches, adjustments, and keys on the personal computer and its support equipment. There will be one more similar exercise at the end of this chapter.

Experienced users may not need to practice this exercise. If in doubt, ask your instructor if you should complete this Job.

PURPOSE

The purpose of Microcomputer Job 3 is to familiarize you with some frequently used function keys. You will purposely enter data containing errors and then correct those errors. You will key in a small computer program that will cause an error condition and use a function key to terminate it, and you will use function keys to cancel processing and reboot the system. As always, read the complete Job instructions before you begin.

PREPARATION

For this Job you will need the following equipment:

1. A computer with a screen and printer

As in the previous Jobs, use only the keys specified in the Job instructions. In this Job, be particularly careful to use the Enter (cursor return) key only when it is called for in the instructions. Remember that the Enter key signals the computer to input the data displayed on the screen, and some of the data we are displaying is not acceptable to the control program we are using. This is an artificial situation that should not occur anywhere except in a training situation, but it is useful here.

PROCEDURE

1. Turn on, or boot, your system and enter the sentences below. Use the Shift keys for capitals. Use the cursor positioning arrows on the numeric keypad to move from line to line. Experiment with using Home and End keys. On Line 6, enter the first two groups of digits with the keys at the top of the keyboard and enter the second two groups with the keys on the numeric keypad (using NumLock).
    1. We are busy on Satrday, but are free on Friday.
    2. We are busy on Saturrday, but are free on Friday.
    3. We are busy on Saturrday, but are free on Friday.
    4. We are busy on Saturrday, but are free on Friday.
    5. We are busy on Saturday,,but are free on Friday.
    6. 0123456789 0123456789 0123456789 012345678902.
2. Print your screen by pressing Alt F, highlighting print, then pressing Enter twice. Then make the following corrections:
    A. In Sentence 1, use INSERT mode to place a *u* between the *t* and the *r* in *Satrday* to spell *Saturday* correctly.

B. In Sentence 2, use the Delete key to remove the extra *r* from *Saturrday* to spell *Saturday* correctly.

C. In Sentence 3, use the left arrow key between the NumLock key and the + key to erase the extra *r*.

D. In Sentence 4, use the space bar to remove the extra *r*.

E. In Sentence 5, remove the extra comma by using the key that is most appropriate.

F. Print your corrected screen by pressing Alt-F, highlighting Print, then pressing Enter twice.

■ STORAGE: THE DRIVE AND THE MEDIUM

To enter data, you select the correct data entry program and then press the keys on the keyboard. The data appears on the screen, where you can examine it visually if you suspect an error. When you have completed a record, you signal the data entry program that is controlling the computer. The program then prepares the machine to accept another record. The data entry program also stores the data by causing the disk drive to write the records onto the surface of the disk. This may be done after each record is entered or after several have been entered, depending on the instructions in the program.

The storage medium: The disk

The disks shown in Figure 3-12 are made of a plastic material that is coated with a metallic oxide. Disks come in two popular sizes: 5 ¼" and 3 ½". The data is recorded on the metallic coating in a code made up of magnetized spots. Because the spots that represent a character can be changed to represent another character, a disk that holds payroll data today can be used to hold inventory data tomorrow. This is an important characteristic of disks; it means that they are both **correctable** and **reusable**.

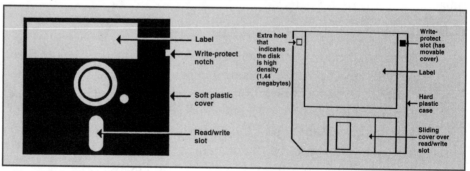

Figure 3-12. 5 ¼" and 3 ½" Disks.

The magnetic spots are very small and quite close together, and things as light as a fingerprint or a film of dust can make them unreadable. To avoid such damage, the disk is permanently sealed in a protective envelope or plastic jacket.

The 5 ¼" disk has three openings. The 3 ½" disk does not show an opening until it is placed in the drive. The shutter opens when the 3 ½" disk is engaged in the drive. On the 5 ¼" disk the round and oval openings are areas needed by the mechanisms that position the disk and read data from it or record data on it. The rectangular read/write notch is for data protection. When a data entry program issues a write instruction, the system checks to see if the notch is covered on the 5¼" disk and checks to see if the notch is open on the 3½" disk. If a protective tab has been placed over the notch on the 5¼" disk or if the notch is open on the 3½" disk, the system will issue a warning to the operator that no data keyed will be recorded. When disks contain programs or data that must not be changed, tabs are put over the notch on the 5¼" disk and the window is open on the 3½" disk for security.

Manufacturers place a label on the envelope, usually in the upper left-hand corner of the 5¼" disk. They also provide stick-on labels for recording notes about the disk to indicate what data it contains, the owner's name, and other information. When you use these labels, be careful to write on the label before placing it on the disk. Otherwise, the pencil or pen may damage the surface. If you must write on a label that is already on the disk, use a felt-tip pen and a light touch to avoid damaging it. When placing the label on the disk, do not block the shutter on the 3½" disk or touch the magnetic area on the 5¼" disk.

The disk must be handled carefully. Keep the 5¼" disk in its sleeve whenever it is not in use. Of course, the disk must never be removed from the inner envelope or it will be ruined. Do not bend it, and keep it away from any source of heat, electricity, or magnetism. Do not touch the exposed areas of the disk when you handle it; hold it at the label corner where the envelope is solid and covers the disk surface. Read the following discussion on "Prolonging the Life of Your Disks" for guidelines on how to protect your disks and extend their life.

Data addressing

The system must use a logical pattern when recording data on disk so that the data can be found quickly when it is needed. To develop a storage pattern, the surface of the disk is divided into two dimensions: **tracks** and **sectors**.

The surface is divided into a series of data recording circles called **tracks**, and each track is assigned a number. In Figure 3-12, the record that contains 3D is on Track 3, 5Z is on Track 5, and 6M is on Track 6. Thus the number of the track gives some idea of where a record is located on the surface of the disk. Many records, however, can be written around one track, so another dimension is needed to make the address more precise. To provide this, the disk is also divided into pie-shaped wedges called sectors, as shown in Figure 3-12. Now we can be more precise about the location of the record containing 3D: It is on Track 3 in Sector 2. This is its **disk address**. Of course, a sector can hold more than one record, but the addressing method has narrowed the area of the disk that must be searched to find the desired record.

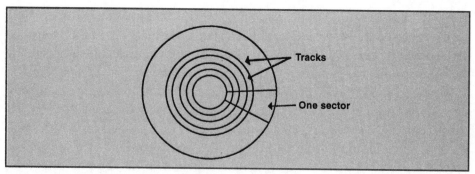

Figure 3-13. Tracks and sectors on a disk.

Although all microcomputers use the track and sector method of data addressing, different micros have slightly different ways of organizing disk space. For example, one system may require eight sectors per surface, whereas another may require nine or sixteen sectors. When a disk comes from the manufacturer, it is not prepared for use by any particular system. The user must run a program to format it, that is, to organize it to accept data from his or her particular system. See Appendix A for instructions on formatting your disk.

The disk drives

As you know, the device called the **disk drive** reads and records data onto the disk using its read/write head. The microcomputer system shown in Figure 3-14 has two drives. Some systems, however, have only one drive, and others have more than two. The drives are identified by letter. In Figure 3-14, the drive on the left is Drive A, and the one on the right is Drive B. If you have more than two drives, ask your instructor for the identification of the others.

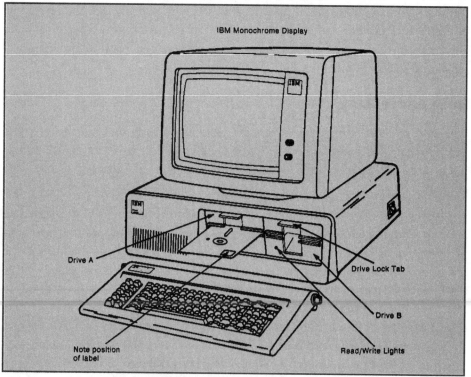

Figure 3-14. Disk drives with disk being inserted, showing Drive Lock Tab and Read/Write lights.

To insert a disk, grasp the disk so that your right thumb is on the manufacturer's label and slip the disk into the slot.

The small light on the upper portion of the drive will glow when the system is either reading data from the disk or recording (writing) data onto it. In a data entry application, the data entry program may accept a number of records before it writes them onto the disk, and the light will signal when the writing occurs. You should avoid inserting or removing a disk when the light is lit. Although some systems tolerate insertion of disks during a read or write operation, others do not. In any case, it is a bad habit to form.

Prolonging the life of your disks

Disks are durable; if handled properly, a disk will endure many hours of read/write time. One moment of carelessness, however, can destroy the programs and data a disk contains and perhaps even damage the disk so that it cannot be used again. Follow these guidelines to prolong the lives of your disks:

1. Keep the 5¼" disk in its protective sleeve when it is not in use. Form the habit of immediately removing the disk from the drive and placing it in the sleeve when you have finished with it. When you put a disk into a drive, lay its sleeve just above the drive on the CPU case. This will help to prevent you from losing sleeves and will assist you in determining which sleeve goes with which disk. When you remove the disk, the sleeve will be readily available. Keep both the 5¼" and the 3½" disks in a case. Cases come in various sizes—one disk, ten disks, and larger.

2. Do not touch the exposed areas on the surface of the 5¼" disk or open the shutter of the 3½" disk. Always handle the 5¼" disk by the label corner, placing your right thumb on the label. This right-thumb-on-the-label procedure will protect the surface and also will ensure that you insert the disk into the drive correctly. With the 3½" disk do not touch the shutter areas. Hold the opposite end from the shutter area. Do not open the shutter.

3. If possible, do not write on a label that already has been glued to the disk. If this is unavoidable, use a felt-tip pen and write with a light touch.

4. Avoid writing on the protective sleeve of the 5¼" disk. Writing on the sleeve can damage the disk it contains. It also can cause confusion because we often change sleeves from one disk to another unintentionally. Writing on the sleeve is a poor method of identifying a disk's contents.

5. Do not insert or remove the disk when the read/write light is lit. Some systems will tolerate this at some points in the read/write process, but others will destroy the disk contents and perhaps damage the disk.

6. Form the habit of checking the drives before you leave the computer. A disk left in a drive can be lost easily, especially if it is not clearly labeled.

7. Do not expose a disk to areas where there is excessive heat, strong sunlight, or an electric or magnetic field such as those created by stereos, television sets, magnets, and so forth. Remember that your system screen is a type of television set, so never lay a disk on top of it.

8. Use common sense when you handle your disk.
    *   Do not bend it,
    *   use a paper clip to fasten anything to it, or
    *   leave it in a car in the summer.

Clearly label your disks when they are ready for use. In a class situation, be sure to include your name and your class or instructor's name along with the contents of the disk on the disk label.

Occasionally, a disk or its contents will be lost despite precautions. One procedure for guarding against losing disks is to make a copy of, or to back up, the disk at appropriate intervals. Appendix A contains instructions for making a back-up copy of your disk.

STUDY QUESTIONS

1   How can data be recorded in the form of magnetized spots if the disk is made of plastic?

2   Can a data item that was previously recorded on a disk be changed?

3   Can a disk be reused for another purpose?

4   The disk is sealed in an envelope for protection, and yet there are holes in the envelope. Explain the purpose of (a) the round and oval openings and (b) the rectangular notch.

5   What is a disk track?

6   What is a sector?

7   Is the address Track 6, Sector 4, the same as Track 4, Sector 6?

8   Do all disks have the same number of sectors?

9   Why don't manufacturers format the disk into sectors rather than leaving it for the purchasers to do?

10 How can you tell if the drive is reading or recording data onto the disk at any given time?

11 Explain one technique for ensuring that you place the disk into the drive properly.

12 List the eight rules for prolonging the life of a disk.

13 How long will a disk last if it is handled with care?

14 Explain what a back-up copy is and why it is needed.

MICROCOMPUTER JOB 4:

PREPARING DISKS FOR USE

This last exercise contains instructions for preparing disks to be used in entering the data in Data Entry Jobs 1 through 25 (Chapter 4).

Experienced users may not need to practice this exercise. If in doubt, ask your instructor which exercises you should complete.

PURPOSE

The purpose of Microcomputer Job 4 is to give you experience in using the disk drives and to teach you to format and copy disks. When a disk is formatted, it is organized in the manner required by the system that will use it. Disks are frequently copied, or backed up, so that all the programs and/or data they contain will not be lost if the original disk is lost or destroyed.

In this exercise you will use a DISKCOPY program to obtain your own copy of the data entry programs. As you work through the Data Entry Jobs, you will frequently make a copy of (or back up) the disk that contains your data so that if some accident destroys one copy you will not lose the hours of work you spent creating the material it contains.

PREPARATION

For this Job you will need the following equipment:

1. A computer with a display screen.
2. A disk that contains programs that will perform the format and copy routines. This is called the Disk Operating System (DOS) disk because it contains many programs that are used to operate the computer. Ask your instructor where to obtain this disk. It may be permanently mounted inside your computer.
3. The disks that contain the data entry programs you will use to enter the data in Chapter 4 of the text. Ask your instructor where to obtain this disk.
4. Two or three work disks. These may be either new or previously used. It is not uncommon to reformat a disk that has been used on another system so that it may be used on the present system.

This exercise contains instructions for preparing a work disk on which to store the data you will be entering from the Data Entry Jobs in Chapter 4. You may choose to put the data on the computer's hard drive or on a network. Ask your instructor or consult the documentation of the software to determine which option is best for you.

If you are not using the software package, ask your instructor for material to copy when the DISKCOPY assignment is done.

Note: Either of the system programs you are about to run (the FORMAT and the DISKCOPY) will completely erase the disk being formatted or copied. Do not use a disk that contains any material you want to keep.

PROCEDURE

1. Turn to Appendix A, locate the instructions for the FORMAT command, and follow those instructions to format one of your two work disks. If you use the data entry programs available with this text, you will be given the option of either storing your data on the disk containing the programs or putting it on a separate disk. (This option is discussed in Appendix C. You need not make this choice now; simply format the disk.) If you store your data on a separate disk, that will be your data disk. If you store your data on the program disk, this can be used when you back up, or copy, your files. Prepare a label for the disk, indicating your name and perhaps the name of your class or instructor. Remember to write on the label before you affix it to the disk.

2. Turn to Appendix B and locate the instructions for the DISKCOPY command. Follow those instructions to copy the data entry programs from the disk provided by your instructor onto your program disk. The instructor's disk should have a write-protect tab over the read/write notch so that you cannot mistakenly erase it by copying the contents of the work disk over the programs. In the future, however, when you use the DISKCOPY program to backup your disks you should follow the instructions in this procedure carefully. If you insert the two disks incorrectly, the wrong disk may be copied, and the good data or programs will be lost.

   A. When the system DISKCOPY program from the DOS disk calls for the source disk, use the disk with the data entry programs you obtained from your instructor.

   B. When the program calls for the object disk, use your work disk.

   C. If a disk has not been formatted previously, the DISKCOPY program will format as it copies. A message to this effect will appear on the screen.

3. After completing the FORMAT and DISKCOPY operations, be sure that your stick-on disk labels reflect the contents of the disks as well as the identity of the owner. If labels have already been affixed and you need to add information to them, be sure to use a felt-tip pen and a gentle touch to avoid damaging the disks.

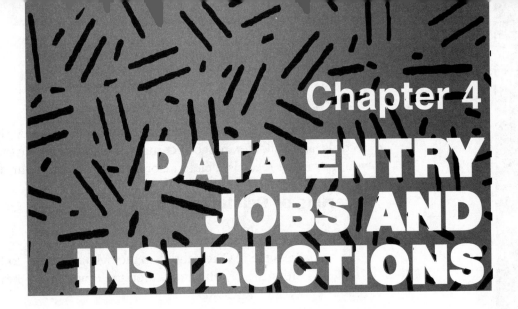

Chapter 4

DATA ENTRY JOBS AND INSTRUCTIONS

This chapter contains job instructions and data for the data entry software package that accompanies this text. The package is designed for IBM microcomputers and compatible systems. In addition to enabling data entry, it allows verification and produces work statistics such as the number of records entered, percentage of errors, and so forth. As an alternative, people with other systems may elect to use a database or word processing package for data entry. Those planning to use a database should proceed to Chapter 6 and the material on databases. Those planning to use a word processing package should proceed to Chapter 7.

We have said that procedures are an important part of any data entry task. This chapter presents the documentation for the procedures you are to follow for each Job, as well as the data for that Job. The procedures assume that you are using an IBM Personal Computer or a compatible system. Before you begin the Jobs, you should study the procedures for using the overall data entry package that is available with your text. As you begin each Job, ask your instructor or supervisor whether you are to enter all records in the Job or a portion of the records in the Job.

In these and all Jobs, it is important to keep the hand with which you are keying floating over the keys. Do not rest the heel of your hand on the frame of the keyboard. Your reach is much freer and faster when your hand hovers just above the keys. On the numeric keypad, keep your hand suspended just above the 4-5-6 line. Reach up and down for other keys as you need them, but your hand should automatically return to the home line after each reach.

Ask your instructor how to load the data entry program or read the program documentation. After you have created and named your student file, the job menu will appear. Highlight the job you wish to key and press cursor return.

The data entry program contains the following options that are available for each Job.

These options allow you to practice speed and accuracy, insert and delete records, and validate and correct input. (Ask your instructor whether or not you may insert records, delete records, and validate your data.)

Inserting or Deleting Records

1. To insert a missed record:
    A. Press the ESC key and then the right arrow key to highlight EDIT.
    B. Press cursor return and then the down arrow key to highlight INSERT RECORD.
    C. Press cursor return.
    D. Press the Up/Down arrows or Keyboard Page Up/ Page Down to move the highlight (place the highlight on the record after the missed record).
    E. Key the missed record and press cursor return.
2. To delete an inaccurate record:
    A. Press the ESC key and then the right arrow key to highlight EDIT.
    B. Press cursor return and then the down arrow key to highlight DELETE RECORD.
    C. Press cursor return.
    D. Press the UP/Down arrows or Keyboard Page Up/Page Down to move the highlight (place the highlight on the record to be deleted).
    E. Press cursor return.

Data Validation

Close the session and return to the main menu. The Job must be completed before Data Validation.

1. To validate data:
    A. Press the ESC key and then the right arrow key to highlight EDIT.
    B. Press cursor return and then the down arrow key to highlight VALIDATE INPUT.
    C. Press cursor return.
        NOTE: Each time the validation screen is accessed, validation attempts increase by one.
2. To print scores only:
    A. Press the TAB key to highlight PRINT.
    B. Press cursor return.
3. To change invalid records:
    A Press the TAB key to highlight CHANGE INVALID RECORDS.
    B. Press cursor return. (The Job screen will appear.)
    C. Key correct record.

Practice Speed and/or Accuracy

Start at the main menu.

1. To practice speed:
   A. Highlight the job you would like to practice.
   B. Press the ESC key and then the right arrow key to highlight PRACTICE.
   C. Press cursor return and then the down arrow key to highlight SPEED.
   D. Press cursor return.
   E. Enter the selected job and begin keying. The timer will beep at 1 minute.
   F. The program will display your goal and speed in strokes per minute.
2. To change yout speed goal:
   A. Follow steps 1A through 1D (unless you are already in the selected job)..
   B. Press Alt-G.
   C. Key new speed goal in highlighted area.
   D. Press cusor return.
3. To practice accuracy:
   A. Highlight the job you would like to practice.
   B. Press the ESC key and then the right arrow key to highlight PRACTICE.
   C. Press cursor return and then the down arrow key to highlight ACCURACY,
   D. Press cursor return.
   E. Enter the selected job and begin keying. The timer will beep at 1 minute.
   F. The program will display your accuracy percentage.
4. To change your accuracy goal:
   A. Follow steps 3A through 3D (unless you are already in the selected job).
   B. Press Alt-G.
   C. Key the new accuracy percentage in the highlighted area.
   D. Press cursor return.

DATA ENTRY JOB 1:
STUDENT MAJOR LIST

PURPOSES

1. To introduce you to the procedures for making selections from the menu presented by the data entry programs
2. To familiarize you with the layout of the keyboard and the general functional characteristics of the data entry programs you will be using

PREPARATION

Begin this Job and all other Jobs by thoroughly reading the Job description and Job instructions and asking questions about any points that are not clear. If you begin with a clear understanding of the Job, you will save much time that would otherwise be spent reentering data that was entered incorrectly the first time.

In reading the instructions for Job 1, you will notice that a great many services that the computer can perform for the operator are not performed for you in this Job. No keying aid is provided. Future Jobs will incorporate other keying aids, such as automatic duplication of the Major from record to record. In the first Jobs, however, you are exploring the keyboard and will do most of the entry manually.

PROCEDURE

Job 1: Student Major List

Data Entry Screen

Job #1

Student Major List

Name	Major	Record
		0

Set-Up

1. Press the CapsLock key to place the alphabetic keys in upper shift.

General Entry

1. For each student record to be entered, follow these steps:
   A. Enter the student Name—press cursor return.
   B. Enter the student's Major—press cursor return.
   C. Enter the Record Number—press cursor return.
   D. The system will accept the record and clear the screen.
2. When you are ready to terminate the entry session:
   A. Press the Escape (ESC) key and cursor return key.

   B. Highlight CLOSE SESSION—press cursor return.

NAME	MAJOR	NUMBER
Inez Allen	Business	001
Donald Baumhauer	Business	002
James Campbell	Business	003
Arnold Davenport	Business	004
Martha Effinger	Business	005
Minerva Farrell	Business	006
Robert Goldstein	Business	007
Gregory Headrick	Business	008
Rebecca Lysinger	Business	009
Arthur Madison	Business	010
George Michaels	Business	011
Dennis Montgomery	Business	012
Jacqueline Packer	Business	013
Valeria Pettinger	Business	014
Frances Pollard	Business	015
Helen Bickerstaff	English	016
Dorothy Blackwell	English	017
Jeraldine Bradley	English	018
Patricia Calvert	English	019
Douglas Chandler	English	020
Rayford Falkenberry	English	021
Douglas Fountain	English	022
Cornelius Harris	English	023
Kenneth Hatcher	English	024
Augusta Hemphill	English	025
Rudolph Holloway	English	026
Theresa Latimer	English	027
Evelyn Russell	English	028
Laura Stephenson	English	029
Diane Wadsworth	English	030
Edward Anthony	Psychology	031
Adrienne Brown	Psychology	032
Phillip Drummond	Psychology	033
Patricia Epperson	Psychology	034
Linda Frazier	Psychology	035
Rachel Jemison	Psychology	036
Cheryl Lois Lacey	Psychology	037
William MacDonald	Psychology	038
Thomas Marshman	Psychology	039
Joseph Mazlett	Psychology	040
Kay Morrison	Psychology	041
Steven Palmer	Psychology	042

NAME	MAJOR	RECORD NUMBER
Carl Pittman	Psychology	043
Martha Powell	Psychology	044
Ralph Richardson	Psychology	045
Wendell Barber	Sociology	046
William Burrows	Sociology	047
Joyce Chandler	Sociology	048
Paula Desmond	Sociology	049
Harold Fleming	Sociology	050
Jasper Fowler	Sociology	051
Milton Funderburg	Sociology	052
Julius Goodall	Sociology	053
Harry Grantland	Sociology	054
David Gregory	Sociology	055
Leon Harrison	Sociology	056
Arthur Hutchinson	Sociology	057
Penny Lightfoot	Sociology	058
David Luenberg	Sociology	059
Marvin Marshman	Sociology	060

DATA ENTRY JOB 2:
REGISTERED VOTERS LIST

PURPOSES

1. To reinforce concepts introduced in Job 1
2. To provide experience with fields that have automatic cursor advance in contrast to fields that require manual advance
3. To illustrate a keying aid that is **transparent to** (**unseen by**) the user

PREPARATION

Job 2 introduces the concept of automatic cursor advance. This means that the data entry program automatically will move the cursor to the beginning of the next field when you have filled the current field. In order for the program to be able to automatically advance the cursor, the data item to be entered into a field must always contain the same number of characters. The program then counts the number of characters that have been entered into the field and advances the cursor at the appropriate time.

In Job 2, the item you enter into the ZIP Code field will always completely fill the field. The data entry program has been designed to advance the cursor automatically to the beginning of the next field when you have keyed the last digit of the ZIP Code. You will not need to press the cursor return key. The Social Security Number field also provides the automatic cursor advance.

The Social Security number appears on the source document and on the screen as three separate fields. The data you key will completely fill each of these fields. Therefore, the program has been designed to advance the cursor automatically to the beginning of the next field when one field has been filled without waiting for the cursor return key to be pressed.

Caution: Using automatic cursor advance requires close concentration. You must not press the cursor return key when it is not required; if you do, you may skip a field. When you have entered the ZIP Code, for example, the cursor automatically advances to the Community field. If you press the cursor return key before you enter the name of the community into the Community field, the cursor will move to the Social Security Number field, and you will find yourself attempting to key a name into the Social Security Number field. Be careful not to press the cursor return key when it is not needed and to press it when it is needed.

The data entry aids provided by the data entry program save the operator many keystrokes. Another keying aid that is not seen by the operator is the way the program handles the Social Security number. The data processing programs that will read these records require the Social Security number to be a string of nine digits with no blanks or other separations between the digits. The data entry program allows the operator to enter the Social Security number as three separate fields and then puts those three fields together to form the solid string required by other programs before it records them on disk. People find it much easier to read and key numbers of four digits than numbers of nine digits, and overall entry is thus improved. A process such as this that occurs without the user's being aware of it is referred to as **transparent to the user**. You should add this phrase to your data entry vocabulary.

STUDY QUESTIONS

1   What is the advantage of automatic cursor advance?
2   What is the disadvantage of automatic cursor advance?
3   What is meant when we say that something is "transparent to the user"?

PROCEDURE

Job 2: Registered Voters List

Data Entry Screen

Job #2
Registered Voters List

ZIP	Community	SSN	Name	Record
00000		000 00 0000		0

Set-Up

1. Press the CapsLock key to place the alphabetic keys in upper shift.

General Entry

1. For each record to be entered, follow these steps:
    A. Enter the ZIP Code.
       The cursor automatically will advance to the Community field.
    B. Enter the Community name—press cursor return.
    C. Enter the Social Security Number.
       The cursor will automatically advance when each field is filled.
    D. Enter the Name—press cursor return.
    E. Enter the Record Number—press cursor return.
2. When you are ready to terminate the session:
    A. Press the Escape (ESC) key and cursor return key.
    B. Highlight CLOSE SESSION—press cursor return.

Caution

1. When working with a record in which the cursor is advanced automatically in some fields but not in others, keep alert to avoid pressing the cursor return key when it is not required. Doing so will cause a field to be skipped.

Keying Aids

1. Automatic cursor advance from
    A. ZIP Code and
    B. Social Security Number

ZIP	COMMUNITY	SOC.SEC.NO.	NAME	RECORD NUMBER
36401	Sparta	422 28 7336	William Hagood	001
		421 74 3213	Edward Hilton	002
		415 26 3075	Elizabeth Yarbrough	003
		416 88 7946	Delane Vincent	004
		416 28 7265	Hester Lawrence	005
		417 22 2863	Benny Levin	006
		421 81 3526	Terrlen Simpson	007
		419 70 0873	Phyllis Honeycutt	008
		416 84 3278	Rosalene North	009
		415 28 8963	Shirley Keith	010
		418 23 1280	Joel P. Rainey	011
		416 34 8612	Henry E. Yarbrough	012
		423 79 6413	Stanley LaMonte	013
		411 22 4467	Janice Swope	014
		416 27 5619	Ruth V. Walters	015
		421 33 4053	Cheryl H. Smith	016
		419 95 5876	Louise Townsend	017
		422 33 4940	Branda Jordon	018
36402	Castleberry	418 51 3987	Chris L. Lee	019
		421 33 4185	Martin Vandeford	020
		416 19 0726	Harry C. Pugh	021
		421 25 2317	Peter B. Acheson	022
		419 81 9925	Roy Koski	023
		418 23 8390	Helen J. Blakely	024
		415 22 3198	Dennis R. Huggins	025
		416 18 9066	Samuel Goggins	026
		419 33 3550	Willis Hambrick	027
		416 18 3109	Donna Booker	028
		416 45 5090	Leon P. Yarbrough	029
		415 92 2615	Lawrence Herrington	030
		418 36 6869	Edith Lee	031
		416 22 9845	Ralph Montgomery	032
		418 52 4893	Kenneth Buzby	033

36403 Evergreen	417 48 9329	Althea Denise Cook	034
	416 19 8544	Martha Hatter	035
	416 14 5366	Tracey M. Gill	036
	426 28 2613	Tina Ramsden	037
	421 52 7254	Charlotte Jenkins	038
	416 18 5097	Dean Lawrence	039
	422 77 6824	Victor C. Hagood	040
	417 23 7955	Scott Moorer	041
	421 85 1564	Leanne Taylor	042
	426 51 4466	Barbara Seals	043
	414 12 3428	George Sload	044
	416 41 5892	Patricia Pollard	045
	416 89 3402	Arthur Madison	046
	415 33 2640	Daniel R. Huggins	047
	419 67 6528	Hugh G. Hagood	048
	421 91 5224	Alan Wilhite	049
	418 51 1328	Gladys Hollifield	050
	419 23 1751	Dorothy Kay Meeks	051
	416 48 2555	Annette Paulson	052
	426 22 2092	Lillian Inez Odum	053
	416 54 5452	Elaine Davis	054
	415 92 9812	Laura Jean Huggins	055
	425 67 7592	Debbie Wilkerson	056
36404 Trumbauerville	421 36 9745	Phillip Fountain	057
	421 33 4521	Douglas Keplinger	058
	416 86 2390	Charles Bullard	059
	412 39 4732	Theresa Littlefield	060
	415 33 9749	Russell Sanders	061
	416 44 3287	Sigmund Wadsworth	062
	415 23 5426	Steven Marshman	063
	414 57 8236	James E. Larkin	064
	421 34 8623	Deborah Paulson	065
	424 22 1196	Alan Chaukey	066
	423 22 5411	Mark North	067
	417 22 9749	David Hacker	068

PURPOSE

1. To gain practice with automatic duplication in a new format

PREPARATION

As you examine the data in Job 3, you will see that it is an extension of Job 1. In Job 3, however, the data entry program will perform automatic duplication of the student's major for you. Compare the amount of time required to enter the data in Job 3 with the amount required in Job 1.

PROCEDURE

Job 3: Student Major List

Data Entry Screen

Job #3
Student Major List (version 2)

| Name | Major | Record |

Set-Up

1. Press the CapsLock key to place the alphabetic keys in upper shift.

General Entry

1. For each record to be entered, follow these steps:
    A. Enter the Name—press cursor return.
    B. IF the data item in the Major field is the same as the item on the last record,
       (1) Press cursor return.

       OR

       (1) Place the cursor at the first position in the Major field.
       (2) Enter the new Major.
       (3) Use the space bar to erase any trailing letters remaining in the field from the previous Major.
       (4) Press cursor return.

    C. Enter the Record Number.

2. When you are ready to end the session:
    A. Press the Escape (ESC) key and cursor return key.
    B. Highlight CLOSE SESSION—press cursor return.

Caution

1. Remember to erase trailing characters when changing the Major field. *Engineering* keyed over *Data Processing* leaves *Engineeringsing* unless the trailing characters are erased with the space bar or DEL key.

Keying Aids

1. Automatic duplication of Major field

NAME	MAJOR	RECORD NUMBER
Thomas Acker	Biology	001
Rene Agee	Biology	002
William Alexander	Biology	003
Thomas A Anderson	Biology	004
James Bailey	Biology	005
C Richard Barnham	Biology	006
Laura Blaylock	Biology	007
Michael Boutwell	Biology	008
James Cox	Biology	009
Harold T Cunningham	Biology	010
Alfonzo Drake	Biology	011
Charles Hagood	Biology	012
Roberta Holland	Biology	013
Harlan Keeton	Biology	014
Mary Ann Shackelford	Biology	015
Ronald Tucker	Biology	016
Lorraine Wadsworth	Biology	017
Paul Warren	Biology	018
John Allmon	Chemistry	019
David Ballentine	Chemistry	020
John Bearden	Chemistry	021
Rufus Blecher	Chemistry	022
Sidney R Clements	Chemistry	023
Richard Cohn	Chemistry	024
Don L Cooper	Chemistry	025
Teresa Easter	Chemistry	026
Monty Elliott	Chemistry	027
John Fiorella	Chemistry	028
Ross Galloway	Chemistry	029
Edward Gilmore	Chemistry	030
Rosemary Hill	Chemistry	031
Jim Jackson	Chemistry	032
James Lewis	Chemistry	033
Carolyn Mack	Chemistry	034
Felton Perry	Chemistry	035
Edward Schrimsher	Chemistry	036
David Turner	Chemistry	037
Millie Willingham	Chemistry	038
Robin Carlisle	Data Processing	039
Christopher Doekel	Data Processing	040

Bruce Franklin	Data Processing	041
Robert Gayles	Data Processing	042
Adam Hancock	Data Processing	043
Patricia Holland	Data Processing	044
Lena Jeffries	Data Processing	045
David Kaetz	Data Processing	046
Howard King	Data Processing	047
Laura Latta	Data Processing	048
Joyce Mitchell	Data Processing	049
Virgil Pearson	Data Processing	050
Curtis Ragland	Data Processing	051
Henry Robertson	Data Processing	052
James Scott	Data Processing	053
Byron C Shaw	Data Processing	054
Martin Street	Data Processing	055
Patrick Thomas	Data Processing	056
E Gene Thrasher	Data Processing	057
Ruby B Underwood	Data Processing	058
Pauline Vaughn	Data Processing	059
Curtis Walls	Data Processing	060
Keith Zinder	Data Processing	061
Irene Aaron	Engineering	062
George Alexander	Engineering	063
Charles Bankhead	Engineering	064
Mark Bolan	Engineering	065
A J Brown	Engineering	066
Wvan Capps	Engineering	067
Martin Chandler	Engineering	068
Sue Cook	Engineering	069
Cliff Doss	Engineering	070
Julia Elgin	Engineering	071
Jerome Flint	Engineering	072
Thomas Freeman	Engineering	073
Jean Goodwin	Engineering	074
Leon Hanes	Engineering	075
Russell Harris	Engineering	076
Fred Hollis	Engineering	077
Yvonne Johnson	Engineering	078
James Kirk	Engineering	079
Annie Lowe	Engineering	080
Perry Morgan	Engineering	081

DATA ENTRY JOB 4:
LIBRARY LIST

PURPOSES

1. To provide practice with material requiring use of the CapsLock key
2. To illustrate handling of data items that are longer than the fields provided for them

PREPARATION

Notice that the data to be entered in Job 4 is different in two ways from the data in the preceding Jobs. First, one field is in all capital letters. Second, some of the items (book titles) are longer than the field provided to hold them.

When the contents of a field will always consist of capital letters, the data entry program can be designed to accept small letters from the keyboard and change them to capitals as an aid to the operator. In order to become familiar with the CapsLock key, however, in this Job you will do the shifting manually.

Another difference between the data in this Job and the data in previous Jobs is that in this Job the data items are longer than the fields allowed for them. This situation was considered, however, when the record layouts were planned. When the person designing the record plans the storage for a data item, he or she usually leaves enough space to hold the longest item that will occur. Thus when the field for the amount of an employee's pay is planned, the designer knows the highest pay in the organization and can provide sufficient space in the Pay field to hold that amount.

In a case such as this library list, however, it is not practical to leave enough space to hold the longest title of any book in the library. Allowing that much space would result in a great deal of unused space in most records, and storage space is expensive. Instead, the planner assigns a field length that is long enough to hold the majority of the data items that will be entered. Items longer than the allotted field are simply chopped short and made to fit.

If you examine Record Number 1 in Job 4, you will see that the title of the book is missing one letter. Enough of the title remains, however, to ensure that it will not be confused with another title. Other records (32, 33, 39, etc.) also have shortened titles. In this practice data, a few titles are still too long to fit into the Title field. A warning beep will sound to alert you when the field is full and you are still keying. When the beep sounds, move to the next field by pressing the cursor return.

Cutting titles short may not seem to provide enough information, but the person who designed the record has considered the amount of data needed, and we now follow this plan.

PROCEDURE

Job 4: Library List

Data Entry Screen

Job #4
Library List
    Number: 00000   Author:
    Name: Record: 0
    Title:

Set-Up

1. No special preparation required.

General Entry

1. For each record to be entered, follow these steps:
   A. IF this is the first record or the Student Number and Name are to be changed,
      (1) Enter the Student Number—cursor return.
      (2) Enter the Name (shifting for capitals).
      (3) Erase any unwanted characters.
      (4) Cursor return.

      OR

      (1) Cursor return to accept the Student Number.
      (2) Cursor return to accept the Name.
2. Press the CapsLock key to place the alphabetic keys in upper shift.
3. Enter the data into the Title field—cursor return.
   A. The title may be too long for the field, so the list may be abbreviated
   B. Press cursor return when you have keyed the last character of the title.
4. Press CapsLock to return the keyboard to lower shift.
5. Enter the Author—cursor return.
6. Enter the Record Number—cursor return.

Cautions:

1. Keep alert when using the CapsLock key. It must be engaged and released at the correct time. Capitals and lowercase letters are represented by different codes when stored inside the system, and you cannot routinely substitute one for the other.
2. When some items fill a field and others do not, you must be even more alert than usual about when to use and when not to use cursor return.

Keying Aids

1. Automatic duplication of Student Number and Name

STUDENT NUMBER	NAME	TITLE	AUTHOR	RECORD NUMBER
09123	Blackwood Robert	WINSLOW HOMER AMERICAS OLD MASTE	Beam P C	001
09123	Blackwood Robert	FAULKNER THE MAJOR YEARS	Backman M	002
09937	Morton Gloria	PRINCIPLES OF RENAL PHYSIOLOGY	Smith H W	003
09937	Morton Gloria	PHYSIOLOGY OF THE KIDNEY AND BOD	Pitts R F	004
12880	Cole Louise	TREASURE ISLAND	Stevenson R L	005
12880	Cole Louise	THE AMERICAN DRAMA SINCE 1918	Krutch J W	006
12880	Cole Louise	THE LEARNER IN EDUCATION FOR THE	Towle C	007
12880	Cole Louise	SOCIAL WELFARE INSTITUTIONS	Zaid M N	008
16895	Ellis Bonnie	THE REAL JESUS HOW HE LIVED AND	Cassels L	009
16895	Ellis Bonnie	THE JOY OF CHILDREN	Buck P S	010
20073	Fox William	WRITE AND SELL IT	Marple A C	011
20073	Fox William	SIX MODERN AMERICAN PLAYS	Star P	012
20073	Fox William	SHAKESPEARES COMEDIES	Perry A	013
20073	Fox William	SHAKESPEARE AND HIS COMEDIES	Brown J	014
20073	Fox William	STORIES FROM SHAKESPEARE	Chute M G	015
21191	Ragland Patricia	TWENTIETH CENTURY MUSIC	Bauer M	016
21191	Ragland Patricia	THE COMPLETE BOOK OF 20TH CENTUR	Ewen D	017
21191	Ragland Patricia	AARON COPLAND	Berger A V	018
23363	Paul Juanita	ECONOMICS OF POLLUTION	Brown G R	019
23363	Paul Juanita	COACHING ATHLETICS AND PSYCHOLOG	Singer R H	020
24067	Armstrong Jennifer	WALT WHITMAN	Allen G W	021
24067	Armstrong Jennifer	THE CIVIL WAR	Street J H	022
24067	Armstrong Jennifer	THE WAR BETWEEN THE STATES	Mullinax H	023
25099	Moore Marvin	PATIENTHOOD IN THE MENTAL HOSPIT	Lewinson D J	024
25099	Moore Marvin	THE ELECTRIC KOOL AID ACID TEST	Wolfe T	025
25099	Moore Marvin	BEHAVIOR MODIFICATION IN MENTAL	Gardner W I	026
25099	Moore Marvin	BEHAVIOR THERAPY TECHNIQUES	Wolpe J	027
25099	Moore Marvin	BEHAVIOR DISORDERS PERSPECTIVES	Milton O	028
25099	Moore Marvin	PRINCIPLES OF BEHAVIOR MODIFICAT	Bandura A	029
25099	Moore Marvin	THE PRACTICE OF BEHAVIOR THERAPY	Wolpe A	030
25099	Moore Marvin	CASE STUDIES IN BEHAVIOR MODIFIC	Ullman L P	031
25099	Moore Marvin	BEHAVIOR MODIFICATION IN CHILD T	Browning R M	032
25639	White Ronald	PERSPECTIVES IN ECOLOGICAL THEOR	Margalef R	033
25639	White Ronald	FIELD BIOLOGY AND ECOLOGY	Benton A H	034
27103	Wilkinson Jeffrey	CRITICAL APPROACHES TO AMERICAN	Browne R B	035
27103	Wilkinson Jeffrey	THE TWENTIES FORDS FLAPPERS AND	Mowry G E	036
27103	Wilkinson Jeffrey	ONLY YESTERDAY	Allen F L	037
27103	Wilkinson Jeffrey	HER MAJESTY THE QUEEN THE STORY	Cathcard H	038
28414	Ford Ronald	THE ISRAEL ARMY	Luttwak E	039
31128	Rhoades Kenny	PHOTOSYNTHESIS	Asimov I	040

31128	Rhoades Kenny	THE ART OF COUNSELING	May R	041
39453	Lavender Dennis	FUNDAMENTALS OF NURSING	Fuerst E V	042
39453	Lavender Dennis	THE DAY LINCOLN WAS SHOT	Bishop J A	043
39453	Lavender Dennis	CARDIAC ARREST AND RESUSCITATION	Stephenson H E	044
40606	Woodward Joseph	NATHANIEL HAWTHORNE	Martin T	045
40606	Woodward Joseph	HAWTHORNE A CRITICAL STUDY	Waggoner H H	046
40725	Tolbert Lovenia	HELPING THE BATTERED CHILD AND H	Kempe C	047
40725	Tolbert Lovenia	VIOLENCE AGAINST CHILDREN	Gil D G	048
40991	Howard Teresa Diane	GENERAL CHEMISTRY	Selwood P W	049
40991	Howard Teresa Diane	ART OF FAULKNERS NOVELS	Swiggart P	050
40991	Howard Teresa Diane	THE NOVELS OF JOHN STEINBECK	Levant H	051
41058	Evans Terry Glenn	SOME CLINICAL APPROACHES TO PSYC	Burd S	052
41058	Evans Terry Glenn	POWER OF WORDS	Chase S	053
42670	Hawthorne Solomon	STRUCTURE OF ARITHMETIC	Minnick J H	054
42670	Hawthorne Solomon	BASIC MATHEMATICS REVIEW	Cooley J A	055
42670	Hawthorne Solomon	FIRST COURSE IN ALGEBRA FOR COLLE	Adams L J	056
42670	Hawthorne Solomon	INTRODUCTION TO COLLEGE ALGEBRA	Hart W L	057
42670	Hawthorne Solomon	ELEMENTARY SET THEORY	Leung K	058
42879	Smith Albert L	SHAW	Ohmann R M	059
42879	Smith Albert L	COMPLETE PLAYS WITH PREFACES	Carpenter C A	060
42879	Smith Albert L	BERNARD SHAW AND THE ART OF DEST	Carpenter C A	061

Notes on Jobs 5-10

These Jobs teach the reaches to the numeric keys. The way you enter numeric data will be determined by whether the source document contains all numeric data or mixed data and by the type of keyboard you are using. If you are using a machine with a keypunch or data entry keyboard, the numerics are the upper shift of the alphabetic keys under your right hand. To enter a numeric character rather than a letter, either (1) you must use the correct shift key, or (2) the program controlling the machine must place the key in numeric shift. Your Job instructions or your instructor should tell you which approach to take.

This approach may vary from one Job to another depending on the layout of the Job to be done. If the machine has a standard typewriter keyboard, the numerics are on the upper row of keys. These keys are used to enter data that is all numeric. You may also be using a microcomputer or another device with numeric keys in two places: (1) along the top row of the central keyboard, where they are the lower characters on the keys, and (2) on a numeric keypad located to the right of the central keyboard.

When your keyboard has numeric keys in two locations, the type of data you are entering will determine which set of numeric keys you use. When the data being entered is totally numeric, as in Jobs 5 through 10, use the numeric keypad. The numeric keypad is designed to place the numeric keys within the reach of one hand. This is done both to increase keying speed and to allow operators to use their other hand to keep their place in the data being keyed.

If your data contains both letters and numbers, it is most efficient to use the numeric keys along the upper row of the central keyboard to enter numeric data, even though you also have a numeric keypad. This is true because when you move your right hand from the home line of the central keyboard to the home line of the keypad you can easily place your hand in the wrong position, and incorrect placement usually results in numerous mistakes before it is detected.

As you work through the numeric Jobs, place a ruler, sheet of paper, or some other marker on the source document. When you finish a line, move the marker to the next line with the hand you are not using to enter data. When entering numeric data that is especially hard to read, you may want to use your index finger as a pointer on the line being keyed.

In these and all exercises, it is important to keep the hand with which you are keying floating over the keys. Do not rest the heel of your hand on the frame of the keyboard. Your reach is much freer and faster when your hand hovers just above the keys. On the numeric keypad, keep your hand suspended just above the 4-5-6 line. Reach up and down for other keys as you need them, but your hand should automatically return to the home line after each reach.

As you examine the data in the exercises, notice that the first Job begins with the **home keys** (4-5-6) and then adds reaches down to the 1-2-3 line. The second Job again begins with 4-5-6 but adds reaches up to the 7-8-9 line. The following Jobs use various mixtures of the three lines for practice.

The beginning Jobs place digits into groups of two so that they are easy to read and remember as you key. Later Jobs group them into fours to give you practice keying longer numbers and to change the rhythm of keying. In a working situation, you will key numbers much longer than four digits, but you can read and enter these as smaller groups for your convenience.

For example, look ahead to Job 10. It contains numbers of four digits. Many people cannot read and remember a four-digit number long enough to key it, so they simply read and key it as a series of two smaller groups. Instead of trying to remember the first product code as 4798, they form the habit of reading it as "forty-seven," followed by "ninety-eight." They read the second product code as "ninety-four," "fifty-two."

Unfortunately, many forms used to capture, or collect, data do not consider the needs of the data entry operator. We can improve the keying job by breaking the numbers apart mentally into smaller groups, as above.

After you have worked through the first group of Jobs, the grading program provided to your instructor or supervisor may reveal that you need more practice on some reaches. Your supervisor or instructor will guide you in determining which of the numeric exercises you should enter to build your keying speeds.

The purpose of the numeric Jobs is to teach you to key digits rapidly and accurately. Therefore, the Jobs are designed to allow you to concentrate on the numeric keys. The software program will generate the record numbers so that you need not break your concentration on the practice data to enter record numbers.

These data entry programs will also provide a service called automatic record advance, which is like the automatic cursor advance you experienced in earlier assignments. When you have keyed the last digit into the last position in a record, or when the program has generated the last character (as in the ones with the Record Numbers), the data entry program will accept the record and clear the screen without requiring you to press the cursor return key. In Jobs 5 through 10, for example, you will enter the digits you are leaving and then press cursor return after you have entered the last digit. Next, the program will generate the Record Number, insert it into the record, and automatically advance the record. The automatic generation of record numbers and use of automatic record advance will allow you to concentrate on pressing the correct number keys.

THE STANDARD ENTRY SCREEN. In the numeric Jobs, the entry screens are designed to display data. They also are designed to discourage the operator from reading the screen. One line appears for all the practice data, which will merge on entry and form a display that is difficult to read. Whether you are entering the two-digit numbers in Job 5 or the four-digit numbers in Job 10, a finished record will display as one long number. Do not look at the screen during these exercises: Keep your eyes on the source document. If you become confused, the record number is clearly displayed, and you can tell from it whether you are keying on the correct line. If it is absolutely necessary to check the data you have keyed, it is readable but intentionally not clear. The screen for all jobs looks like the one below. The Job Numbers, of course, will vary.

Job #5

Numerical Exercises

Number	Record
000000000000000000000000000000	1

When you have finished keying all except the final digit of Record 1, the screen will look like the one below.

Job #5

Numerical Exercises

Number	Record
54464465565554654656454546565444564	1

When you enter the final digit, press the cursor return. The record will be accepted, the Number area on the screen will clear, and the Record Number field will display the digit 2.

PURPOSES

1. To introduce the numeric keypad home line (4, 5, and 6)
2. To introduce the 1, 2, 3 reaches
3. To illustrate automatic data generation
4. To introduce automatic record advance
5. To introduce the use of the NumLock key

PREPARATION

In examining the data for Job 5, you will see that it first drills on the home keys (4, 5, and 6) and then adds reaches down to the 1, 2, and 3 keys. Numbers are two digits long so that they can be remembered easily.

Use a ruler, sheet of paper, or some other line marker to keep your place in the data. When using the keypad, move the marker along with your left hand as you key with your right hand.

In Job 5, you will be concentrating on the digits in your assignment data. To avoid interrupting your concentration on keying the assignment data, the data entry program automatically will generate Record Numbers for you; you will not enter them. Notice that this data is generated automatically rather than copied from a previous record.

When you have entered the last digit of a line and pressed the cursor return, the system will accept the record and the screen will clear automatically. You will not key the Record Number. The data entry program will provide an automatic record advance service.

In this Job, you will be locking the keypad into numeric shift by pressing the NumLock key. As you know, it is possible to have the data entry program go into numeric shift automatically when a numeric field is to be entered. In these numeric Jobs, however, you will use the NumLock key to lock the keypad into numeric shift and then to unlock it. This will give you practice in using the function in these Jobs in which an error is less likely.

PROCEDURE

Job 5: Numerical Exercises (4, 5, and 6 with 1, 2, and 3)

After you have selected Job 5, the standard screen for all numeric exercises (described in "Notes on Jobs 5-10" on page 90) will appear.

Set-Up

1. Place the keypad in numeric shift by pressing NumLock.
2. Place your hand above the numeric keypad in the home position:
   A. Forefinger hovers over 4 and will reach down to 1.
   B. Middle finger hovers over 5 and will reach down to 2.
   C. Ring finger hovers over 6 and will reach down to 3.

General Entry

1. For each line to be entered:
   A. Enter the line—auto advance provided.
2. When you are ready to terminate the entry session:
   A. Press NumLock to release the keyboard from numeric shift.
   B. Press the Escape (ESC) key and cursor return.
   C. Highlight CLOSE SESSION—press cursor return.

Keying Aids

1. Automatic generation of Record Number
2. Automatic record advance

```
54  46  44  65  56  55  54  65  46  56  45  45  46  56  54  44  56  45
45  44  54  44  54  64  66  54  55  44  46  46  44  65  55  66  66  46
64  56  54  65  56  55  56  65  44  54  45  46  64  44  56  56  46  45
56  65  65  65  54  44  45  64  64  46  64  44  46  46  45  44  46  55
44  45  64  56  46  65  66  64  46  45  65  45  46  54  45  46  64  56

33  54  46  63  36  45  46  63  66  63  36  56  54  46  63  56  63  53
55  54  46  63  54  63  44  54  53  65  44  65  36  33  45  34  64  45
54  43  55  65  63  36  36  43  45  63  35  36  44  64  65  44  43  46
45  34  46  64  56  33  64  66  34  46  44  36  33  65  63  45  65  53
36  65  43  65  34  35  55  34  64  63  65  66  34  66  43  34  44  45

45  56  63  52  45  52  36  25  45  46  36  25  63  52  45  46  63  52
65  66  25  33  25  66  65  53  64  35  46  43  64  46  24  56  64  63
46  36  52  64  23  66  34  25  25  46  45  22  34  36  63  44  66  56
53  44  43  54  36  55  63  45  52  56  66  65  35  56  52  25  22  56
64  52  56  24  22  62  66  25  46  42  46  26  54  63  24  65  56  22

45  46  41  45  52  63  41  45  46  63  25  46  41  45  45  46  36  25
56  24  65  21  16  42  11  42  65  31  44  63  22  14  35  25  24  26
22  25  34  55  41  54  12  31  41  22  55  52  32  12  44  45  21  41
52  13  22  63  52  41  23  35  46  56  65  63  14  33  55  63  31  16
24  23  12  34  63  24  45  33  32  26  23  45  24  65  45  56  65  55

62  14  53  56  44  16  53  16  63  45  52  13  14  53  61  11  26  12
36  63  63  42  55  15  23  52  12  14  24  42  22  33  11  35  14  52
14  21  66  56  65  36  35  24  33  35  21  12  11  46  32  41  33  16
24  42  56  65  34  62  65  56  62  63  41  52  62  43  51  15  25  61
41  25  63  52  14  36  61  43  52  51  53  62  16  35  24  45  64  56
```

DATA ENTRY JOB 6:
NUMERICAL EXERCISE (4, 5, 6 WITH 7, 8, 9)

PURPOSES

1. To practice the numeric keypad home line (4, 5, 6)
2. To introduce the 7, 8, 9 reaches
3. To illustrate automatic data generation
4. To illustrate automatic record advance
5. To practice the use of the Numeric Lock feature

PREPARATION

As you examine the data for Job 6, you will see that it first drills on the home keys of the numeric keypad (4, 5, and 6) and then adds reaches up to the 7, 8, and 9 keys. As in Job 5, numbers are two digits long so that they can be remembered easily.

Use a line marker to keep your place in the data. Depending on how your source document will be positioned, it is sometimes more convenient to place the marker above rather than beneath the line to be keyed.

As in Job 5, Record Numbers will be generated automatically to help you maintain your concentration, and records will be advanced automatically.

PROCEDURE

Job 6: Numerical Exercises (4, 5, and 6 with 7, 8, and 9)

After you have selected Job 6, the standard screen for numeric exercises will appear.

Set-Up

1. Place the keypad in numeric shift by pressing NumLock.
2. Place your right hand above the numeric keypad in the home position:
   A. Forefinger hovers over 4 and will reach up to 7.
   B. Middle finger hovers over 5 and will reach up to 8.
   C. Ring finger hovers over 6 and will reach up to 9.

General Entry

1. For each line to be entered:
   A. Enter the line—auto advance provided.
2. When you are ready to terminate the entry session:
   A. Press NumLock to release the keyboard from numeric shift.
   B. Press the Escape (ESC) key and the cursor return key.
   C. Highlight CLOSE SESSION—press the cursor return key.

Keying Aids

1. Automatic generation of Record Number
2. Automatic record advance

```
45  56  44  45  44  44  65  45  55  45  65  54  54  64  64  46  55  44
54  66  65  54  46  54  55  44  46  55  55  66  44  54  56  65  64  46
44  46  54  66  56  65  56  46  46  55  44  64  44  65  55  56  65  46
46  64  46  55  54  65  66  56  66  44  66  54  44  54  55  65  44  55
66  45  56  54  66  56  55  45  46  65  54  45  44  66  55  56  66  54

45  44  47  46  74  46  47  45  46  64  54  74  47  44  45  46  47  56
74  44  55  65  45  66  44  47  74  44  75  44  46  44  64  66  74  54
47  55  46  64  47  47  57  76  57  74  54  74  57  67  66  46  46  56
47  67  76  55  54  75  55  67  54  55  75  66  56  45  65  74  54  67
66  64  57  74  44  47  45  74  64  45  54  56  75  56  54  56  75  77

54  56  47  58  56  58  47  58  45  56  58  46  47  58  47  74  58  85
84  55  44  76  87  78  68  76  65  57  85  86  55  64  74  85  84  48
88  84  44  88  54  58  68  77  66  56  66  56  84  64  77  88  74  85
77  45  77  64  86  67  56  56  76  64  77  66  48  66  58  77  86  54
54  57  54  56  47  78  67  76  88  56  58  66  57  54  45  57  44  55

46  65  69  58  47  69  47  74  58  85  69  96  46  48  56  59  69  96
67  58  69  47  87  49  97  96  56  87  78  67  94  75  45  96  89  96
88  95  94  76  97  94  55  95  98  69  45  76  58  98  77  58  69  56
65  45  74  69  97  44  98  59  64  94  95  96  68  44  46  79  47  96
65  66  67  78  59  58  44  79  95  46  57  49  95  77  47  97  89  85

45  69  67  74  49  68  65  48  95  94  49  87  46  49  77  95  86  85
74  59  44  74  79  55  98  86  65  54  64  69  79  89  77  69  59  74
56  85  69  75  68  49  88  89  87  44  79  46  64  84  54  85  65  44
49  97  88  64  54  79  75  44  46  56  87  75  58  77  88  59  88  49
89  55  97  46  54  45  49  59  49  76  97  44  88  84  45  48  84  68
```

DATA ENTRY JOB 7:
NUMERICAL EXERCISE (1 THROUGH 9)

PURPOSES

1. To practice the digits already learned (1, 2, 3, 4, 5, 6, 7, 8, 9)
2. To illustrate automatic data generation
3. To illustrate automatic record advance

PREPARATION

As you examine the data for Job 7, you will see that it contains no digits that you have not keyed before. In this exercise, you will practice the reaches previously learned. As before, you will find a line marker helpful. Helps provided by the program are automatic record number and automatic record advance.

PROCEDURE

Job 7: Numerical Exercises (1 through 9 keys)

After you have selected Job 7, the standard screen for numeric exercises will appear.

Set-Up

1. Place the keypad in numeric shift by pressing NumLock.
2. Place your right hand over the home keys. Remember not to rest your hand on the frame of the keyboard, or you will reduce your keying speed.

General Entry

1. For each line to be entered:
   A. Enter the line—auto advance provided.
2. When you are ready to terminate the entry session:
   A. Press NumLock to release the keyboard from numeric shift.
   B. Press the Escape (ESC) key and the cursor return key.
   C. Highlight CLOSE SESSION—cursor return.

Keying Aids

1. Automatic generation of Record Number
2. Automatic record advance

```
45  44  46  65  44  45  56  55  54  44  45  47  56  65  63  46  47  63
45  55  54  46  54  63  45  65  45  47  74  63  45  65  46  47  63  46
65  54  54  64  64  46  55  44  56  64  63  47  56  46  53  57  73  47
46  63  47  56  46  54  63  36  74  56  36  74  56  46  54  37  73  74
65  56  64  55  64  44  56  63  74  47  36  54  64  37  73  74  36  54

74  63  74  47  55  37  75  77  63  34  67  55  44  54  53  67  43  56
75  34  43  35  66  73  65  44  45  64  74  73  63  75  66  55  76  74
63  44  74  66  37  55  37  73  76  75  47  64  46  35  36  43  34  76
73  47  57  35  54  34  33  55  73  63  45  54  33  66  34  37  64  37
64  43  36  67  73  76  53  47  56  53  64  43  36  67  73  76  53  47

43  27  73  28  42  32  35  65  78  46  47  73  54  85  64  62  77  66
46  38  83  27  42  66  56  58  26  62  25  78  74  34  53  88  22  37
74  52  42  87  84  74  28  87  22  77  48  88  84  65  63  34  22  53
24  27  34  83  65  25  37  74  33  27  53  77  56  48  78  43  74  57
68  63  87  87  55  72  44  24  63  68  56  37  75  28  62  42  43  26

28  15  64  43  34  66  28  72  18  65  47  16  48  82  93  16  84  51
14  15  22  84  35  84  82  74  94  54  87  17  18  69  51  94  54  76
34  55  78  55  62  32  22  51  24  44  52  81  57  54  86  63  98  64
63  32  55  53  45  41  82  95  46  66  59  22  35  46  57  49  38  34
83  67  99  93  65  32  92  17  26  48  58  37  74  66  87  67  52  38
```

DATA ENTRY JOB 8:

NUMERICAL EXERCISE (THE 0 [ZERO] REACH)

PURPOSES

1. To introduce the zero reach
2. To practice the use of the Numeric Lock feature

PREPARATION

Job 8 introduces the final digit: the 0 (zero). The reach to the zero depends on the layout of the keyboard you are using. On a numeric keypad, you may have one of two layouts:

1. If the zero key is above the 3 key, reach up with your ring finger.
2. If the zero key is below and to the right of the 1 key, press it with your thumb.

The zero reach is not difficult, but it does require practice. As before, you will find a line marker helpful.

PROCEDURE

Job 8: Numerical Exercises (Adding the 0 [zero] Reach)

After you have selected Job 8, the standard screen for numeric exercises will appear.

Set-Up

1. Place the keypad in numeric shift by pressing NumLock.
2. Place your right hand over the home keys. Remember not to rest your hand on the frame of the keyboard, or you will reduce your keying speed.

General Entry

1. For each line to be entered:
   A. Enter the line—auto advance provided.
2. When you are ready to terminate the entry session:
   A. Press NumLock to release the keyboard from numeric shift.
   B. Press the Escape (ESC) key and the cursor return key.
   C. Highlight CLOSE SESSION—cursor return.

Keying Aids

1. Automatic generation of Record Number
2. Automatic record advance
3. Warning beep when nonnumeric data is entered in numeric field

```
45  46  63  60  63  64  65  45  36  35  60  06  64  36  45  60  63  64
64  63  60  65  45  54  64  35  46  60  63  54  52  45  53  14  30  60
46  63  06  65  45  53  52  41  45  63  60  63  30  06  36  03  56  60
34  42  55  60  43  45  53  32  45  06  51  32  63  16  32  13  46  60
50  20  36  32  43  45  53  32  30  06  36  45  12  42  31  34  14  44

11  52  15  52  53  20  40  12  05  32  26  30  40  55  54  11  14  36
32  20  16  05  43  24  55  02  20  43  42  36  63  04  44  41  46  36
66  42  56  13  65  33  53  51  60  50  41  64  04  42  52  63  20  64
56  36  34  52  64  53  02  30  36  21  64  11  03  42  52  63  20  64
56  36  34  52  64  53  02  30  36  21  64  11  03  14  60  13  34  24

46  64  65  69  65  96  46  69  58  64  47  45  64  69  96  36  64  69
46  41  54  52  56  63  64  69  58  47  85  96  46  56  64  69  68  96
68  51  47  24  53  35  14  93  11  44  54  14  80  75  42  39  05  11
46  38  09  46  93  64  72  59  21  13  78  79  91  96  29  42  35  54
16  89  68  18  69  34  06  25  18  16  01  38  49  90  89  57  28  84

21  44  70  16  20  72  77  78  82  75  42  18  04  29  77  40  24  30
82  15  38  39  26  61  52  48  83  89  95  02  08  24  17  96  91  70
58  48  60  86  24  96  71  49  25  53  05  83  89  07  81  54  87  75
26  63  34  95  17  88  38  23  15  10  12  47  71  66  24  68  59  27
75  93  85  48  95  52  40  27  62  17  99  63  50  01  16  25  38  80

99  18  56  68  94  95  59  83  50  62  50  35  12  51  12  96  86  90
17  10  45  78  38  31  16  35  18  65  95  97  06  00  84  03  08  15
11  66  10  23  24  42  09  34  12  96  45  67  91  24  06  94  04  71
53  82  65  59  82  28  20  52  58  34  96  00  24  17  08  12  68  06
30  33  44  38  79  18  90  01  42  65  62  70  87  62  91  20  77  61
```

DATA ENTRY JOB 9:
NUMERICAL EXERCISE (THE 0, 3, 6, and 9 REACH)

PURPOSES

1. To practice all digits and emphasize the 0 reach
2. To provide experience entering longer numbers

PREPARATION

Examining the data for Job 9 reveals that it stresses the correct fingering for the zero reach. This reach is not difficult but does require practice. As always, you will find a line marker helpful. Helps provided by the program are automatic record number and automatic record advance.

PROCEDURE

Job 9: Numerical Exercises (Longer Numbers Emphasizing the 0 Reach)

After you have selected Job 9, the standard screen for numeric exercises will appear.

Set-Up

1. Place the keypad in numeric shift by pressing NumLock.
2. Place your right hand over the home keys. Remember not to rest your hand on the frame of the keyboard, or you will reduce your keying speed.

General Entry

1. For each line to be entered:
   A. Enter the line—auto advance provided.
2. When you are ready to terminate the entry session:
   A. Press NumLock to release the keyboard from numeric shift.
   B. Press the Escape (ESC) key and the cursor return key.
   C. Highlight CLOSE SESSION—press cursor return.

Keying Aids

1. Automatic generation of Record Number
2. Automatic record advance

```
46  63  69  60  64  36  96  06  96  09  54  56  52  63  41  96  09  30
22  53  11  55  64  60  03  54  34  00  24  01  55  65  00  55  60  03
32  36  50  60  22  41  35  36  60  14  34  36  63  60  90  06  96  03
53  56  01  03  06  61  41  10  33  36  60  46  90  06  63  46  52  60
56  54  05  33  41  51  31  40  10  41  56  03  64  23  50  11  60  54

64  69  63  69  58  74  56  69  67  63  69  03  06  09  46  56  63  69
59  70  66  63  55  79  90  58  89  96  09  96  63  60  30  96  74  36
41  63  74  85  93  63  09  17  72  91  73  57  16  04  03  63  64  69
89  49  27  12  50  50  21  36  69  78  65  69  63  30  60  69  96  93
01  40  43  80  26  79  27  29  69  63  60  41  47  48  91  96  90  69

24  83  21  16  21  90  00  17  38  69  49  25  35  57  65  88  36  69
12  98  37  36  69  63  60  69  60  69  90  96  63  36  45  46  36  69
13  46  78  81  54  85  11  21  85  71  15  37  36  96  93  63  36  39
66  56  40  24  04  43  46  54  32  48  65  40  19  59  03  08  57  96
11  84  20  39  60  71  83  34  85  43  21  26  00  19  66  85  68  69

43  73  47  42  14  05  38  96  97  54  75  41  96  36  63  30  60  90
42  32  36  69  56  58  47  24  23  08  70  69  25  92  12  32  51  07
19  02  18  32  98  07  60  54  03  11  96  63  72  96  32  89  63  58
96  80  57  97  75  26  10  62  00  44  29  04  35  07  84  81  74  69
93  28  92  24  56  12  33  87  61  22  19  45  72  63  40  75  69  60
```

DATA ENTRY JOB 10:
NUMERICAL EXERCISE (ALL DIGITS)

PURPOSES

1. To practice keying all digits
2. To provide experience entering longer numbers

PREPARATION

The major difference in the data for Job 10 is obvious: The numbers are longer. Whereas two-digit numbers are useful when you are learning keys, most numbers you will enter in a working situation will be longer—sometimes much longer.

In Job 10, you will be able to remember the groups of four digits in the data. When Jobs contain longer numbers, you can read them as smaller groups of two, three, or four digits. If you can remember a group of four, you can handle long numbers by subdividing them. As always, you will find a line marker helpful.

PROCEDURE

Job 10: Numerical Exercises (Practice with All Digits)

After you have selected Job 10, the standard screen for numeric exercises will appear.

Set-Up

1. Place the keypad in numeric shift by pressing NumLock.
2. Place your right hand over the home keys. Remember not to rest your hand on the frame of the keyboard, or you will reduce your keying speed.

General Entry

1. For each line to be entered:
   A. Enter the line.
2. When you are ready to terminate the entry session:
   A. Press NumLock to release the keyboard from numeric shift.
   B. Press the Escape (ESC) key and the cursor return key.
   C. Highlight CLOSE SESSION—press cursor return.

Keying Aids

1. Automatic generation of Record Number
2. Automatic record advance

4798	9452	8638	5680	6270	7852	2118	2912	0046	5684	6214	6946
4476	9217	2693	6105	7000	6687	6831	0470	3504	5623	9526	3220
9498	7200	1497	8033	9587	9896	6102	1569	3843	8649	7761	2355
1047	6610	5727	1606	1983	0282	1948	5479	8719	2868	8416	5366
3293	2668	6433	2791	1330	3803	6768	7838	3370	9061	0724	4736
3074	3795	6137	6752	0887	4833	3599	1527	3736	4536	1508	7121
0108	9942	3161	1265	7503	4849	0643	9785	2410	1929	5780	7363
7871	8846	0653	0585	5042	0995	4365	8499	8589	1827	0745	4902
7781	8168	2071	2020	8572	8035	7267	4656	6504	7141	5974	3650
3630	4071	9751	3356	7467	1822	6589	5808	0961	7827	8272	9006
8236	0041	4696	1047	5587	5402	5739	0760	4376	7838	9706	9321
4350	7317	7509	3517	6341	1751	0072	4723	0149	9238	1078	9549
6695	3103	5129	0943	0315	8737	8671	5642	4084	3481	6098	0830
7132	7334	8961	7096	0450	1362	8628	9457	5126	7652	4771	9881
3307	0474	4071	6535	1928	5661	7235	1934	2345	0889	7126	1776

DATA ENTRY JOB 11:
DAILY TRANSACTIONS

PURPOSES

1. To provide practice entering numeric material
2. To provide practice entering automatically duplicated items
3. To provide practice with a mixture of automatically advanced and manually advanced fields

PREPARATION

Notice that the material to be entered in Job 11 contains two types of data: (1) data that is to be repeated on each record prepared from the source document and (2) data that is to be entered into only one record created from the source document.

Look at the first sheet of data for Job 11. The Store Number, Date, and Transaction Codes (at the bottom of the page) are repeated on all records entered from this sheet. Thus Record 1 will contain the Store Number, the Date, the 1 that indicates a sales transaction, and the data from the first line on the source document. Record 2 will contain the same Store Number, the same Date, the same Code, and the data from the second line on the document.

As a keying aid, the program for Job 11 will automatically duplicate these three fields for you. You must take care, however, to change the data in the duplicated fields when the data on the source document changes.

The program will also provide automatic record number generation and automatic record advance. On this job, a reading marker will be particularly helpful.

A new problem exists in this Job: a mixture of numeric fields in which some advance automatically and others require manual advance. This is another awkward situation that is best handled by simply concentrating on what you are doing. Check the notes under "General Entry" carefully before beginning to key.

Job 11 contains some of the difficult-to-remember numbers we have discussed. The Product Code is nine digits long, and few people can remember and key a number of that length. Before you begin the job, study the Product Code Number and decide how it can be comfortably broken up. Is it simpler for you to remember it as 152 915 712, as 15 291 5712, as 1529 15 712, or as some other configuration of digits? Choose the reading pattern that is easiest for you and stick to it.

Fortunately, the analysts who design forms for data capture are becoming aware that long numbers pose a problem, and they are now designing forms that minimize the problem. Notice how much easier it is to read and remember the Store Number than the Product Code Number. The Store Number is also a long number but is divided with a hyphen. Longer numbers still remain in many jobs, however, and we must cope with them efficiently.

Note: The date should be entered as four digits. For example, June 1, 1995, should be entered as 0601. The program will edit in slashes and display 06/01.

PROCEDURE

Job 11: Daily Transactions

Data Entry Screen

Job #11

PJ's			Store:	000000
Daily Transactions			Date:	00/00/00
			Trans:	0

Product	Size	Quan	Dept	Record
000000000	00 00	000	00	1

Set-Up

1. Use NumLock to place the keypad in numeric shift.
2. Place your hand over the home keys. No resting your hand on the keyboard!

General Entry

1. IF the Store Number, Date, or Transaction Code is to be changed:
   A. Press Alt-A to place the cursor under the first automatically duplicated field.
   B. Enter the new contents into each field to be changed—cursor return.
   OR
   A. Cursor return to accept the displayed fields.
2. Enter Product Code—do not press cursor return; auto advance is provided.
3. Enter Waist Size 1—auto advance provided.
4. Enter Inseam Size 1—auto advance provided.
5. Enter Quantity 1—press cursor return.
6. Enter Department 1—auto advance provided.

Caution

1. Keep alert when entering the Quantities. Although it may seem strange that the data entry program provides automatic advance for some items and not for others, there are reasons for coding the program in this way. Building good habits to cope with situations like this is an important part of data entry training.

Keying Aids

1. Automatic duplication of Store Number, Date, and Transaction Code
2. Automatic cursor advance from Product, Size, and Dept
3. Automatic generation of Record Number

PJ's
Everything in Pants and Jeans
DAILY TRANSACTIONS

STORE NO. 237-046
DATE 12-17
PAGE 1 OF 4

SIGNATURE: B. Bugby

Return original to : **Central Merchandising
San Francisco**

PRODUCT CODE	SIZE	QUAN.	DEPT.
1529 5712	30X32	001	16
1536 4821	30X32	001	16
1546 7649	34X30	002	16
1529 5714	31X32	001	16
1595 4821	31X33	001	16
1512 4892	34X30	001	16
1436 7741	24X28	002	16
1526 5715	31X31	001	16
1529 5712	29X33	002	16
1536 4824	30X31	001	16
1608 5738	29X29	001	16
1608 5742	29X29	001	16
1515 4638	31X32	001	16
1529 5712	29X33	002	16
1536 5715	34X30	001	16
1536 5712	34X30	001	16
1529 5714	30X29	001	16
2419 2740	24X28	001	16
2416 2793	34X28	001	16
1604 5738	29X34	001	16
3523 6856	32X33	001	16
3523 6229	32X33	001	16
1604 6411	26X30	002	16
1536 0748	28X32	001	16
1523 6977	32X31	001	16
1523 6393	32X31	001	16
1523 6328	32X31	002	16
1516 7929	30X30	001	16
1529 5716	32X31	001	16
2416 2733	26X28	001	16
1536 5712	30X31	001	16
1436 2683	25X29	001	16

PRODUCT CODE	SIZE	QUAN.	DEPT.
1523 6393	30X29	001	16
1523 6977	30X29	001	16
1523 6393	34X30	001	16
1523 6328	34X30	001	16
1595 4821	33X31	002	16
2413 2738	28X26	001	16
2413 2733	28X26	001	16
1515 5779	33X29	001	16
1515 4091	33X30	001	16
1609 2894	33X29	001	16
1609 2886	32X29	001	16
3528 6856	32X36	001	16
1608 5712	30X28	001	16
1529 4392	30X30	002	16
1529 4228	32X31	001	16
1536 4228	31X32	001	16
1529 5738	34X31	002	16
1529 5720	34X36	001	16
1515 4638	31X32	002	16
2416 2733	26X26	002	16
2413 2738	26X28	003	16
1436 2741	28X28	001	16
1512 4833	34X30	001	16
1608 5738	31X33	001	16
1529 5712	36X32	001	16
1523 6393	32X31	001	16
2416 2738	28X28	002	16
1536 5712	36X30	002	16
1436 2683	29X28	001	16
1604 6411	31X31	001	16
3523 6229	32X33	001	16
1609 4837	34X30	002	16

CODES

1 Sales	4 Return to Vendor	7 Transfer Out	
2 Inventory	5 Customer Returns	8 Miscellaneous In	
3 Receipt from Vendor	6 Transfer In	9 Miscellaneous Out	

PJ's
Everything in Pants and Jeans
DAILY TRANSACTIONS

SIGNATURE: B. Bugby

Return original to: **Central Merchandising**
San Francisco

PRODUCT CODE	SIZE	QUAN.	DEPT.
1545122553	30X31	001	23
1545111390	36X34	001	23
1545122263	34X32	001	23
2545120575	38X33	002	23
1541109074	40X32	001	23
2543200055	36X34	001	23
1543100095	34X31	001	23
1602183104	34X36	001	16
1611100843	33X35	002	16
1604257058	30X34	001	23
1604169244	29X32	002	23
1604269164	28X32	001	16
2611105974	30X36	003	23
1604114044	32X36	001	23
1523161294	30X32	001	16
2416217384	26X28	062	16
1611105224	29X30	001	16
1611206055	36X32	002	23
1604177814	28X32	001	16
1602297304	27X29	003	16
2611206134	30X34	001	14
2602197305	1X34	001	18
1602200765	32X36	001	16
1603122554	30X28	001	16
1604113905	32X32	002	23
1543297305	33X32	001	18
2611206115	28X29	001	18
1612177814	34X36	001	16
1543261294	34X36	001	23
1528205975	33X34	002	16
1543169164	30X30	001	16
2416283104	32X31	001	16

PRODUCT CODE	SIZE	QUAN.	DEPT.
1604113905	26X30	001	18
1611222575	40X36	001	18
2543106415	31X36	001	16
1545200385	39X36	001	16
1541222575	28X34	002	16
1611150585	34X36	001	18
3604169165	32X36	001	18
1602205975	32X36	001	18
2523161295	33X37	002	16
1602517385	29X30	002	18
1611305225	34X35	001	18
3604106055	36X36	001	18
1545297365	33X34	001	16
2523100675	32X34	001	23
2528122575	32X34	001	23
1611122595	33X34	003	18
1604161295	31X33	001	18
1611105975	33X34	001	18
1523269165	29X30	001	23
1528183105	28X32	001	23
1543300955	29X32	001	23
2611113905	30X34	001	18
1604109073	1X33	001	18
3416287165	33X34	001	14

CODES

1 Sales	4 Return to Vendor	7 Transfer Out
2 Inventory	5 Customer Returns	8 Miscellaneous In
3 Receipt from Vendor	6 Transfer In	9 Miscellaneous Out

PJ's
Everything in Pants and Jeans

DAILY TRANSACTIONS

STORE NO 237-046
DATE 12-17
PAGE 3 OF 4

SIGNATURE: B. Bugby

Return original to : **Central Merchandising**
San Francisco

PRODUCT CODE	SIZE	QUAN.	DEPT.
154512255	28X32	612	23
154512255	28X34	012	23
154512255	30X32	012	23
154512255	30X33	012	23
154512255	30X34	024	23
154512255	32X36	006	23
160218310	34X36	024	16
160216916	34X36	024	16
160411404	30X34	012	18
160411404	32X36	006	18
160411404	34X36	006	18
152316129	28X30	012	16
152316129	28X32	012	16
152316129	28X34	024	16
152316129	30X34	018	16
160312255	30X30	012	18
160312255	30X34	012	18
160312255	32X30	012	18
160312255	32X32	012	18
160312255	32X34	006	18
160312255	34X34	012	18
160417781	30X34	006	23
261120613	28X30	006	14
261120613	28X34	006	14
261120613	28X36	006	14
261120613	34X34	006	14
261120613	36X32	006	14
261120613	36X34	006	14
161217781	29X28	006	16
161217781	30X32	012	16
161217781	31X32	012	16
161217781	32X32	006	16

PRODUCT CODE	SIZE	QUAN.	DEPT.
160411390	28X32	006	18
160411390	29X32	012	18
160411390	32X32	018	18
160411390	34X30	012	18
160411390	36X32	012	18
160411390	36X34	012	18
160231738	30X32	006	18
160231738	31X32	006	18
160231738	32X34	006	18
160231738	34X34	006	18
160410907	28X34	006	16
160410907	29X32	012	16
160410907	30X30	012	16
160410907	30X32	012	16
160410907	30X34	012	16
160410907	32X32	006	16
160410907	32X34	012	16
160410907	32X29	012	16
341628716	28X30	006	14
341628716	28X32	006	14
341628716	30X28	006	14
341628716	30X32	006	14
341628716	30X34	012	14
341628716	32X32	012	14
341628716	34X32	006	14
261111390	30X32	006	16
261111390	32X32	006	16
260410907	28X30	006	18
	X		
	X		
	X		
	X		

CODES

1 Sales	4 Return to Vendor	7 Transfer Out
2 Inventory	5 Customer Returns	8 Miscellaneous In
③ Receipt from Vendor	6 Transfer In	9 Miscellaneous Out

PJ's

Everything in Pants and Jeans

DAILY TRANSACTIONS

SIGNATURE: _B. Bugby_

Return original to : **Central Merchandising**
San Francisco

PRODUCT CODE	SIZE	QUAN.	DEPT.
1546 764 9	34 X 30	001	16
151 2 4832	34 X 30	001	16
1608 5738	29 X 29	001	16
1529 5712	29 X 39	002	16
1556 5712	34 X 30	001	16
1604 5738	29 X 34	001	16
241 32 740	24 X 26	001	18
1609 2894	51 X 30	001	14
241 62 733	34 X 26	002	18
3523 6856	51 X 30	001	14
1609 2894	31 X 30	001	16
1529 5712	29 X 31	001	16
2413 2733	24 X 28	001	18
1608 5738	51 X 33	001	16
1604 6411	30 X 32	001	16
3523 6229	38 X 30	001	14
2116 2641	26 X 28	002	18
3528 6856	51 X 32	001	18
241 6 7133	28 X 28	002	14
3523 6229	52 X 33	001	18
1608 5172	34 X 30	002	16
2413 6229	30 X 29	001	14
2416 2733	26 X 28	001	18
1515 4091	34 X 29	001	16
2416 7133	26 X 28	002	18
3523 6229	28 X 30	001	14
1515 4821	33 X 31	001	16
2413 2733	26 X 28	001	18
3523 6856	52 X 30	002	14
1529 4592	52 X 32	001	16
2416 2733	24 X 26	001	18
3523 6856	54 X 30	001	14

PRODUCT CODE	SIZE	QUAN.	DEPT.
2424 1 154	58 X 50	001	29
2416 1293	56 X 31	001	16
1609 5712	31 X 30	001	18
1608 5865	96 X 29	001	14
1608 2856	32 X 30	001	18
2416 2733	24 X 28	001	16
1604 6411	30 X 32	002	14
1546 7649	34 X 30	001	16
1529 5714	31 X 32	001	16
2413 2229	30 X 29	001	14
2416 733	26 X 28	002	14
1515 4091	34 X 29	001	16
	X		
	X		
	X		
	X		
	X		
	X		
	X		
	X		
	X		
	X		
	X		
	X		
	X		
	X		
	X		
	X		
	X		
	X		
	X		

CODES

1 Sales	4 Return to Vendor	7 Transfer Out
2 Inventory	5 Customer Returns	8 Miscellaneous In
3 Receipt from Vendor	6 Transfer In	9 Miscellaneous Out

DATA ENTRY JOB 12:

ORDER FORMS

PURPOSES

1. To provide practice entering numeric material
2. To provide practice with automatically duplicated items

PREPARATION

Like Job 11, Job 12 contains data that is to be repeated on each record prepared from the source document and data that is to be entered into only one record created from the source document.

Look at the first sheet of data for Job 12. The Date and Store Number are repeated on all records entered from this sheet. Thus Record 1 will contain the Date and Store Number from the top of the first sheet of the exercise, followed by the five Quantity and Code Numbers from the first line of the sheet. The second record will contain the same Date and Store Number, along with the data from Line 2 of the sheet.

As a keying aid, the program for Job 12 will duplicate these Date and Store Number fields for you automatically. You must take care, however, to change the data in the duplicated fields when the data on the source document changes.

Again in Job 12, use your strategy of reading numbers that are difficult to remember as groups of shorter numbers. Before you begin the job, decide whether there are any numbers you will want to break up and how you will divide them.

In this Job and all others, the Date always needs a leading zero for months before October. For example, March is 03. Do not use a leading zero for the Store No. and Quantity. Press the cursor return to advance entries of only one or two digits.

PROCEDURE

Job 12: Order Forms

Data Entry Screen

Job #12
ORDER FORM

Date: 00/00
Store No.: 000

Qty	Code	Qty	Code	Qty	Code	Qty	Code	Qty	Code	Rec
000	000000	000	000000	000	000000	000	000000	000	000000	1

Set-Up

1. Use NumLock to place the keypad in numeric shift.
2. Place your hand over the home keys.

General Entry

1. IF the Date or Store Number is to be changed:
   A. Press Alt-A to place the cursor under the first automatically duplicated field.
   B. Enter new data or press cursor return to accept the displayed data.
2. Enter Quantity 1—auto advance provided.
3. Enter Code 1—auto advance provided.
4. Enter Quantity 2—auto advance provided.
5. Enter Code 2—auto advance provided.
6. Enter Quantity 3—auto advance provided.
7. Enter Code 3—auto advance provided.
8. Enter Quantity 4—auto advance provided.
9. Enter Code 4—auto advance provided.
10. Enter Quantity 5—auto advance provided.
11. Enter Code 5—auto advance provided.

Keying Aids

1. Automatic duplication of Date and Store Number
2. Automatic cursor advance from Code and Qty when field is full
3. Automatic record generation and advance

ORDER FORM

DATE _____ 6-12 _____ STORE NAME _____ DALE BROS. _____

PUNCHED BY _____ STORE NO. _____ 23 _____

QTY	CODE	QTY	CODE	QTY	CODE	QTY	CODE	QTY	CODE
120	000141	90	000232	100	000265	10	000661	20	000703
16	000745	10	000752	25	001248	30	001255	50	001271
54	001289	60	001305	75	002212	50	002345	25	002360
96	002741	100	003103	10	003186	10	002642	20	002865
81	002907	75	003228	60	003780	50	004085	20	004089
20	004499	20	004556	20	004572	25	004606	16	004889
50	004929	40	005082	20	005264	10	005298	10	005595
10	005603	15	005611	10	005769	20	005801	30	005884
50	005959	50	005967	25	005983	25	005991	10	006007
10	006023	10	006031	10	006072	30	006171	25	006189
50	006288	50	006296	50	006312	50	006320	50	006338
50	006346	50	006352	50	006361	100	006403	100	006437
30	005314	75	005322	10	005330	75	005348	25	005355
45	005363	90	005371	30	005389	45	005397	20	005405
20	005413	40	006924	55	006965	25	007047	30	007088
50	007120	50	007203	65	007229	70	007245	65	007328
65	007336	20	007443	10	007484	10	007526	10	007567
10	007641	10	007682	15	007765	50	007922	10	008045
10	008086	20	008128	20	008169	20	008201	20	008219
20	008243	20	008284	25	008326	25	008334	125	008409
150	008524	100	008607	100	008615	100	008649	30	008722
35	008896	20	008904	10	008987	10	009027	10	009043
10	009050	10	009068	30	009142	30	009217	15	009225
20	331728	50	010017	30	010033	25	010041	40	010058
15	010066	50	010074	110	010082	20	010090	25	010116

ORDER FORM

DATE _____6-02_____ STORE NAME _QUALITY MEATS_

PUNCHED BY _____ STORE NO. _485_

QTY	CODE	QTY	CODE	QTY	CODE	QTY	CODE	QTY	CODE
125	130005	100	130047	100	130088	150	130179	75	130195
220	130203	20	130286	50	130328	50	130393	25	130534
100	130724	100	130732	100	131003	20	131342	20	131425
20	131466	20	131474	20	131490	50	131508	50	131649
50	131664	150	131763	200	131797	150	131805	150	131888
70	132001	70	132035	70	132068	70	132092	70	132191
70	132522	70	132548	70	132555	100	132589	80	132761
90	132985	90	132993	20	133009	20	133132	20	133157
20	133181	20	133215	20	133520	20	133793	25	133942
50	134122	40	134338	40	134684	35	134726	100	135129
100	135145	100	135384	100	135608	100	135806	100	135889
25	136002	25	136010	15	136023	15	136507	20	136598
40	136291	30	136416	15	136515	15	136549	20	136556
25	136572	20	136663	10	136721	10	136879	10	136887
10	136895	20	136903	15	136911						

ORDER FORM

DATE 6-15 STORE NAME GREEN & GREEN

PUNCHED BY _____ STORE NO. 114

QTY	CODE	QTY	CODE	QTY	CODE	QTY	CODE	QTY	CODE
2	501601	2	501676	1	501700	2	501825	2	501833
2	501841	3	501854	3	502112	5	502146	1	502245
1	502468	1	502476	8	502484	2	502526	2	502559
3	502617	6	502632	6	502849	2	502853	2	503649
1	503672	3	503706	8	504126	9	504761	9	505461
6	505479	1	505487	7	507566	8	507848	2	507943
2	507962	9	508002	9	508010	1	508192	1	509166
1	509174	1	509182	7	509570	7	509620	7	510412
8	510438	7	510453	2	510487	4	510495	4	510511
3	510560	123	510636	100	510644	2	511063	2	511303
2	511337	2	511220	2	513416	1	515593	1	515627
1	515668	1	517452	1	517482	1	517581	1	523134
1	524009	1	524165	5	524264	5	524272	7	524397
7	524603	8	525220	8	526327	6	526368	4	526459
3	526509	3	526681	2	526707	1	526749	2	526780
3	526798	1	526806	2	526822	10	526848	10	526988
23	527010	23	527028	20	527044	22	529719	15	529800
15	530055	8	530089	8	530147	6	530485	7	530543
7	530550	5	530816	14	530832	13	530865	10	598821
15	599092	4	599621	4	598839	3	599100	1	598847
1	599118	1	599126	2	599183	2	599415	2	599209
6	599217	6	599225	5	599720	1	599761	1	599241
1	599258	2	599274	2	599316	1	599357	6	599381
6	599379	5	599423	5	599449	5	599456	4	599480
4	599498	1	599506	3	599563	3	599639	3	600742

ORDER FORM

DATE __6-17__ STORE NAME __EVERGREEN GROCERY__
PUNCHED BY _____ STORE NO. __755__

QTY	CODE	QTY	CODE	QTY	CODE	QTY	CODE	QTY	CODE
5	096560	5	096602	5	096610	5	096628	5	096883
1	096644	4	097667	2	097832	2	098244	6	098491
6	099283	6	099317	20	100214	20	100503	20	100512
5	101469	5	101667	2	102384	2	102582	3	103150
2	102996	1	103002	4	103077	1	103119	3	103648
2	103887	2	103937	1	104000	1	104224	1	104422
1	105163	1	105247	1	105288	1	105338	1	105486
1	105528	1	105767	1	106161	1	106203	1	106245
1	106310	2	106468	1	107185	5	107425	20	107433
20	107508	25	107573	6	107649	2	107680	10	107714
10	107904	15	107946	7	107987	5	108043	5	108084
4	108092	3	108183	4	108266	4	108308	5	108563
5	108647	1	108720	3	108985	3	109033	3	109041
4	109561	10	109769	15	109967	20	110163	20	110197
10	110205	10	110221	5	110262	5	110312	20	110148
4	111104	2	111112	2	111294	3	112383	1	112664
1	112714	1	113068	1	113126	1	113324	1	113449
2	113589	3	113704	2	114746	2	114827	3	114942
5	114967	5	115055	9	115147	2	115162	2	115196
2	115204	2	115238	2	115253	2	115261	2	115279
5	115303	5	115469	3	115501	2	115584	3	115626
5	116103	3	116277	4	117085	4	117168	4	118588
1	118661	1	118836	1	118943	2	119305	2	119513
20	121574	20	121723	4	121764	10	122028	15	122127
20	122481	6	122523	6	122606	4	122689	5	122960

DATA ENTRY JOBS AND INSTRUCTIONS

ORDER FORM

DATE __6-15__   STORE NAME __BALLARD AND WILBOURN__

PUNCHED BY _____   STORE NO. __120__

QTY	CODE	QTY	CODE	QTY	CODE	QTY	CODE	QTY	CODE
2	000141	20	000224	20	000232	20	000448	15	000497
10	000604	20	001271	20	001305	20	002212	16	002238
5	002873	25	002881	13	003384	2	003467	7	003707
20	002824	20	003103	10	003145	20	003186	20	003343
10	003350	8	002865	10	002907	20	002949	11	022335
125	022194	10	022244	15	022277	18	022285	15	126565
15	127407	16	338863	10	022707	20	022913	20	022962
20	023069	15	023077	9	023143	10	024414	4	024307
1	024315	20	024323	10	024356	10	024364	10	026245
15	026252	2	026203	10	026112	15	026484	1	026948
19	027037	10	027185	20	027748	15	028530	20	028787
20	029397	100	029520	100	029827	20	029926	10	030007
3	030049	20	031526	5	032110	20	033563	6	033589
15	033597	10	033647	15	051144	9	051185	10	050740
20	051714	7	052365	10	053124	20	084137	15	085563
10	085720	15	086264	10	092512	15	092528	10	093922
6	094367	20	094441	12	095802	20	095869	3	096040
20	096131	15	096180	15	096248	14	096486	10	096560
15	096768	10	103358	15	103606	20	104422	15	104703
20	105163	7	105288	10	105320	15	107573	10	107607
15	107649	20	107714	20	107789	20	108092	15	108563
13	109009	9	109066	10	109504	8	110163	9	110171
7	110205	17	110148	20	110924	20	110965	115	111229
4	111211	15	111724	120	111864	150	112136	15	112540
10	113324	20	113886	15	114025	200	114827	75	114967

ORDER FORM

DATE _6-15_   STORE NAME _KODER'S_

PUNCHED BY _____   STORE NO. _145_

QTY	CODE	QTY	CODE	QTY	CODE	QTY	CODE	QTY	CODE
6	340109	5	340117	10	340133	16	340141	7	340158
9	340166	25	340174	10	340182	11	340190	15	340208
20	340216	25	340224	30	340240	10	340257	10	340265
10	340281	10	340299	16	340307	20	340364	10	340372
10	340380	5	002741	5	002824	5	002642	5	002659
14	003301	7	003343	10	003350	6	007268	15	007443
20	007526	6	007567	4	008128	2	008201	3	008219
10	008284	15	008987	5	009043	20	009050	8	009068
10	009217	10	009225	2	010348	2	010389	5	010421
5	010462	5	010488	10	010595	10	010660	10	011361
6	011429	6	011452	5	011460	5	011809	6	015032
2	015909	10	017806	2	017848	2	020248	10	020289
1	021527	1	021535	10	022293	5	029371	4	029413
10	029439	5	029447	3	029603	6	029611	10	031542
15	031583	10	031666	30	031708	16	032219	15	032367
8	032516	5	032540	5	046623	20	072041		

DATA ENTRY JOB 13:

TELEPHONE COMPANY CUSTOMERS

PURPOSES

1. To provide experience with jobs having mixed fields
2. To provide experience with fields having upper- and lower-case letters

PREPARATION

Examine the data for Job 13. The content of records in Jobs 5 through 12 was entirely numeric. In Job 13, you again work with records that have some alphabetic and some numeric fields. For this practice exercise, the data is provided in a familiar format.

Remember: This Job provides automatic duplication of ZIP Code as well as automatic generation of Record Number. It also provides automatic cursor advance on ZIP Code.

PROCEDURE

Job 13 Telephone Company Customers

Data Entry Screen

Job #13
Telephone Company Customers

ZIP	Phone Number	Name	Record
00000	000 0000	000000 000000	1

Set-Up

1. No special preparation required.

General Entry

1. For each record to be entered:
   A. IF the ZIP Code is to be changed:
      (1) Press Alt-A to place the cursor under the first automatically duplicated field.
      (2) Enter new data or press cursor return to accept the displayed data.
   B. Enter the Phone Number.
      The cursor automatically will advance when each field is filled.
   C. Enter the Name—cursor return.
      The record automatically will advance.
2. When you are ready to terminate the session:
   A. Press the Escape (ESC) key and the cursor key.
   B. Highlight CLOSE SESSION—press cursor return.

Cautions

1. When changing the data in an automatically duplicated field, be sure to erase any characters that may remain from the previous field contents.

2. When working with a record in which the cursor automatically is advanced in some fields but not in others, keep alert to avoid pressing the cursor return when it is not required. Pressing the cursor return when it is not required will cause a field to be skipped.

Keying Aids

1. Automatic duplication of ZIP Code
2. Automatic cursor advance from
   A. ZIP Code
   B. Phone Number
3. Automatic generation of Record Number
4. Warning beep on numeric fields

ZIP	PHONE NUMBER	NAME
36405	487-5294	Janie Johnson
	487-5982	Andy Gross
	487-8930	Robert Hill
	487-2847	Bertha Hill
	487-2987	Bessie Whatley
	613-3457	Lester Stewart
	613-3907	Nolan Hudson
	613-9364	Kenneth Brown
	613-3928	Joe T. Brown
	613-7563	Robert Chafin
	520-3410	Randolph Dees
	520-8240	Howard Hill
	520-0389	Betty Howard
	520-9264	Errol Maguire
	520-2497	Mildred Maguire
	312-4298	Virgil Pearson
	312-2167	Clements Lee
	312-4289	Virginia Lee
	312-3704	Frank Lee
	312-9237	Michael Stewart
36406	422-3847	John Snodgrass
	422-3476	Anita Dees
	422-0571	Ronald Joiner
	422-0616	Harold West
	422-7382	Brenda Hudson
	834-2618	Ray Joiner
	834-3826	Jerry Pritchett
	834-1026	Kelton Pritchett
	834-3740	Bettina Whatley
	834-2861	Thomas Howard
	286-9284	Benjamin York
	286-2632	Maud Stevens
	286-7832	Herbert Murphy
	286-2739	William Pruett
	286-8273	Ethel West
	415-1253	Conrad Murphy
	415-9786	Kathleen Hughes
	415-3057	Dennis Knight
	415-8743	Glenn Lawrence
	415-2134	Billy Kizziah

36407	333-4523	John Carter
	333-9071	Byron McDonald
	333-2138	Claude McDonald
	333-9200	Anita Jones
	333-0889	Edna Adams
	921-4927	Robert Neal
	921-3957	Mary Neal
	921-1836	Debra Stewart
	921-5387	Albert Miller
	921-1906	Arthur Carter
	364-2376	Jessie Mae Miles
	364-3819	Eugene Webb
	364-1978	Dewey Weaver
	364-2094	Letty Price
	364-1298	Lula Bell Price
	542-2368	Eleanor Myers
	542-1927	Reginald Bass
	542-4932	Curtis Hagood
	542-3928	Robert R. Carter
	542-3190	Lucinda Carter
36408	410-2817	Pauline Thigpen
	410-9374	Wayne Thigpen
	410-2837	Quinton Hudson
	410-1829	James D. Lowery
	410-1726	Valeria Pearson
	261-8476	Nelson Tucker
	261-8274	Carla York
	261-2841	Eric Miles
	261-0983	Edna Earle Lowery
	261-5619	Ronald L. Johnson
	728-2635	Ida Burnett
	728-8702	Nell Lovelace
	728-1172	Robert N. Lovelace
	728-3083	Sandra Price
	728-1720	Angus Dees
	912-8125	Theodora Lovelace
	912-4569	Douglas Ballenger
	912-0369	Clifford Pruett
	912-4280	Tracy Dawkins
	912-2188	Elton Finley

DATA ENTRY JOB 14:
INVENTORY ADDITIONS AND CHANGES

PURPOSES

1. To provide experience entering data for jobs with mixed numeric and alphabetic fields
2. To provide experience entering data for jobs with automatically and manually advanced fields

PREPARATION

Examine the data for Job 14. It is written on a form with fields divided by lines and then further divided with shorter lines to indicate character positions within the fields. Such forms are used frequently for data capture when there is a bulk of data for key entry. They are intended to make the source document more readable for the entry operator.

You also will notice that in some fields—the Add (A) or Change (C) Code, the Vendor Number, the Buyer Number, and the Unit—lines have been drawn down the column from one entry to another. These lines indicate that the data item will be the same for all these entries and should be duplicated.

In Job 14, you again have the situation in which some fields are programmed to advance automatically and others are not. The Date, the Add/Change Code, the Vendor Number, and the Buyer Number will advance automatically. Other fields—the Unit, the FOB Cost, and the Retail Price—require cursor advance.

Notice that all alphabetic fields are in capital letters. As in Job 12, the data entry program will insert slashes into the Date field automatically.

PROCEDURE

Job 14: Inventory Additions and Changes

Data Entry Screen

Job #14
INVENTORY

Additions & Changes						Date: 00/00/00		
A/C	Vendor	Byr	Item	Description	Unit	Cost	Retail	Rec
000	000000	00	000000		000	000000	000000	000

Set-Up

1. Use NumLock to place the keypad in numeric shift.
2. Use CapsLock to shift the alphabetic keys into upper shift.

General Entry

1. For each record to be entered:
   A. IF the Date is to be changed,
      (1) Press Alt-A to place the cursor under the Date field.
      (2) Enter the new Date or press cursor return to accept the displayed Date.
   B. Enter the Item Number—automatic advance.
   C. Enter the Description—cursor return.
   D. Enter the Unit—cursor return.
   E. Enter the FOB Cost—cursor return.
   F. Enter the Retail Price—cursor return.
2. When you are ready to terminate the session:
   A. Press the Escape (ESC) key and the cursor return key.
   B. Highlight CLOSE SESSION—press cursor return.

Caution

1. When working with a record in which the cursor is automatically advanced in some fields but not in others, keep alert to avoid pressing the cursor return when it is not required. Pressing the cursor return when it is not required will cause a field to be skipped.

Keying Aids

1. Automatic duplication of
   A. Date
   B. Add/Change Code
   C. Vendor Number
   D. Buyer Number
2. Automatic leading zero fill on numeric fields
3. Automatic cursor advance from Date, A/C, Vendor, Byr, and Item Number
4. Automatic generation of Record Number
5. Warning beep on numeric fields
6. Automatic insertion of slashes in Date field

INVENTORY
ADDITIONS & CHANGES

A/C	VENDOR	BYR	ITEM	DESCRIPTION	UNIT	FOB COST	RETAIL
ADD/184055		33	2973735	POWER MOWER SPARK PLUG	EA	4800	12900
			2961147	WIZARD TERRARIUM		401000	129500
			2962122	PLASTIC PLANT STAND		71000	179500
			2983910	FLOOR MODEL TERRARIUM		55000	139500
	157661		2808511	LAWN EDGER		311700	54900
			2841143	EDGER BLADE		22300	39900
			2846711	MOWER REPLACEMENT BLADES		47500	69900
			2854121	REPLACEMENT SPOOL		13900	24900
	157681		2928987	TOOL HOLDER MODEL 6		3900	6900
			2929155	CORD REEL		727700	129900
	158243		2964022	POTTING SOIL 2 QT		2500	5900
			2964110	POTTING SOIL 4 QT		4000	8900
			2964362	POTTING SOIL 8 QT		6500	13900
			2964469	POTTING SOIL 25 LB		12500	24900
			2964711	AFRICAN VIOLET SOIL 2 QT		2500	3900
			2943655	LAWN LIME		44163	116900
			2971269	WHITE MARBLE CHIPS		73112	179900
			2972235	KIDDIELAND PLAY SAND		61163	199900
			2983209	AIR FERN		9000	18900
			2982159	AMARYLLIS BULBS		18700	39900

INVENTORY
ADDITIONS & CHANGES

JOB NAME INV,D,I,O   DATE 09/15

A/C	VENDOR	BYR	ITEM	DESCRIPTION	UNIT	FOB COST	RETAIL
ADD	2123375A		287732	TRACTOR TIRES	PR	450000	829500
			287757	TURNING PLOW	EA	163000	279500
			287765	CULTIVATOR		288000	479500
			287773	WISHBONE HARROW		204000	359500
			287799	EXTENSION TINES		18000	324600
			281230	SWIVEL HOOK NO 1		2795	6910
			281240	SWIVEL HOOK NO 2		3969	9800
			281255	SWIVEL HOOK EYE NO 1		1985	4900
			281263	SWIVEL HOOK EYE NO 2		3605	8900
			281271	MOUNT BRACKET		3969	9800
			281289	WALL BRACKET		15350	37700
			281305	SWIVEL CEILING HOOK		56300	139000
	241602		281453	BURGESS SPRAYER		213800	499500
			281545	FOGGER		87000	19500
			281552	MISTER		8200	12500
			281578	VAPOR SPRAYER		30000	17900
			281628	DUSTER		11300	247900
			281651	HOSE CLAMP		1850	12000
			281727	PUMP CYLINDER GASKET		12160	3000
			281750	PUMP ASSEMBLY		206000	49000

INVENTORY

ADDITIONS & CHANGES

JOB NAME: INV0110   DATE: 0920

A/C	VENDOR	BYR	ITEM	DESCRIPTION	UNIT	FOB COST	RETAIL
ADD	3762523 1		2926256	6-7 FT PEACH TREE	EA	325 00	595 00
			2931934	-5 FT WHITE BIRCH TREE		140 00	249 00
			2932194	-5 FT SILVER MAPLE TREE		140 00	249 00
			2932274	-5 FT SWEET GUM TREE		140 00	249 00
			2932764	-5 FT GREEN ASH TREE		140 00	249 00
	3764 52		8559245	SIZE 7 MOORE RUBBER BOOT	PR	636 00	1395 00
			8559325	SIZE 8 MOORE RUBBER BOOT		636 00	1395 00
			8559405	SIZE 9 MOORE RUBBER BOOT		636 00	1395 00
			8559575	SIZE 10 MOORE RUBBER BOOT		636 00	1395 00
	39708 1		2915933	FURROWER	EA	368 00	749 00
	43A110		2919324	GAS CAP		14 00	39 00
			2919325	STARTER HANDLE		44 00	129 00
			2919400	MUFFLER		60 00	159 00
			2919735	LEVER CONTROL		30 00	299 00
			2919381	TUNE UP KIT		140 00	399 00
			2917350	SINGLE EDGE RIDER BLADES		320 63	895 00
	43A409		2974000	MOORE BLADE		194 09	499 00
			2965010	03 IN CLAY POT		10 35	19 00
			2965190	08 IN CLAY POT		12 65	29 00
			2965270	10 IN CLAY POT		20 70	39 00

INVENTORY
ADDITIONS & CHANGES

A/C	VENDOR	BYR	ITEM	DESCRIPTION	UNIT	FOB COST	RETAIL
ADD	5689521/6	280026	TROWEL		EA	71.25	149.00
		2810034	FORK			85.00	155.00
		2800059	HOE			71.25	149.00
		2800067	RAKE			85.00	155.00
		2800836	CULTIVATOR			71.25	149.00
		2801255	SIDEWALK CLEANER			162.45	349.00
		28105A7	HEDGE SHEAR			251.75	529.00
		2806112	LOPPING SHEAR A-103			641.25	1349.00
		2806210	LOPPING SHEAR A-122			399.00	899.00
	5689713	2811363	COAL SHOVEL CT 2			555.75	1169.00
		281404	SPADE DP 16			745.75	1569.00
		2811446	LONG BLADE GARDEN SPADE			451.25	947.00
		2823013	GRAIN SCOOP ALUMINUM			665.00	1399.00
		2823386	COTTON SEED FORK			1263.50	2737.00
CHG		2824436	HAY FORK			555.0A	1239.00
		2824793	MORTAR HOE			595.65	1317.00
		2826242	POTATO HOOK			527.96	1229.00
		2825163	CHOPPER AXE			351.98	779.00

INVENTORY
ADDITIONS & CHANGES

JOB NAME INVYOLD   DATE 09/16

A/C	VENDOR	BYR	ITEM	DESCRIPTION	UNIT	FOB COST	RETAIL
ADD	5174017	013	2827177	DIGGING FORK	EA	380000	79700
			2827158	PRUNING TOOL		16625	34900
			2835700	WEED CUTTER		23916	52900
			2836656	GRASS CUTTER		20306	44900
			2836681	BUSH HOOK		68875	151700
			2838483	GRASS HOOK		16245	35900
			2855795	GRASS SHEAR		31825	66900
			2856111	PRUNING SHEAR		27550	62900
			2856729	HEDGE SHEAR		39900	89900
			2891100	GRAIN SCOOP		76000	159900
			2862205	SHOVEL HANDLE		11875	11900
CHG	5719003		2788416	IRRIGATING SPADE		503510	111700
			2905036	GARDEN MATTOCK		42000	104900
			2266649	PRUNING SAW		21000	41900
			2126763	HAND PRUNING SAW		32500	69900
			2301333	MEADOW HOE		21000	59500
			2301666	PLANTERS HOE		22800	47900
			2805339	ROSE AND GARDEN SHEAR		13000	34900
CHG	5800111		2891595	SAW CHAIN		2750004	4975000
			2891233	GUIDE BAR		49700	99500

DATA ENTRY JOB 15:
EMPLOYEE EDUCATIONAL HISTORY

PURPOSES

1. To provide further examination of design and keying strategies for jobs having both automatically and manually advanced fields
2. To provide additional practice with
   A. Mixed field advance
   B. Mixed format fields
   C. Data entry forms

PREPARATION

As in Job 14, the data for Job 15 is written on a form with fields divided by lines and then further divided with shorter lines to indicate character positions within the fields.

In Job 15, you again have the situation in which some fields will always be completely filled by keyed data and others will not, but the keying is handled in two different ways. Let us compare the Degree Level field with the Major and Minor fields. In the Degree Level field, few items in the data will fill the field. In the Major and Minor fields, however, most data items will fill the fields. For this reason, different keying patterns are specified, and each is intended to require the least number of keystrokes for the data being entered. Notice that the data entry form makes it easy to see how many blank spaces remain in fields that are not full.

Because the Major and Minor data items will almost always fill the field, the program has been designed to advance them automatically. When operators encounter an item that does not fill the field, such as the HPR major in Record 9, they enter a blank to fill the field, and the record advances. If the field had been programmed for manual advance, the operators would need to press the cursor return 20 times in entering the data on the first page. With automatic advance, they will press the space bar to enter blanks twice, thereby saving 18 keystrokes on the Major field alone.

On the other hand, the data for the Degree Level field usually does not fill the field. If the operator keyed blanks, most fields would require one keystroke, and the great majority would require two. Therefore, the field is programmed for manual advance so that the operator can hit the cursor return once rather than hitting the space bar once or twice. Examine the data and you will see that using the cursor return, as opposed to entering blanks, saves 13 keystrokes on the first page alone.

PROCEDURE

Job 15: Employee Educational History

Data Entry Screen

Job #15
EMPLOYEE EDUCATIONAL HISTORY

Date: 00/00/00

SSN	A/C	From	Thru	Code	Institution Name	Cd Maj	Cd Min	Lev	Rec
000000000		0000	0000	000		00	00		1

Set-Up

1. Use NumLock to place the keypad in numeric shift.
2. Use CapsLock to shift the alphabetic keys into upper shift.

General Entry

1. For each record to be entered:
   A. Enter the Social Security Number—auto advance.
   B. IF the Action Code (A/C) is to be changed,
      (1) Enter the Action Code—auto advance.
      OR
      (1) Press cursor return to accept the displayed code.
   C. Enter the From Date—cursor return.
      Do not enter slashes; the program will insert them.
   D. Enter the Thru Date—cursor return.
      Do not enter slashes.
   E. Enter Institute Code—cursor return.
   F. Enter the Institute Name—cursor return.
   G. Enter the Major Code—auto advance.
   H. Enter the Major.
      IF the data item fills the field,
      (1) The cursor will automatically advance to the next field.
      OR
      (1) Enter blanks to fill the field—auto advance.
   I. Enter the Minor Code—auto advance.
   J. Enter the Minor.
      IF the data item fills the field,
      (1) The cursor will automatically advance to the next field.
      OR
      (1) Enter blanks to fill the field—auto advance.
   K. Enter the Degree Level—cursor return.

2. When you are ready to terminate the session:
   A. Press the Escape (ESC) key and the cursor return.
   B. Highlight CLOSE SESSION—press cursor return.

Note: The Institution Name seems out of place when the screen is compared to the source document, but it is keyed in the same order as the source document.

Keying Aids

1. Automatic duplication of Action Code and Date
2. Automatic leading zero fill on numeric fields
3. Automatic cursor advance from Social Security Number, Action Code, Major Code, Major, and Minor Code
4. Automatic generation of Record Number
5. Warning beep on numeric fields
6. Warning beep when field limit is exceeded in manually advanced fields

EMPLOYEE EDUCATIONAL HISTORY

Prepared by L. Moulton   Date 0191 / 61

*Action Code
ADD
CHG
DEL

600

Soc Sec No	A/C 13	From 16	Thru 20	Code 24	Institution Name 27	Code 45	Major 47	Code 51	Minor 53	Level 57
415 16 3075	ADD	0970	0678	493	UNIV WISCONSIN-MAD	44	NOED	413	SCED	PHD
418 53 2278		0968	0678	421	UNIV OF TENNESSEE	5	BADM	13	CSCI	DBA
421 74 8213		0969	0375	102	GEORGIA STATE UNIV	23	MATH	24	PHYS	MS
416 26 7447		0961	0674	015	AUBURN UNIVERSITY	44	HYOED	413	SCED	EDD
422 28 7336		0674	0679	35	BOB JONES UNIV	51	ACCT	53	BADM	MS
354 72 9316		0973	0678	491	UNIV OF WISCONSIN	51	ACCT	53	MGT	MS
423 53 3962		0161	0667	092	FLORIDA STATE UNIV	32	PSCI	33	PSY	LLD
416 88 7846		0970	0978	091	UNIV OF FLORIDA	34	SOC	33	PSY	PHD
421 91 5882		0970	0676	173	WEST KENTUCKY UNIV	42	HPR	413	SCED	MS
416 28 7265		0971	0676	011	UNIV OF ALABAMA	15	ENG	13	CSCI	MS
425 65 4395		0368	0677	013	ALABAMA-BIRMINGHAM	33	PSY	34	SOC	LLD
356 24 3765		0670	0976	35	OHIO STATE UNIV	14	ENG	23	MATH	MS
206 14 2762		0368	0578	381	UNIV OF PENN	3 H	SOC	33	PSY	LLD
417 22 2863		0167	0978	326	COLUMBIA UNIVERSITY	44	HYOED	31	EH	EDD
418 42 6078		0971	0676	435	EAST TEXAS STATE	13	CSCI	53	BADM	MS
421 81 3526		0971	0679	332	NORTH CAROLINA ST	21	BIOL	22	CHEM	PHD
426 52 5900		0972	0677	171	UNIV OF KENTUCKY	13	PSCI	42	HPR	MA
419 70 0873		0671	0377	015	AUBURN UNIVERSITY	51	BADM	51	ACCT	MS
354 61 2378		0970	0678	317	CORNELL UNIVERSITY	33	PSY	34	SOC	PHD
364 72 3768		0971	0672	22	MICHIGAN STATE UM	15	ENG	23	MATH	MS

EMPLOYEE EDUCATIONAL HISTORY

Date 0901 — 61
Prepared by L. Moulton

*Action Code
ADD
CHG
DEL

600

Soc Sec No 01	A/C 13	From 16	Thru 20	Code 24	Institution Name 27	Code 45	Major 47	Code 51	Minor 53	Level 57
416159817	ADD	0971	0676	182	LOUISIANA ST UNIV	91	ART	34	SOC	MA
421851564		0970	0677	018	SAMFORD UNIVERSITY	52	ADM	34	SOC	MBA
419859627		0971	0677	101	UNIV OF GEORGIA	14	EENG	23	MATH	MS
421514466		0362	0869	012	ALABAMA A+M	15	MENS	52	ADM	PHD
418229002		0972	0667	092	FLORIDA STATE UM	15	MENS	23	MATH	MS
416185097		0672	0577	148	PURDUE UNIVERSITY	11	AEME	22	CHEM	MS
419987126		0971	0679	242	MISSISSIPPI STATE	34	SOC	32	PSCI	PHD
422776824		0370	0578	182	LOUISIANA ST UNIV	32	PSCI	14	ELED	PAD
418235700		0170	0679	171	UNIV OF KENTUCKY	42	HPR	14	ELED	EDD
417237956		0971	0577	173	WEST KENTUCKY UNIV	31	EH	21	BJO	PHD
415255386		0170	0783	321	NEW YORK UNIV	32	PSCI	34	SOC	LLD
426286613		0971	0976	329	FORDHAM UNIVERSITY	31	EH	32	PSCI	MA
419386231		0971	0676	092	FLORIDA STATE UNIV	13	CSCI	23	MATH	MS
421527252		0970	0376	365	AUBURN UNIVERSITY	33	ASYI	32	PSCI	MA
416231812		0969	0675	361	OKLAHOMA CITY UNIV	52	BADM	51	ACCT	MBA
365217921		0670	0375	361	UNIV OF OKLAHOMA	13	CSCI	51	ACCT	MS
354873726		0969	0675	361	UNIV OF OKLAHOMA	22	CHEM	23	MATH	PHD
346441927		0970	0675	387	DREXEL INST TECH	14	EENG	23	MATH	PHD
211846.1		0368	0777	387	DREXEL INST TECH	14	EENG	23	MATH	PHD
212327883		0971	0676	388	VILLANOVA UNIV	15	MENS	23	MATH	MS

Action Code
ADD
CHG
DEL

Prepared by *L. Mouton*

Date 01 | 0901

01 Soc Sec No	600	A/C 13	From 16	Thru 20	Code 24	Institution Name 27	Code 45 / Major 47	Code 51 / Minor 53	Level 57
422 87 8365		CHG	0975	0980	33	2 NORTH CAROLINA ST	1 HEENG	23 MATH	MS
416 18 3109			0674	0880	38	2 PENN STATE UNIV	11 AENG	21 BIO	MS
417 52 8198			0375	0980	44	21 UNIV OF TENNESSEE	2 12 CHEM	23 MATH	MS
419 33 3550			0971	0680	11	1 UNIV OF ALABAMA	1 HEENG	24 PHYS	PHD
421 25 5350			0670	0802	21	UNIV OF MICHIGAN	33 PSY	31 EH	KLD
416 18 9066			0969	0680	01	5 AUBURN UNIVERSITY	33 PSY	32 PSCI	PHD
416 13 2020			0971	0580	32	SOUTHERN METHODIST	3 30 14 HEENG	22 CHEM	MS
417 22 53 04			0974	0680	35	20 OHIO STATE UNIV	13 CSCI	23 MATH	MS
418 23 8390			0973	0980	44	33 TEXAS CHRISTIAN	52 BADM	51 ACCT	MBA
418 22 6609			0672	0980	36	1 UNIV OF OKLAHOMA	44 VOED	34 SOC	EDD
417 13 9831			0674	0680	42	13 MEMPHIS STATE UNIV	15 MGT	53 MGT	MBA
415 23 9083			0974	0880	10	3 GEORGIA INST TECH	15 MGT	13 CSCI	MS
416 81 0226			0974	0880	35	10 OHIO STATE UNIV	1 HEENG	23 MATH	MS
417 32 9038			0974	0980	33	2 NORTH CAROLINA ST	44 VOED	24 PK	MS
212 71 21 65			0974	0680	51	3 IOWA STATE UNIV	53 MGT	51 ACCT	MBA
209 73 16 29			0975	0980	21	2 MASS INST TECH	1 HEENG	23 MATH	MS
212 03 71 31			0974	0380	21	1 HARVARD UNIV	32 PSCI	34 SOC	MA
354 61 73 12			0673	0380	35	20 OHIO STATE UNIV	52 BADM	13 CSCI	MBA
364 52 01 03			0974	0680	13	4 SOUTH ILLINOIS UNIV	52 BADM	51 ACCT	MBA
			0975	0680	22	2 MICHIGAN STATE UM	15 MENG	52 BADM	MS

EMPLOYEE EDUCATIONAL HISTORY

Prepared by L. Moulton
Date 0901 / 61

Soc Sec No 01	A/C 13	From 16	Thru 20	Code 24	Institution Name 27	Code 45 / Major 47	Code 51 / Minor 53	Level 57
423 26 1652	CHG	0974	0980	317	CORNELL UNIVERSITY	34 SOC	32 PSCI	MA
418 67 6528		0674	0880	471	WASHINGTON UNIV	32 PSCI	34 SOC	MS
418 70 1255		0975	0680	171	UNIV OF NEBRASKA	21 BIO	22 CHEM	MS
415 13 2640		0973	0680	103	GEORGIA INST TECH	12 CENG	52 BADM	MS
416 91 2843		0671	0690	18	SAMFORD UNIVERSITY	33 PSY	34 SOC	PHD
423 42 0655		0674	0880	362	OKLAHOMA STATE UNI	52 BADM	23 MATH	MBA
418 51 1328		0973	0890	182	LOUISIANA STATE UNI	51 ACCT	53 MGT	MS
416 95 0917		0974	0880	141	INDIANA UNIVERSITY	11 AENG	21 BIO	MS
421 91 5124		0875	0303	04	NORTH TEXAS STATE	13 CSCI	23 MATH	MS
424 74 3455		0675	0380	131	ILLINOIS UNIVERSITY	43 SCED	34 SOC	MS
426 22 2092		0371	0680	11	HARVARD UNIVERSITY	32 PSCI	34 SOC	PHD
417 23 4337		0972	0680	32	NEW YORK UNIV	33 PSY	34 SOC	PHD
416 48 2555		0975	0690	09	UNIV OF FLORIDA	11 AENG	23 MATH	MS
425 32 5511		0975	0880	22	UNIV OF MICHIGAN	14 EENG	21 BIO	MS
425 67 7592		0675	0880	22	MICHIGAN STATE UNI	21 BIO	22 CHEM	MS
415 92 9812		0875	0680	384	BLOOMSBURG STATE	44 HVDED	52 BADM	MS
417 91 3060		0975	0680	433	EAST TEXAS STATE	13 CSCI	52 BADM	MS
41 16 54 4532		0975	0680	183	TULANE UNIVERSITY	13 PSCI	51 ACCT	MS
01 72 08 90		0172	0890	015	AUBURN UNIVERSITY	32 PSCI	34 SOC	PHD
		0973	0303	0162	KANSAS STATE UNIV	52 BADM	53 MGT	MBA

EMPLOYEE EDUCATIONAL HISTORY

Prepared by *L. Moulton*

Date 61 | 090.1

*Action Code
ADD
CHG
DEL

600

Soc Sec No	A/C 13	From 16	Thru 20	Code 24	Institution Name 27	Code 45 Major 47	Code 51 Minor 53	Level 57
414 575 236	DEL	0972	0676	016	JACKSONVILLE ST UN	34 SOC	33 PSY	BA
415 23 8897		0974	0678	362	OKLAHOMA STATE UN	44 VOED	23 MATH	AS
421 34 8623		0671	0679	01	ATHENS COLLEGE	41 SCED	23 MATH	EDD
422 93 1510		0972	0676	011	UNIV OF ALABAMA	13 CSCI	51 ACCT	MS
424 43 2133		0971	0678	11	UNIV OF ALABAMA	23 MATH	24 PHYS	MA
417 22 9749		0368	0673	015	AUBURN UNIVERSITY	33 PSY	32 PSY	LLD
421 45 7508		0966	0676	40	OKLAHOMA BAPTIST	31 EH	34 SOC	PHD
423 22 5411		0971	0676	363	CENTRAL STATE UN	13 CSCI	51 ACCT	MS
412 62 2074		0972	0678	141	INDIANA UNIVERSITY	52 BADM	51 ACCT	MA
414 26 3321		0368	0679	183	TULANE UNIVERSITY	33 PSY	34 SOC	PHD
415 75 9788		0671	0879	311	UNIV OF NEW MEXICO	42 HPR	44 VOED	EDD
421 39 5031		0972	0674	34	UNIV OF HOUSTON	51 ACCT	52 BADM	BS
423 29 1611		0974	0780	11	UNIV OF COLORADO	52 BADM	51 ACCT	MS
424 12 2379		0975	0679	363	CENTRAL STATE UN	13 CSCI	51 ACCT	MS
411 22 0875		0166	0676	161	UNIV OF KANSAS	32 PSY	34 SOC	PHD
433 45 9719		0968	0678	382	PENN STATE UNIV	14 ENG	24 PHYS	PHD
421 21 331?		0968	0677	326	COLUMBIA UNIV	32 PSY	34 SOC	PHD
411 74 37403		0972	0777	386	SLIPPERY ROCK ST	52 BADM	51 ACCT	MOA
424 41 1154		0972	0679	231	UNIV OF MINNESOTA	44 VOED	52 BADM	EDD
		0973	0679	22	MICHIGAN STATE UN	11 AENG	24 PHYS	MS

DATA ENTRY JOB 16:

PAYROLL REGISTER—TEMPORARY EMPLOYEES

PURPOSE

1. To provide practice with concepts already introduced

PREPARATION

In examining the data for Job 16, notice that four fields repeat their contents: the Date and three sections of the Employee Number. The Employee Number is broken into four subfields (Code, Branch, Dept, and Sales Representative), each of which provides some information about the employee. This is a frequent practice with identification numbers, and it leads to repeated data in portions of those numbers.

PROCEDURE

Job 16: Payroll Register—Temporary Employees

Data Entry Screen

Job #16
PAYROLL REGISTER
Temporary Employees

Date: 00/00

Employee	SSN	Name	Rate	Reg	Over	Total	Rec
00 00 000	000 00 0000		000	0000	0000	0000	1

Set-Up

1. Use NumLock to place the keypad in numeric shift.
2. Use CapsLock to shift the alphabetic keys into upper shift.

General Entry

1. For each record to be entered:
   A. IF the Date, Code, Branch, or Dept data changes,
      (1) Press Alt-A and enter the new data (no slashes in date)—cursor return.
      OR
      (1) Cursor return.
   B. Enter Social Security Number—auto advance.
   C. Enter Name, including the comma after the last name and the period after the middle initial—cursor return.
   D. Enter Pay Rate—auto advance.
   E. Enter Regular Hours—auto advance.
   F. Enter Overtime Hours—cursor return.

G. Enter Total Hours—cursor return.

Do not enter slashes; the program will insert them.

2. When you are ready to terminate the session:

A. Press the Escape (ESC) key and the cursor return key.

B. Highlight CLOSE SESSION—press cursor return.

Keying Aids

1. Automatic duplication of Date, Code, Branch, and Department
2. Automatic leading zero fill on numeric fields
3. Automatic cursor advance from Social Security Number, Pay Rate, and Regular Hours
4. Automatic generation of Record Number
5. Warning beep on numeric fields

PAYROLL REGISTER — TEMPORARY EMPLOYEES

Code	Branch	Dept	Sales Rep	Soc Sec No	Name	Rate	Regular	Overtime	Total
C	15	03	043	425 16 5427	SULLIVAN, ARCHIBALD	350	1750	—	1750
			044	418 08 4011	WEAVER, RUSSELL	390	1275	—	1275
			047	419 19 3526	CARTWRIGHT, BRUCE	400	3500	—	3500
			048	205 22 5934	RIALS, EDWIN	325	3000	—	3000
			050	421 18 1421	STEIN, JOHN S.	350	4000	250	4250
			051	421 28 2631	YOUNG, REBECCA	375	1900	—	1900
			053	421 51 1882	BONNER, THOMAS	375	2500	—	2500
			054	425 71 9435	FAUST, KIRK	425	1450	—	1450
			055	415 32 1421	CIULLA, VITO	350	4000	—	4000
			058	418 04 5229	PERYEAR, DERECK	325	1875	—	1875
			060	419 65 4003	TEBO, RICHARD	325	4000	700	4700
			061	425 21 5418	JIMMERSON, RAYMOND	350	4000	1000	5000
			062	427 13 3219	LANCE, CHESTER	425	1200	—	1200
			065	421 12 8147	CHANLER, ORMAND	400	3000	—	3000
			066	421 03 2881	DINAR, NATHANIEL	325	3500	—	3500
			067	425 31 3775	LIBOWSKY, MARTIN	375	3100	—	3100
		04	069	419 34 8779	ADAMS, CHARLES	375	2500	—	2500
			070	216 13 2143	JAFFEE, ABRAHAM	350	2000	—	2000
			071	408 12 1492	BONNER, TERRACE	375	4000	1250	5250
			073	354 27 8622	PLOTINE, MONROE	350	4000	—	4000

Week Ending __12/20__

PAYROLL REGISTER — TEMPORARY EMPLOYEES

| Employee Number | | | | Soc Sec No | Name | Rate | Hours | | |
Code	Branch	Dept	Sales Rep				Regular	Overtime	Total
C	15	04	075	421 04 2614	GARRIS, WAYNE	385	1350	—	1350
			076	418 62 7176	PASCOE, ELIZABETH	325	1450	—	1450
			079	408 13 3233	FONTENOT, PAUL E.	350	1775	—	1775
			080	420 34 6541	HARRIS, MAURICE	325	1500	—	1500
			081	421 23 0124	ENGEL, GORDON	420	1275	—	1275
			082	418 21 5025	BRACKEN, MAJOR	375	4000	0750	4750
			083	408 88 2934	CALERA, EUNICE P.	375	1200	—	1200
			084	419 94 4161	KEEN, ALLAN	325	4000	0500	4500
			087	419 16 3672	LENTZ, DEN	350	1275	—	1275
			088	418 03 7091	DIXON, RODNEY	390	3500	—	3500
			090	418 64 1027	KIMBRELL, LARRY	410	3000	—	3000
			091	427 35 9367	OLSEN, MARK T.	400	3500	—	3500
			092	421 27 4117	NGUYEN, MOHIT	375	2500	—	2500
			094	420 72 5992	ACTON, MERLE	325	2000	—	2000
			095	419 60 1649	MAZOR, LAWRENCE	375	1500	—	1500
			096	419 12 8176	HILL, DAVID F.	390	3000	—	3000
			099	425 21 6222	STADDARD, AARON	325	2500	—	2500
		1	100	235 18 9038	JACKSON, ARTHUR	325	2500	—	2500
	1		101	351 46 6449	TEMPLE, NEAL	350	2000	—	2000
1			102	418 22 1875	ALLEN, THOMAS	350	1875	—	1875

PAYROLL REGISTER — TEMPORARY EMPLOYEES

Code	Branch	Dept	Sales Rep	Soc Sec No	Name	Rate	Regular	Overtime	Total
C	15	06	163	526 54 1563	GRAY, PHILIP M.	325	3500	—	3500
			164	329 32 2399	GOLDERT, JAMES	455	3000	—	3000
			165	416 92 5943	IRBY, JANICE	375	1550	—	1550
			167	418 33 6601	LAMBERT, CHARLES	375	4000	0800	4800
			168	421 96 1450	UPDIKE, BRENDA	325	1500	—	1500
			170	421 06 4360	KRANITSKY, KALVIN	375	1875	—	1875
			174	428 60 2877	RODRIGUEZ, MARCUS	350	3500	—	3500
			175	421 25 8090	LISTER, RUFUS	390	1650	—	1650
			176	419 52 2505	FANT, HUBERT	350	2500	—	2500
			177	419 36 1656	HAMBY, PRICE J.	350	3600	—	3600
			178	408 30 7096	PUYA, RUTHANN	425	2725	—	2725
			179	418 43 4357	JOHNSON, GARY	375	4000	—	4000
			180	425 82 1495	MAPLES, TERESA	410	3500	—	3500
			181	418 79 8361	ALLEY, EARNEST	400	4000	0200	4200
			182	418 13 4255	SHARMON, TALMADGE	375	1250	—	1250
			184	426 76 5814	KABASE, HARVEY	425	4000	0250	4250
			185	418 40 4269	CHASTEEN, ANDREW	390	1700	—	1700
		07	188	420 37 0624	LENOIR, KENNETH	350	1275	—	1275
		1	189	421 74 7479	BASTON, ROBERT N.	350	2725	—	2725
	1	1	191	423 88 9092	HAGGON, WALTER	325	2000	—	2000

PAYROLL REGISTER — TEMPORARY EMPLOYEES

Code	Branch	Dept	Sales Rep	Soc Sec No	Name	Rate	Hours Regular	Overtime	Total
C	15	07	193	422 62 5167	HOLMES, ROGER	4 25	35 00	—	35 00
			194	419 88 3221	DISMUKES, HAROLD	3 50	40 00	06 00	46 00
			197	419 33 6262	STABB, MICHEAL	3 50	30 00	—	30 00
			198	421 74 5226	FARMER, MONROE	3 50	16 50	—	16 50
			199	626 36 9649	ECHOLS, KAREN	3 75	15 00	—	15 00
			201	411 56 2006	SPIRIDIGLIOZZI, VICTOR	4 25	25 00	—	25 00
			202	418 71 1711	LOCKE, WILLIAM	3 75	35 00	—	35 00
			206	418 26 3250	INSTONE, MORTON	3 25	40 00	12 50	52 50
			207	423 20 5843	McCOLLISTER, JOHN D.	4 10	20 00	—	20 00
			208	636 50 9880	ELROD, MICHEAL	3 25	26 00	—	26 00
			209	205 34 8131	HARVELL, YOLANDA	3 50	25 00	—	25 00
			213	417 55 1856	LANE, SPENCER	3 90	19 75	—	19 75
		08	214	414 41 2323	PLEMMENS, RALPH	3 50	29 00	—	29 00
			216	426 85 1975	ZIMMERMAN, MILTON	3 75	14 25	—	14 25
			217	595 29 6066	ABBST, LAWERENCE	4 00	40 00	05 00	45 00
			218	415 49 5416	BOLVIG, ANTHONY	3 25	35 00	—	35 00
			219	418 54 8623	SPRADLEY, FLINT	3 75	18 75	—	18 75
			220	418 68 2169	MIZELL, BENJAMEN	3 50	20 00	—	20 00
			221	418 94 9116	COATES, BETTY	3 50	17 25	—	17 25
			222	421 23 7227	ENISE, GEORGE	3 50	25 00	—	25 00

PAYROLL REGISTER — TEMPORARY EMPLOYEES

| Employee Number | | | | Soc Sec No | Name | Rate | Hours | | |
Code	Branch	Dept	Sales Rep				Regular	Overtime	Total
C	15	08	253	425 75 0792	LONERGAN, DONALD	375	15 00	— —	15 00
			254	421 26 6083	DYAL, BERRY T.	350	30 00	—	30 00
		1	255	421 30 6225	MOGAB, OLA R.	390	20 00	—	20 00
		09	256	421 14 2417	CALHOUN, SAMUEL	425	35 00	—	35 00
			259	418 32 6291	SISSON, THOMAS	425	35 00	—	35 00
			260	420 91 4209	DOWNING, FRANK	375	40 00	11 00	51 00
			261	420 37 1275	KEARNS, PAUL	350	40 00	06 00	46 00
			262	418 41 6241	SPEARS, WILLIAM	350	20 00	—	20 00
			263	418 76 7524	EADS, TROY	325	25 00	—	25 00
			266	426 23 8228	CASADAY, STERLING	410	25 00	—	25 00
			267	452 15 4126	KAYLOR, GYLE	350	16 00	—	16 00
			268	421 80 3213	DORER, LINCOLN	375	12 50	—	12 50
			269	421 71 6747	AINSWORTH, CARRIE	310	20 00	—	20 00
			270	422 29 3697	SHAHID, GENEVA	375	12 75	—	12 75
			272	419 64 4800	NEWSOME, JOSEPH	375	16 00	—	16 00
			274	420 26 5155	ARVIN, RACHAEL	425	20 00	—	20 00
			275	528 59 7863	RASCO, NEWMAN	350	25 00	—	25 00
		1	276	821 90 1475	VORHEES, COLONEL	350	14 50	—	14 50
		10	277	416 87 2772	NERO, SIDNEY T.	325	15 00	—	15 00
1	1	1	278	415 14 7916	SEKHON, SARAH	325	15 00	—	15 00

DATA ENTRY JOB 17:

TELEPHONE ORDERS (CHARGE TO ACCOUNT)

PURPOSE

1. To provide practice with the use of multiple screens

PREPARATION

As you examine the data for Job 17, you will see that it contains two types of records: a detail record and a total record. Like Job 16, it contains a data item that is made up of both digits and letters: the Customer Number. The first three portions of the Customer Number are numeric, but the final character is an S, an R, or an E. The data entry program provides the proper format for you, but you must use the Shift key to enter a capital letter.

Job 17 will test your ability to concentrate. Like Job 16, it contains a mixture of manually and automatically advanced fields. The Description and Color/Finish fields require shifting for capital letters. If the Description is too long for the field length, a warning beep will sound when the field is full. Move to the next field by pressing cursor return.

PROCEDURE

Job 17: Telephone Orders

Job 17 contains two types of records: (1) a detail record containing information about an item that has been ordered and (2) a total record containing totals on Clerk Number, Quantity, and Price. Of course, a total of Clerk Numbers makes no sense arithmetically, but it is a hash total used for data control. The Totals on Quantity and Price are batch totals for data control.

Because Job 17 has two types of records, it presents two screens. Both the detail screen and the total screen are illustrated below.

Data Entry Screen (Detail)

```
Job #17
TELEPHONE ORDERS          Charge to Account     Date    00/00
        Clerk: 0000                                     Pounds: 0000
Customer: 00000000        Description:                  Ounces: 00
        Item: 00000               Size:                 Price: 0000
Quantity: 000        Color/Finish:          Record: 1
```

Set-Up

1. Use NumLock to place the keypad in numeric shift.

General Entry

1. IF a detail record is to be entered:
   A. IF the Date, Clerk Number, or Item Number is to be changed,
      (1) Press Alt-A and enter the new data item. The Date and Item Number will advance automatically. Press cursor return to advance Clerk Number.
   B. Enter Quantity—cursor return.
   C. Enter Item Description—cursor return.
   D. Enter Item Size—cursor return.
   E. Enter Color or Finish—cursor return.
   F. Enter Pounds—cursor return.
   G. Enter Ounces—cursor return.
   H. Enter Item Price—cursor return.

   OR

   A. Press Alt + R to select the screen for totals. The screen below will display:

Data Entry Screen (Total)

Job #17
TELEPHONE ORDERS
Charge to Account

Total Clerk:	Total Qty:	Total Price:
000000	00000	00000000

   B. Enter Clerk Total—cursor return.
   C. Enter Quantity Total—cursor return.
   D. Enter Price Total—cursor return.
   E. The system will return to the previous screen.

2. When you are ready to terminate the session:
   A. Press the Escape (ESC) key and the cursor return key.
   B. Highlight CLOSE SESSION-press the cursor return.

Note: Key the alphabetic items as they appear, with capitals and lowercase letters as indicated. When you select the Insert Records option, the last detail record entered will display. The total record is on disk, but the last detail record displays because it provides more information.

Keying Aids

1. Automatic duplication of Date, Clerk Number, and Customer Number
2. Automatic leading zero fill on numeric fields
3. Automatic cursor advance from selected fields
4. Automatic advance from total screen to detail screen
5. Automatic generation of Record Number
6. Warning beep on numeric fields
7. Warning beep when field limit is exceeded in manually advanced fields

TELEPHONE ORDERS
Charge to Account

Date: 1 / 14
mo. / da.

Clerk Number	Customer Number	Item Number	Qty	Description	Size	Color/Finish	Weight Lbs.	Weight Oz.	Price
1024	6301 6147	E 6 5290	1	Pair mens pants	34b	Cloud blue	2	3	32.90
		6 8395	1	Pair mens pants	34b	Tan	2	7	10.99
		6 0014	1	Mens jacket	38	Brown	2	0	25.00
	8 319 0030 R	0 1207	1	Sewing machine			24	0	219.95
	5 230 4698 5	5 9439	1	Womans blouse				8	10.98
		5 1072	1	Pants suit	10	Red	1	7	35.00
		5 4854	1	Dress	10	Beige	1	0	17.50
		0 1940	1	Hair dryer	10	Black	11	0	29.88
	7 272 4428 5	7 9943	1	Pair draperies	—	Yellow	11	10	95.99
		9 2512	1	Rocking chair	14t	Goldenrod	60	0	169.99
		9 2847	1	Grandfather clock	—	Maple	52	0	289.99
	6 504 6362 E	4 1454	2	Pkgs mens plate	—	Maple	1	14	5.19
		4 1918	2	Pkgs mens undershorts	38	white	1	9	6.98
		4 0612	1	Pair mens pajamas	42	white	1	0	9.00
					42	Blue			
						Green			
		5 2093	1	Ladies girdle	34	Yellow	0	8	7.25
		7 4755	1	Expandable closet rod	72	Stainless	2	12	5.95
	18432		20						990.54

TELEPHONE ORDERS
Charge to Account

Date: _1_ / _14_
mo. / da.

Clerk Number	Customer Number	Item Number	Qty	Description	Size	Color/Finish	Weight Lbs.	Oz.	Price
1024	7066 7235 R	4 3868	1	Man shirt	40	Berry	0	7	7.99
		4 4902	2	Mens sweatshirt	40	Gray	1	5	12.99
		4 2212	1	Pkg. sport socks	—	White	0	6	3.99
	5 1776 1192 R	7 2006	1	Shower head	—	—	1	12	21.99
	6 2027 7781 R	7 1278	2	Bedspread	TWN	Poppy	3	2	19.99
		7 1279	1	Pair drapes	48	Poppy	2	3	15.99
	5 653 6160 E	0 2358	2	Skateboard	—	Red	3	0	16.50
	5 465 A3915	9 5783	1	TV stand	36	Walnut	22	0	27.95
	4 804 9057 R	D 7324	1	Folding door	13D	Oak	27	0	34.95
	6 967 1579 R	2 4854	1	Pr. boys hats	12	Brown	1	10	15.99
		2 8625	4	Pr. boys jeans	12	Denim	1	0	10.49
		2 9211	1	Belt buckle	—	Copper	0	4	3.50
		0 4239	1	Towel bar	24	Stainless	1	4	7.49
	8 123 7819 R	4 7749	1	Pr. mens shorts	9D	Chocolate	1	15	17.99
		5 4609	1	Pr. womens shoes	75A	Beige	1	6	17.00
		5 5463	1	Pr. womens slippers	8	Pink	1	0	5.39
		2 1462	1	Pr. boys shoes	3C	Brown	1	8	10.99
		2 1462	1	Pr. boys shoes	1C	Brown	1	8	10.99

18432   24   26 2.17

TELEPHONE ORDERS
Charge to Account

Date: 2 / 15 (mo. / da.)

Clerk Number	Customer Number	Item Number	Qty	Description	Size	Color/Finish	Weight Lbs.	Oz.	Price
1037	6 360 2838 R	9 6585	1	Entertainment Center	—	Walnut	65	0	79.99
	8 021 6593 R	7 0619	1	Clock	—	Brass	6	0	34.95
		7 2035	1	Mirror	—	—	10	8	21.99
		9 5544	1	Piano Lamp	—	Brass	5	8	34.99
	8713 5613 R	7 3997	1	Wastebasket	—	Bamboo	1	6	9.50
		7 4433	1	Clothes Hamper	—	Bamboo	10	0	25.00
		7 3922	1	Towel Stand	—	Bamboo	10	8	24.00
		7 4458	1	Wall Cabinet	—	Bamboo	6	4	30.00
	2 377 1974 R	3 4055	1	Leotard	M	Sun Yellow / Burgundy / Jade	0	8	9.92
		3 1188	1	Pr. Jazz Shoes	7	Black	1	12	13.92
		5 4305	1	Girdle	6	White	0	8	12.70
		5 6399	1	Jumpsuit	18	Medium Blue	0	14	24.00
		1 7741	1	Watch	—	Gold			14.88
	4 299 4656 R	9 2193	1	Musical Mobile	—	—	2	0	15.99
	6 900 0696 R	0 2205	1	Washburn Faucet	—	Chrome	2	3	14.95
		9 2026	1	Franklin Stove	4FT	Black	402	0	610.00
		9 1593	2	Rocking Chair	—	Mustard	76	0	149.92
		7 4360	4	Foam Pillows	REG	Blue	2	0	7.50

27   20740   1154.31

TELEPHONE ORDERS
Charge to Account

Date: __2__/__15__
mo. / da.

Clerk Number	Customer Number	Item Number	Qty	Description	Size	Color/Finish	Weight Lbs.	Oz.	Price
2/15	5012 4754	5 0 8692	1	Upright vacuum cleaner	—	Yellow	14	8	97.95
	A 032 1427 R 1	6445	1	Ladies bangle watch	—	Gold	0	8	42.95
		5 2851	1	Swim suit	12	Blue check	1	0	23.00
		5 2610	1	Raincoat	12	Parchment	1	12	49.99
		5 1013	1	Folding umbrella	—	Parchment	1	3	7.95
		5 1026	1	Rain hat	M	Parchment	0	4	15.29
		5 1417	1	Strapless bra	34B	Black	0	4	7.50
	6 070 8852 R	0 6491	1	Suitcase	P	Red	13	2	89.00
		0 6495	1	Tote bag	—	Red	3	4	58.00
	4 803 2567 R	5 2820	1	Swim suit	18	Green	0	12	30.00
		5 2889	1	Beach coat	18	Green	0	4	9.50
		5 1071	1	Terry turban	L	White	1	0	5.00
	2 476 9141 R	9 7052	1	Rug	6x9	Blue	23	0	75.00
		9 3487	1	Chandelier	9LT	Brass	22	0	169.99
		9 7203	2	Cotton blanket	DBL	White	3	4	17.50
		9 7184	1	Bedspread	DBL	White	6	8	59.99
		9 7993	1	Brass bed	DBL	Antique	100	0	999.99
36805			18				1758		60

154

CHAPTER 4

TELEPHONE ORDERS
Charge to Account

Date: 2/15 (mo./da.)

Clerk Number	Customer Number	Item Number	Qty	Description	Size	Color/Finish	Weight Lbs.	Weight Oz.	Price
3075	3564 0148 R5	2824	1	Blouse	18	Green	0	9	17 00
	2	5 2831	1	Skirt	18	Peal	1	0	21 00
	2952 2453 54	4 4071	1	Pair pajamas	B	Red	0	6	7 50
		4 4071	1	Pair pajamas	C	Blue	0	6	7 50
		5 3041	2	Leotard	S	Black	0	8	15 00
		5 3073	1	Nightgown	7	Pink	0	11	9 00
	5544 8460 E	0 9275	1	Boy's bicycle	—	Red	43	0	124 99
	1290 5793 R	0 8112	1	Lawn mower	—	—	90	0	269 99
		0 9037	1	Ceiling fan	—	Brass	23	0	299 99
		0 9055	1	Skylight	—	Smoke	18	0	75 95
		7 7714	1	Clock	—	Walnut	15	0	35 99
	6412 1287 R0	8550	1	Television set	12	Pewter	16	0	94 00
		4 4152	1	Pair jeans	4	Tan	0	12	9 50
		4 4122	1	Star trek log	M	Tan	0	7	3 50

43050   /15   990 96

DATA ENTRY JOB 18:

ADVANCED REGISTRATION

This job contains some intentional errors provided for use in search operations on the 3740 series. Ask your instructor how to key this data.

PURPOSES

1. To provide practice with the use of multiple screens
2. To introduce mental conversion of source document fields and handling of exceptional data

PREPARATION

Job 18 also contains records of two types, but these are both detail records. The first record contains data about the person registering for the conference; the second record contains data about the organization the person represents. Instead of having a group of detail records followed by a total record, Job 18 has one format detail record that is followed by another format detail record. In this case, the Job contains two different data entry screens, and the data entry program will change screens for you automatically because it knows when the next screen is wanted.

This Job requires extra operator attention in three fields: the Date, ZIP Code, and State fields. The Date on the source document is in mixed letters and digits, whereas the Date on the screen is all numeric. You must make this conversion in your head, substituting 3 for March, and so on.

The State Name on the source document is spelled out, but the screen allows only two character positions for the state. You must substitute the correct abbreviation for the state as you key. Prepare for this by determining the correct abbreviations for the states before you begin work.

The alphabetic data is to be entered as it appears, with a mixture of capital and lowercase letters. In the alphabetic fields, shifting must be done by the operator.

PROCEDURE

Job 18: Advanced Registration

Data Entry Screen One

Job #18
ADVANCED REGISTRATION

Reg: 00000   Date: 0000   Name:
Title:
Phone: EXT   Record 001

Set-Up

1. Use NumLock to place the keypad in numeric shift.

General Entry

1. For each participant in the conference:
   A. Enter the participant's detail record:
      (1) Enter Registration Number—auto advance.
      (2) Enter Date—cursor return.
      (3) Enter Name—cursor return.
      (4) Enter Title—cursor return.
      (5) Enter Phone—auto advance.
      (6) Enter Extension—auto advance.
   B. The program will accept the participant's record and display the screen for the organization's record (Screen Two).

Data Entry Screen Two

Job # 18
ADVANCED REGISTRATION

FIRM:
ADDRESS:
CITY:
STATE: ZIP: 00000   RECORD: 002

      (1) Enter Firm Name—cursor return.
      (2) Enter Address—cursor return.
      (3) Enter City—cursor return.
      (4) Enter State abbreviation—auto advance.
      (5) Enter ZIP Code—auto advance.

C. The program will accept the record and display the screen for the participant's record (Screen One).

2. When you are ready to terminate the session,
   A. Press the Escape (ESC) key and the cursor return key.
   B. Highlight CLOSE SESSION—press cursor return.

Note: Key the alphabetic items as they appear, with capital and lowercase letters as indicated. When you select the Add Records option, the last record presently in the file will display. In Job 18, that will frequently be the organization's record. This is not an error. It is the last record entered.

Keying Aids

1. Automatic duplication of Date
2. Automatic cursor advance from selected fields
3. Automatic generation of Record Number
4. Warning beep on numeric fields

ADVANCED REGISTRATION

Conference Title <u>Distributed Data Entry vs. Centralized Data Entry</u>

Page <u>1</u> of <u>6</u>

Reg. No. 12001   **Date** March 4

Name Charles Mulford

Title Director of Data Processing

Phone 205-853-2100 **Ext.** 237

Firm Jefferson State Junior College

Address 2601 Carson Road

City Birmingham

State Alabama   **Zip** 35215

Reg. No. 12002   **Date** March 4

Name Marcia Moulton

Title Associate Professor

Phone 215-643-5000 **Ext.** 123

Firm Montgomery County Community College

Address 1976 DeKalb Pike

City Blue Bell

State Pennsylvania **Zip** 19422

Reg. No. 12003   **Date** March 4

Name Linda Morgan

Title Coordinator of Data Processing

Phone 815-838-1500 **Ext.** 338

Firm Lewis University

Address Route 53

City Lockport

State Illinois   **Zip** 60441

Reg. No. 12004   **Date** March 4

Name Paul Morgan

Title Instructor

Phone 215-884-5300 **Ext.** 244

Firm Beaver College

Address 2500 Philadelphia Avenue

City Glenside

State Pennsylvania **Zip** 19038

Reg. No. 12005   **Date** March 4

Name Donald R. Murtha

Title Coordinator of Data Entry

Phone 206-587-3238 **Ext.** 312

Firm Seattle Central Community College

Address 1710 Broadway

City Seattle

State Washington   **Zip** 98122

ADVANCED REGISTRATION

Reg. No. 12006   **Date** March 4

Name Martin Ed. Myers

Title Instructor

Phone 618-943-6321 **Ext.** 237

Firm Ambraw Valley Vocational Center

Address 714 Tenth Street

City Lawrenceville

State Illinois   **Zip** 62439

Reg. No. 12007   **Date** March 4

Name Denise A. Nass

Title Data Entry Instructor

Phone 515-832-6123 **Ext.** 595

Firm Iowa Central Community College

Address 1725 Beach Street

City Webster City

State Iowa   **Zip** 50595

Reg. No. 12008   **Date** March 4

Name Edwin Pierce

Title Coordinator of Data Entry

Phone 405-449-3391 **Ext.** 309

Firm Mid-America AVTS

Address Box H

City Wayne

State Oklahoma   **Zip** 73095

Reg. No. 12009   **Date** March 4

Name Lillian B. Morgan

Title Instructor, Data Entry

Phone 214-593-4410 **Ext.** 107

Firm Tyler Junior College

Address 5th Avenue

City Tyler

State Texas   **Zip** 75701

Reg. No. 12010   **Date** March 4

Name Steve Preston

Title Asst. Prof., Computer Science

Phone 918-587-5616 **Ext.** 163

Firm Tulsa Junior College

Address 909 South Boston

City Tulsa

State Oklahoma   **Zip** 74119

ADVANCED REGISTRATION

Reg. No. __12011__   Date __March 4__   Firm ____Hutchinson Community Junior College__

Name ____David L. Pryor____   Address ____1300 North Plum Street____

Title ____Director, Data Processing____   City ____Hutchinson____

Phone ____316-663-7815__ Ext. __107__   State ____Kansas____ Zip ____67501____

Reg. No. __12012__   Date __March 4__   Firm ____Southern Area Vocational Tech.____

Name ____John W. Preston____   Address ____Highway 70, East____

Title ____Coordinator of Computer Science____   City ____Ardmore____

Phone ____405-223-2700__ Ext. __205__   State ____Oklahoma____ Zip ____73401____

Reg. No. __12013__   Date __March 4__   Firm ____Jackson State Community College____

Name ____Otto Richardson____   Address ____P. O. Box 2467____

Title ____Director Data Processing____   City ____Jackson____

Phone ____901-424-3520__ Ext. __214__   State ____Tennessee____ Zip ____38301____

Reg. No. __12014__   Date __March 4__   Firm ____Ricks College____

Name ____Edmund A. Rahm____   Address ____COB 412, Business Department____

Title ____Associate Professor____   City ____Rexburg____

Phone ____208-356-4176__ Ext. __321__   State ____Idaho____ Zip ____83440____

Reg. No. __12015__   Date __March 4__   Firm ____Laurel Oaks Community College____

Name ____Denise Roberts____   Address ____Old State Route 73____

Title ____Coordinator, Data Entry____   City ____Wilmington____

Phone ____513-382-4111__ Ext. __148__   State ____Ohio____ Zip ____45177____

ADVANCED REGISTRATION

Reg. No. __12016__   **Date** __March 4__   **Firm** __Community College of Denver__

Name __Joan M. Ritenour__   **Address** __1001 E. 62nd Avenue__

Title __Instructor, Data Processing__   **City** __Denver__

Phone __303-287-3311__ **Ext.** __312__   **State** __Colorado__ **Zip** __80216__

Reg. No. __12017__   **Date** __March 4__   **Firm** __South Oklahoma City Junior College__

Name __Betty S. Ross__   **Address** __7777 South May__

Title __Instructor, Data Entry__   **City** __Oklahoma City__

Phone __405-682-6111__ **Ext.** __333__   **State** __Oklahoma__ **Zip** __73159__

Reg. No. __12018__   **Date** __March 4__   **Firm** __Clarion State College__

Name __Elizabeth Rogers__   **Address** __400 South Pennsylvania Avenue__

Title __Assistant Professor__   **City** __Clarion__

Phone __814-226-7000__ **Ext.** __179__   **State** __Pennsylvania__ **Zip** __16214__

Reg. No. __12019__   **Date** __March 4__   **Firm** __Fort Lewis College__

Name __Dennis E. Taft__   **Address** __1400 Mountain Drive__

Title __Instructor, Computer Science__   **City** __Durango__

Phone __303-247-7433__ **Ext.** __349__   **State** __Texas__ **Zip** __81301__

Reg. No. __12020__   **Date** __March 4__   **Firm** __Gordon Cooper Area Vocational Tech.__

Name __Wanda W. Hinson__   **Address** __Box 848__

Title __Data Entry Instructor__   **City** __Shawnee__

Phone __405-273-7493__ **Ext.** __380__   **State** __Oklahoma__ **Zip** __74801__

ADVANCED REGISTRATION

Reg. No. 12021   **Date** March 4   **Firm** Univ. of Science & Arts of Okla.

Name Betty W. Gowder   **Address** Box 3387

Title Data Entry Instructor   **City** Chickasha

Phone 405-224-3140 **Ext.** 271   **State** Oklahoma **Zip** 73018

Reg. No. 12022   **Date** March 4   **Firm** Oklahoma Christian College

Name Charlotte W. Howell   **Address** Rt. 1, Box 141

Title Instructor, Computer Science   **City** Oklahoma City

Phone 405-478-1616 **Ext.** 544   **State** Oklahoma **Zip** 73111

Reg. No. 12023   **Date** March 4   **Firm** Missouri State University

Name Betty Hamilton   **Address** 900 Normal Avenue

Title Associate Professor, Data Entry   **City** Cape Girardeau

Phone 314-334-8211 **Ext.** 457   **State** Missouri **Zip** 63701

Reg. No. 12024   **Date** March 4   **Firm** Foster Estes Technical College

Name William E. Hanna   **Address** 4901 South Bryant

Title Coordinator Computer Science   **City** Oklahoma City

Phone 405-672-3217 **Ext.** 397   **State** Oklahoma **Zip** 73109

Reg. No. 12025   **Date** March 8   **Firm** College of the Sequoias

Name Ruth J. Howeth   **Address** 915 South Mooney Blvd.

Title Associate Professor   **City** Visalia

Phone 209-733-2005 **Ext.** 528   **State** California **Zip** 93277

ADVANCED REGISTRATION

Reg. No. 12026   Date March 8   Firm _____ Hendrix College

Name _____ Mark N. Howell   Address _____ 450 Razorback Avenue

Title _____ Director Data Processing   City _____ Conway

Phone _____ 501-329-6822 Ext. 380   State _____ Arkansas   Zip _____ 72032

Reg. No. 12027   Date March 8   Firm _____ Iowa Western Community College

Name _____ Barbara J. Humphrey   Address _____ 2700 West College Road

Title _____ Coordinator Data Entry   City _____ Council Bluffs

Phone _____ 712-328-8313 Ext. 353   State _____ Iowa   Zip _____ 51501

Reg. No. 12028   Date March 8   Firm _____ Kennedy-King College

Name _____ Amos T. Harrington   Address _____ 6800 South Wentworth

Title _____ Chairman, Computer Science   City _____ Chicago

Phone _____ 312-762-2223 Ext. 385   State _____ Illinois   Zip _____ 60621

Reg. No. 12029   Date March 8   Firm _____ Clarke College

Name _____ Dorothy E. Hathaway   Address _____ 100 College Avenue

Title _____ Data Entry Instructor   City _____ Dubuque

Phone _____ 319-588-3600 Ext. 423   State _____ Iowa   Zip _____ 51002

Reg. No. 12030   Date March 8   Firm _____ Cameron University

Name _____ Marianne E. Jones   Address _____ 2800 West Gore Street

Title _____ Director Data Entry   City _____ Lawton

Phone _____ 405-248-2000 Ext. 47   State _____ Oklahoma   Zip _____ 73501

DATA ENTRY JOB 19:

ACCOUNTS PAYABLE

PURPOSES

1. To practice sorting invoices by number
2. To provide experience entering data from sales invoices

PREPARATION

1. Examine the data for Job 19. Remove the ten sales invoices. Arrange the invoices in numeric order according to the Sales Invoice Number. (Do not use the Customer Number or the Fax Number.)
2. In Job 19, you will have the situation in which some fields are programmed to advance automatically and others are not. The Item # and Price fields will automatically advance. The Page, Quantity, and Description fields require cursor advance.

PROCEDURE

Job 19: Accounts Payable

Data Entry Screen

Job #19: Accounts Payable

INVOICE: DATE: CUSTOMER NUMBER:

MICHAEL DONAHOE, 14034 DARTMOUTH PL, PHILADELPHIA, PA, 32165

   PAGE ITEM QTY UNIT PRICE TOTAL   DESCRIPTION   GR TOT REC

Set-Up

1. Press the Caps Lock key for all alphabetic fields.

General Entry

1. Enter Invoice Number—auto advance.
2. Enter Date—auto advance.
3. Enter Customer Number—auto advance.
4. Enter Page—cursor return.
5. Enter Item number—auto advance.
6. Enter Quantity—cursor return.
7. Enter Unit—auto advance.
8. Enter Price—cursor return.
9. Program will enter total—auto advance.
10. Enter Description—cursor return.
11. If Invoice number, Date, or customer numbers are to be changed,
    A. Press Alt-A and enter the new data.

Keying Aids

1. Program generates record.
2. As you key in the customer number from the invoice, the customer name and address will appear automatically.
3. Key in the data for the Page, Item#, Price, and Description fields. After the Price and Quantity are entered, the computer will automatically display the Total for each item and the Grand Total for that customer.

WILSON'S OFFICE SUPPLY

ORDER FORM

INVOICE NUMBER 00029   DATE __09/22__

SHIP TO:

CUSTOMER NUMBER __0219__

CUSTOMER NAME __Doris Schleppinger__

STREET ADDRESS __277 Casa Way__

CITY __Phoenix__

STATE __AZ__   ZIP CODE __01329__

PAGE	ITEM #	QUANTITY	PRICE	TOTAL	DESCRIPTION
52	P5-261	4 cartons	15.95	63.80	hanging files

GRAND TOTAL __$63.80__

WILSON'S OFFICE SUPPLY

ORDER FORM

INVOICE NUMBER 00038   DATE _7-27_

SHIP TO:

CUSTOMER NUMBER _1110_

CUSTOMER NAME _Melissa Weaver_

STREET ADDRESS _1989 Oak Knoll Dr._

CITY _Philadelphia_

STATE _PA_   ZIP CODE _321655_

PAGE	ITEM #	QUANTITY	PRICE	TOTAL	DESCRIPTION
322	M3-483	1	21.95	21.95	Pencil Sharpener

GRAND TOTAL _$21.95_

WILSON'S OFFICE SUPPLY

ORDER FORM

INVOICE NUMBER 00027   DATE _07/09_

SHIP TO:

CUSTOMER NUMBER _1037_

CUSTOMER NAME _Brent Lockway_

STREET ADDRESS _2161 Highland Ave._

CITY _Kansas City_

STATE _KS_   ZIP CODE _84103_

PAGE	ITEM #	QUANTITY	PRICE	TOTAL	DESCRIPTION
322	M3-483	1	263.00	263.00	2-drawer file cabinet

GRAND TOTAL _$263.00_

WILSON'S OFFICE SUPPLY

ORDER FORM

INVOICE NUMBER 00028   DATE _08-21_

SHIP TO:

CUSTOMER NUMBER _1463_

CUSTOMER NAME _Peggy Jones_

STREET ADDRESS _1672 Robert St._

CITY _St. Paul_

STATE _MN_   ZIP CODE _55102_

PAGE	ITEM #	QUANTITY	PRICE	TOTAL	DESCRIPTION
241	CO-123	1 boxes	12.50	12.50	Drawing Pencils

GRAND TOTAL _$12.50_

WILSON'S OFFICE SUPPLY

ORDER FORM

INVOICE NUMBER 00039   DATE **7-24**

SHIP TO:

CUSTOMER NUMBER **1702**

CUSTOMER NAME **Allen Seidl**

STREET ADDRESS **70325 Cherokee**

CITY **Wellsley**

STATE **NE**   ZIP CODE **47290**

PAGE	ITEM #	QUANTITY	PRICE	TOTAL	DESCRIPTION
409	N2-207	5 boxes	4.09	20.45	Fine Point Pens
421	N4-850	3 boxes	3.98	11.94	Automatic Pencils
435	P2-168	10 packs	2.70	27.00	Clasp Envelopes
451	Q1-425	25 pads	1.15	28.75	Legal Pads

GRAND TOTAL **$88.14**

WILSON'S OFFICE SUPPLY

ORDER FORM

INVOICE NUMBER 00035   DATE 7-3

SHIP TO:

CUSTOMER NUMBER 3337

CUSTOMER NAME Constance Hall

STREET ADDRESS 14034 Dartmouth Pl.

CITY Roseville

STATE SD   ZIP CODE 50390

PAGE	ITEM #	QUANTITY	PRICE	TOTAL	DESCRIPTION
150	A5-350	1	32.35	32.35	Tape Labeler
150	A5-275	4 rolls	6.07	24.28	Magnetic Tape
151	A5-410	5 rolls	3.58	17.90	Adhesive Labels

GRAND TOTAL $74.53

WILSON'S OFFICE SUPPLY

ORDER FORM

INVOICE NUMBER 00033   DATE 7-1

SHIP TO:

CUSTOMER NUMBER 2173

CUSTOMER NAME Michael Donahue

STREET ADDRESS 821 Birchwood St.

CITY Dayton

STATE OH   ZIP CODE 36420

PAGE	ITEM #	QUANTITY	PRICE	TOTAL	DESCRIPTION
216	D1-970	1	68.25	68.25	Drawing Board
209	M3-106	1	139.00	139.00	Light Box
221	E9-203	3	10.95	32.85	T-Squares

GRAND TOTAL $240.10

WILSON'S OFFICE SUPPLY

ORDER FORM

INVOICE NUMBER 00030 DATE _06/21_

SHIP TO:

CUSTOMER NUMBER _5125_

CUSTOMER NAME _Melvin Miller_

STREET ADDRESS _2265 Belton Ave._

CITY _Boston_

STATE _MA_ ZIP CODE _01023_

PAGE	ITEM #	QUANTITY	PRICE	TOTAL	DESCRIPTION
467	T5-192	1 unit	39.50	39.50	2 tier shelves

GRAND TOTAL _$39.50_

WILSON'S OFFICE SUPPLY

ORDER FORM

INVOICE NUMBER 00036   DATE _7-21_

SHIP TO:

CUSTOMER NUMBER _0930_

CUSTOMER NAME _John Peiffer_

STREET ADDRESS _2137 Fremont Ave._

CITY _Kettle Falls_

STATE _ME_   ZIP CODE _20317_

PAGE	ITEM #	QUANTITY	PRICE	TOTAL	DESCRIPTION
93	A1-215	1	263.00	263.00	2-Drawer File Cabinet
274	F3-752	4 boxes	14.75	59.00	File Folders

GRAND TOTAL ___$322.00___

WILSON'S OFFICE SUPPLY

ORDER FORM

INVOICE NUMBER 00042 DATE _7-13_

SHIP TO:

CUSTOMER NUMBER _2550_

CUSTOMER NAME _Harold Bohen_

STREET ADDRESS _61896 Oxford Ave N._

CITY _Danbury_

STATE _CT_ ZIP CODE _74401_

PAGE	ITEM #	QUANTITY	PRICE	TOTAL	DESCRIPTION
375	K4-710	4	49.95	199.80	Calendar/Clock

GRAND TOTAL _$199.80_

DATA ENTRY JOB 20:
MEDICAL RECORDS

PURPOSES

1. To provide experience entering data from medical records where some fields are not used

PREPARATION

1. Examine the data from Job 20. Remove the twenty medical forms.
2. In Job 20, you will have some data that is larger than the allotted field. Enter as much as possible. Also some fields will not have data to be entered. You will advance through fields you do not have data to enter by pressing cursor return. Do not enter N/A or anything else in these fields. Be sure to key the hyphen in each Identification # field.

PROCEDURE

Job #20: Medical Records
Data Entry Screen (Personal Record)

Job 20: Medical Records

LAST NAME: FREDERICKSON   FIRST NAME: CRISTOPH   MI: S

ADDRESS: 1243 PIKE   CITY: KEN   STATE: NJ   ZIP: 08231

HOME: 6165553216   WORK: 6165553216

SS#: 713428906   SEX: M   BIRTH: 061285   RECORD: 001

Data Entry Screen (Insurer Record)

Job 20: Medical Records

EMPLOYER: HASTINGS MANUFAC   ADDRESS: 2310 COUNTY RD 7

PRIMARY INS: BLUE CROSS/BLUE   ID#: 6301482

SECONDARY INS: PREFERREDPLUS   ID#: 6301482   RECORD: 002

Set-Up

1. Press the Caps Lock key for all alphabetic fields.

General Entry

1. Enter Last Name—cursor return.
2. Enter First Name—cursor return.
3. Enter MI—cursor return.
4. Enter Address—cursor return.
5. Enter City—cursor return.
6. Enter State—cursor return.
7. Enter Zip—cursor return.
8. Enter Home Phone Number—auto advance.

9. Enter Work Phone Number—auto advance.
10. Enter SS#—cursor return.
11. Enter Sex—cursor return.
12. Enter Birthdate—cursor return.
13. Enter Employer—cursor return.
14. Enter Address—cursor return.
15. Enter Primary Ins—cursor return.
16. Enter ID#—auto advance.
17. Enter Secondary Ins—cursor return.
18. Enter ID#—auto advance.

Keying Aids

1. Program generates Record Number.

PATIENT REGISTRATION FORM

Patient Name ___Dailey___ ___Michele___ ___M.___
                       LAST   FIRST   MI

Address ___1090 Quincy Lane, Kendall Park NJ 08824___

Home Phone ___(616)555-3216___ Work Phone ___N/A___

SS# ___713-42-8906___ Sex ___F___ Date of Birth ___6___-___12___-___85___

Employer Name ___N/A___

Employer Address ___N/A___

Primary Insurance Co. ___Aetna___

Identification # ___630148-21___

Secondary Insurance Co. _____

Identification # _____

PATIENT REGISTRATION FORM

Patient Name ___Malek___ ___John___ ___T.___
                       LAST   FIRST   MI

Address ___619 Stuart Lane, Yardley PA 19067___

Home Phone ___(204) 555-4319___ Work Phone ___N/A___

SS# ___157-17-8516___ Sex ___M___ Date of Birth ___3___-___23___-___81___

Employer Name ___N/A___

Employer Address ___N/A___

Primary Insurance Co. ___Blue Cross/Blue Shield___

Identification # ___47695-75___

Secondary Insurance Co. _____

Identification # _____

PATIENT REGISTRATION FORM

Patient Name _Lindenberg_ _____ _Cristopher_ ___ _S._
                        LAST   FIRST   MI

Address _904 Osceola Dr., Winterpark, FL. 34261_

Home Phone _(210) 555-3261_ Work Phone _N/A_

SS# _131-45-6827_ Sex _M_ Date of Birth _8 - 24 - 77_

Employer Name _N/A_

Employer Address _N/A_

Primary Insurance Co. _Burlington Medical_

Identification # _4256-25_

Secondary Insurance Co. _____

Identification # _____

PATIENT REGISTRATION FORM

Patient Name _Turner_ _____ _Derek_ ___ _L._
                        LAST   FIRST   MI

Address _43 Firtree Road, Somerville, NJ 08876_

Home Phone _(616)555-8876_ Work Phone _N/A_

SS# _142-70-6955_ Sex _M_ Date of Birth _5-15-76_

Employer Name _N/A_

Employer Address _N/A_

Primary Insurance Co. _Preferred Plus Medical_

Identification # _692364-93_

Secondary Insurance Co. _____

Identification # _____

PATIENT REGISTRATION FORM

Patient Name _Randolph_ ____ _Aaron_ ____ _T._
 _____LAST_____ FIRST ____ MI

Address _542 Cornell Road, Burlington, NJ 08016_

Home Phone _(616) 555-4328_ Work Phone _N/A_

SS# _626-13-2001_ Sex _M_ Date of Birth _9-27-75_

Employer Name _N/A_

Employer Address _N/A_

Primary Insurance Co. _Aetna_

Identification # _732651-05_

Secondary Insurance Co. _____

Identification # _____

PATIENT REGISTRATION FORM

Patient Name _Komuro_ ____ _Yoko_ ____ _I._
 _____LAST_____ FIRST ____ MI

Address _280 Deer Trail Drive, Princeton, NJ 08540_

Home Phone _(616) 555-4503_ Work Phone _N/A_

SS# _014-72-8564_ Sex _F_ Date of Birth _4-9-75_

Employer Name _N/A_

Employer Address _N/A_

Primary Insurance Co. _Preferred Providers_

Identification # _321-78_

Secondary Insurance Co. _____

Identification # _____

PATIENT REGISTRATION FORM

Patient Name ___Shea___ ___Kathy___ ___E___
                  LAST   FIRST   MI

Address ___17 Crystal Dr., Lakeview, NJ 08952___

Home Phone ___(616) 555-8770___ Work Phone ___N/A___

SS# ___502-36-4756___ Sex ___F___ Date of Birth ___5-15-74___

Employer Name ___N/A___

Employer Address ___N/A___

Primary Insurance Co. ___Appleton Medical___

Identification # ___6314-92___

Secondary Insurance Co. _____

Identification # _____

PATIENT REGISTRATION FORM

Patient Name ___Roberts___ ___Bryon___ ___A.___
                  LAST   FIRST   MI

Address ___3244 W. First St., Kimberly, NJ 08601___

Home Phone ___(616)555-5982___ Work Phone ___(616)555-7216___

SS# ___492-15-6260___ Sex ___M___ Date of Birth ___11-17-73___

Employer Name ___Middleton Electronics___

Employer Address ___110011 Lake Rd___

Primary Insurance Co. ___Aetna___

Identification # ___430629-49___

Secondary Insurance Co. _____

Identification # _____

PATIENT REGISTRATION FORM

Patient Name ___Terrill_____ ___Kelly_____ _E__
                        LAST   FIRST   MI
Address __9 Artic Circle, Neenah, NJ 08626_____

Home Phone __(616) 555-8888__ Work Phone __(616) 555-3235__

SS# __202-20-2400_____ Sex _F_ Date of Birth __11-1-70__

Employer Name __Gerten Greenhouses_____

Employer Address __5500 Blaine Avenue_____

Primary Insurance Co. __Gillette HMO_____

Identification # __2928-48_____

Secondary Insurance Co. _____

Identification # _____

PATIENT REGISTRATION FORM

Patient Name ___Walden_____ ___Arthur_____ ____
                        LAST   FIRST   MI
Address __1243 Pike Lake Dr., New Brighton, NJ 08231_____

Home Phone __(616)555-0547____ Work Phone __(616) 555-7751__

SS# __502-46-2020_____ Sex _M_ Date of Birth __8-28-70__

Employer Name __Hastings Manafacturing_____

Employer Address __1000 E. 80 St._____

Primary Insurance Co. __N/A_____

Identification # _____

Secondary Insurance Co. _____

Identification # _____

PATIENT REGISTRATION FORM

Patient Name ___Frederickson___ ___Sarah___ ___A.___
                     LAST   FIRST   MI

Address ___1993 Plaza Park Pl., Lincoln, NJ 08218___

Home Phone ___(616) 555-1695___ Work Phone ___(616) 555-1270___

SS# ___398-60-4562___ Sex ___F___ Date of Birth ___12___-___1___-___69___

Employer Name ___Rocco Hair Stylists___

Employer Address ___665 Rissotta Street___

Primary Insurance Co. ___Burlington Medical___

Identification # ___1672-91___

Secondary Insurance Co. _____

Identification # _____

PATIENT REGISTRATION FORM

Patient Name ___Saldana___ ___Craig___ ___M.___
                     LAST   FIRST   MI

Address ___2002 Pleasant St., Avalon, NJ 08619___

Home Phone ___(616) 555-2172___ Work Phone ___(616) 555-7158___

SS# ___321-22-8200___ Sex ___M___ Date of Birth ___5___-___3___-___64___

Employer Name ___Southwest Bank___

Employer Address ___1639 Rosehill Blvd.___

Primary Insurance Co. ___Alpha Medical___

Identification # ___00102-69___

Secondary Insurance Co. _____

Identification # _____

PATIENT REGISTRATION FORM

Patient Name <u>Pershing</u>   <u>Gary</u>   <u>B.</u>
                                  LAST   FIRST   MI

Address <u>992 Seventh St., Diamond Falls, NJ 08611</u>

Home Phone <u>(616) 555-0247</u> Work Phone <u>(616) 555-4198</u>

SS# <u>414-56-2861</u>   Sex <u>M</u> Date of Birth <u>3 -30-64</u>

Employer Name <u>Stevenson, Edwards & Associates</u>

Employer Address <u>2310 County Road 7</u>

Primary Insurance Co. <u>Blue Cross</u>

Identification # <u>787240-53</u>

Secondary Insurance Co. _____

Identification # _____

PATIENT REGISTRATION FORM

Patient Name <u>Quilling</u>   <u>Dorothy</u>   <u>P.</u>
                                  LAST   FIRST   MI

Address <u>8737 Rosegarden Pl, Imperial, NJ 08411</u>

Home Phone <u>(616) 555-9358</u> Work Phone <u>(616) 555-8330</u>

SS# <u>661-23-4915</u>   Sex <u>F</u> Date of Birth <u>2 -28-62</u>

Employer Name <u>Imperial Animal Center</u>

Employer Address <u>1534 Larpenter Dr..</u>

Primary Insurance Co. <u>Aetna</u>

Identification # <u>931016-41</u>

Secondary Insurance Co. _____

Identification # _____

PATIENT REGISTRATION FORM

Patient Name   **Eberhardt**   **Judy**   **T.**
                  LAST   FIRST   MI

Address   **8329 Adams Lane, Brewster, NJ 08992**

Home Phone   **(616) 555-2513**   Work Phone   **(616) 555-3277**

SS#   **555-82-2092**   Sex **F**   Date of Birth   **9 -4 -61**

Employer Name   **Ryco Supply Co.**

Employer Address   **1733 NE Osborne Rd.**

Primary Insurance Co.   **Preferred Providers**

Identification #   **618-27**

Secondary Insurance Co. _____

Identification # _____

PATIENT REGISTRATION FORM

Patient Name   *Fairchild*   *Amanda*
                  LAST   FIRST   MI

Address   *7654 Rushford Blvd, Spring Park, NY 43022*

Home Phone   *(616) 555-1124*   Work Phone   *(616) 555-3849*

SS#   *391-71-6195*   Sex *F*   Date of Birth   *10-18 -60*

Employer Name   *Capitol Credit Union*

Employer Address   *95 Sherburne Ave.*

Primary Insurance Co.   *Aetna*

Identification #   *112471-53*

Secondary Insurance Co. _____

Identification # _____

PATIENT REGISTRATION FORM

Patient Name ___Jackson_____ ___Jeffrey_____ __R__
                          LAST   FIRST   MI
Address __4334 Eighth Ave., Resnick, NY 43712_____

Home Phone __(215) 555-7462___ Work Phone __(215) 555-5178___

SS# __221-80-4689_____ Sex _M_ Date of Birth __12-7 -59__

Employer Name __Renaissance Foundation_____

Employer Address __1006 Rice St._____

Primary Insurance Co. __Blue Cross_____

Identification # __05684-99_____

Secondary Insurance Co. _____

Identification # _____

PATIENT REGISTRATION FORM

Patient Name ___Richner_____ ___Susan_____ __A.__
                          LAST   FIRST   MI
Address __1413 Marquette Ave., Greeley, NJ 08615_____

Home Phone __(616) 555-2458___ Work Phone __(616) 555-2183___

SS# __193-46-7698_____ Sex _F_ Date of Birth __1 -30-55__

Employer Name N/A_____

Employer Address N/A_____

Primary Insurance Co. N/A_____

Identification # N/A_____

Secondary Insurance Co. _____

Identification # _____

PATIENT REGISTRATION FORM

Patient Name _____O'Brien_____ ___Vincent___ __T.__
                    LAST   FIRST   MI

Address _1045 Westgate Dr., Roseville, NJ 08612_____

Home Phone _(616) 555-0021___ Work Phone _(616) 555-0889_

SS# _492-36-2456_____ Sex _M_ Date of Birth _4 - 9 - 44_

Employer Name _Oakland Travel_____

Employer Address _7623 Hudson Rd._____

Primary Insurance Co. _Aetna_____

Identification # _261103-45_____

Secondary Insurance Co. _Preferred Plus Medical_____

Identification # _6214-97_____

PATIENT REGISTRATION FORM

Patient Name _____Humbert_____ ___Joan____ __C.__
                     LAST   FIRST   MI

Address _19 Summit Lane, Butler, NJ 08692_____

Home Phone _(616) 555-0629___ Work Phone _(616) 555-2342_

SS# __398-64-2050_____ Sex _F_ Date of Birth _6-18-42_

Employer Name _Omega Marketing_____

Employer Address _17 Charlton Ave._____

Primary Insurance Co. _Appleton Medical_____

Identification # _____

Secondary Insurance Co. _____

Identification # _____

DATA ENTRY JOB 21:

COUPON REDEMPTION

PURPOSES

1. To practice entering data from coupons where customers have entered their names and addresses and product price
2. To provide experience in reading difficult handwritten material written in a small area

PREPARATION

1. In Job 21, sort the 48 coupons by product, and then sort within product by customer last name. When sorting the coupons by product, the Cola ones should be first, then Milk, then Mustard.
2. When entering the Item name, enter Cola, Milk, or Mustard, using the Shift key for the first letter of each.
3. The Units should also be entered with the first letter capitalized, as follows: Can (for Cola), Car (for Milk carton), Jar (for Mustard).
4. To enter the QTY, enter the number of the Item shown on the coupon (3 Cola, 3 Milk, 2 Mustard).
2. Note each coupon has a bar code that would be scanned if equipment were available.

PROCEDURE

Job #21: Coupon Redemption

Data Entry Screen

Job 21: Coupon Redemption with Imaging

ITEM	QTY	UNIT	DISCOUNT			
NAME		ADDRESS	CITY	STATE	ZIP	REC

General Entry

1. Enter Item—cursor return.
   (1) Press Alt-A to place the cursor at the first position in the Item field.
2. IF the data in the QTY field is the same as the item on the last record,
   (1) Press cursor return
   OR
   (1) Press Alt-A to place the cursor at the first position in the ITEM field and cursor return to QTY field.
   (2) Enter the QTY
   (3) Press cursor return
3. IF the data in the UNIT field is the same as the item on the last record,
   (1) Press cursor return
   OR
   (1) Press Alt-A to place the cursor at the first position in the ITEM field and cursor return to the UNIT field
   (2) Enter the Unit
   (3) Press cursor return

4. IF the data in the DISCOUNT field is the same as the item on the last record,
   (1) Press cursor return.
   OR
   (1) Press Alt-A to place the cursor at the first position in the ITEM field and cursor return to the DISCOUNT field.
   (2) Enter the Discount.
   (3) Press cursor return.
5. Enter Name—cursor return.
6. Enter Address—cursor return.
7. Enter City—cursor return.
8. Enter State—auto advance.
9. Enter Zip—auto advance.

Keying Aids

1. Program generates Record Number.

COUPONS

25¢ OFF
COLA
5145

Please clearly print your name and address below before redeeming coupon. By providing this information you will be added to our preferred customer mailing list.
Thank you.

Name __Jerry Anderson__

Address __1962 King Ave. S.__

City __Scranton__ State __PA__ Zip __91247__

25¢ OFF
COLA
5145

Please clearly print your name and address below before redeeming coupon. By providing this information you will be added to our preferred customer mailing list.
Thank you.

Name __Don Chryn__

Address __803 University Ave. W.__

City __Camden__ State __NJ__ Zip __80641__

25¢ OFF
COLA
5145

Please clearly print your name and address below before redeeming coupon. By providing this information you will be added to our preferred customer mailing list.
Thank you.

Name __Anne Farrell__

Address __9032 Fillmore Ave. NW__

City __Lansing__ State __MI__ Zip __59106__

25¢ OFF
COLA
5145

Please clearly print your name and address below before redeeming coupon. By providing this information you will be added to our preferred customer mailing list.
Thank you.

Name __Karyn Geach__

Address __101 E. Washburn St.__

City __Dodge City__ State __KS__ Zip __61141__

30¢ OFF
5145

Please clearly print your name and address below before redeeming coupon. By providing this information you will be added to our preferred customer mailing list.
Thank you.

Name __Anthony Thoe__

Address __7196 Rowland Rd.__

City __Gage__ State __OK__ Zip __73843__

30¢ OFF
5145

Please clearly print your name and address below before redeeming coupon. By providing this information you will be added to our preferred customer mailing list.
Thank you.

Name __Larisa Wolterstorff__

Address __2655 Bryant Trail__

City __Madison__ State __WI__ Zip __56701__

35¢ OFF
5145

Please clearly print your name and address below before redeeming coupon. By providing this information you will be added to our preferred customer mailing list.
Thank you.

Name __Cory Ediker__

Address __3593 Drexel Ave NW__

City __Union City__ State __MI__ Zip __49094__

35¢ OFF
5145

Please clearly print your name and address below before redeeming coupon. By providing this information you will be added to our preferred customer mailing list.
Thank you.

Name __Irving Flasch__

Address __27 Bittersweat Trail__

City __Stuttgart__ State __KS__ Zip __67670__

COUPONS

 25¢ OFF
COLA
6145

Please clearly print your name and address below before redeeming coupon. By providing this information you will be added to our preferred customer mailing list. Thank you.

Name _Carol Peasley_

Address _6837 Garrett Circle_

City _Memphis_   State _TN_ Zip _42213_

 25¢ OFF
COLA
6145

Please clearly print your name and address below before redeeming coupon. By providing this information you will be added to our preferred customer mailing list. Thank you.

Name _Conrad Richards_

Address _125 Eitel Lane_

City _Lincoln_   State _NE_ Zip _31947_

 25¢ OFF
COLA
6145

Please clearly print your name and address below before redeeming coupon. By providing this information you will be added to our preferred customer mailing list. Thank you.

Name _Celeste Reeves_

Address _3317 Selkirk Ave._

City _Honolulu_   State _HI_ Zip _96800_

 25¢ OFF
COLA
6145

Please clearly print your name and address below before redeeming coupon. By providing this information you will be added to our preferred customer mailing list. Thank you.

Name _Anthony Tomazko_

Address _5540 Carlson Pkwy_

City _Provo_   State _UT_ Zip _82010_

 25¢ OFF
COLA
6145

Please clearly print your name and address below before redeeming coupon. By providing this information you will be added to our preferred customer mailing list. Thank you.

Name _Lionel Abny_

Address _1450 Venable Square_

City _Hampton_   State _VA_ Zip _22015_

 25¢ OFF
COLA
6145

Please clearly print your name and address below before redeeming coupon. By providing this information you will be added to our preferred customer mailing list. Thank you.

Name _William Basefield_

Address _4520 NW Palm St._

City _Bluff_   State _UT_ Zip _84512_

 25¢ OFF
COLA
6145

Please clearly print your name and address below before redeeming coupon. By providing this information you will be added to our preferred customer mailing list. Thank you.

Name _Steven Dold_

Address _6349 Boone Ave._

City _Kenney_   State _TX_ Zip _78119_

  25¢ OFF
COLA
6145

Please clearly print your name and address below before redeeming coupon. By providing this information you will be added to our preferred customer mailing list. Thank you.

Name _Carol Hildebrandt_

Address _9119 Xerxes Trail_

City _Mercer_   State _TN_ Zip _38393_

COUPONS

  30¢ OFF

5145

Please clearly print your name and address below before redeeming coupon. By providing this information you will be added to our preferred customer mailing list.
Thank you.

Name **Susan Kolins**

Address **7240 Hidden Lane**

City **Delmont** State **SD** Zip **57330**

  30¢ OFF

5145

Please clearly print your name and address below before redeeming coupon. By providing this information you will be added to our preferred customer mailing list.
Thank you.

Name **Anna Mae Pavek**

Address **41 Groveland Terr.**

City **Oswego** State **SC** Zip **29150**

  30¢ OFF

5145

Please clearly print your name and address below before redeeming coupon. By providing this information you will be added to our preferred customer mailing list.
Thank you.

Name **Frederic Riebe**

Address **6750 Cherry Hill Ln.**

City **Van Meter** State **PA** Zip **15487**

  30¢ OFF

5145

Please clearly print your name and address below before redeeming coupon. By providing this information you will be added to our preferred customer mailing list.
Thank you.

Name **Donald Smurser**

Address **4716 Wellington Cir.**

City **Kemo** State **OR** Zip **97627**

  25¢ OFF COLA

5145

Please clearly print your name and address below before redeeming coupon. By providing this information you will be added to our preferred customer mailing list.
Thank you.

Name **Cyril Severson**

Address **65113 Colonial Way**

City **Barstow** State **CA** Zip **10119**

  25¢ OFF COLA

5145

Please clearly print your name and address below before redeeming coupon. By providing this information you will be added to our preferred customer mailing list.
Thank you.

Name **Rosemarie Kellar**

Address **1006 Stinson Blvd.**

City **Boston** State **MA** Zip **74415**

  25¢ OFF COLA

5145

Please clearly print your name and address below before redeeming coupon. By providing this information you will be added to our preferred customer mailing list.
Thank you.

Name **Allen Matthies**

Address **10113 Rolling Oaks Rd.**

City **Tyler** State **TX** Zip **60731**

  25¢ OFF COLA

5145

Please clearly print your name and address below before redeeming coupon. By providing this information you will be added to our preferred customer mailing list.
Thank you.

Name **Frances Odermann**

Address **6679 Parklawn Ave.**

City **Yakima** State **WA** Zip **15793**

COUPONS

30¢ OFF

Please clearly print your name and address below before redeeming coupon. By providing this information you will be added to our preferred customer mailing list.
Thank you.

6145

Name _Cheri Blair_

Address _6323 Black Friars Ln._

City _Rawson_ State _OH_ Zip _45881_

30¢ OFF

Please clearly print your name and address below before redeeming coupon. By providing this information you will be added to our preferred customer mailing list.
Thank you.

6145

Name _Frank Cannamore_

Address _21861 Spoon Ridge_

City _Suncook_ State _NH_ Zip _03275_

30¢ OFF

Please clearly print your name and address below before redeeming coupon. By providing this information you will be added to our preferred customer mailing list.
Thank you.

6145

Name _Firoz Dawood_

Address _8638 N. 63rd Court_

City _Souris_ State _ND_ Zip _58783_

30¢ OFF

Please clearly print your name and address below before redeeming coupon. By providing this information you will be added to our preferred customer mailing list.
Thank you.

6145

Name _Allison Ebertowski_

Address _22296 Aspen Way_

City _E. Las Vegas_ State _NV_ Zip _89112_

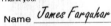

30¢ OFF

Please clearly print your name and address below before redeeming coupon. By providing this information you will be added to our preferred customer mailing list.
Thank you.

6145

Name _James Farquhar_

Address _RR3_

City _Voss_ State _NC_ Zip _28394_

30¢ OFF

Please clearly print your name and address below before redeeming coupon. By providing this information you will be added to our preferred customer mailing list.
Thank you.

6145

Name _Gayle Gaukel_

Address _24911 Chesnut Terr._

City _St. Edward_ State _NE_ Zip _68660_

30¢ OFF

Please clearly print your name and address below before redeeming coupon. By providing this information you will be added to our preferred customer mailing list.
Thank you.

6145

Name _Veikko Harakh_

Address _25732 Hampshire Blvd_

City _Mt. Dale_ State _NY_ Zip _12763_

30¢ OFF

Please clearly print your name and address below before redeeming coupon. By providing this information you will be added to our preferred customer mailing list.
Thank you.

6145

Name _Bernard Irmiter_

Address _27 Garner Court_

City _Glasgow_ State _MT_ Zip _59230_

COUPONS

 35¢ OFF

Please clearly print your name and address below before redeeming coupon. By providing this information you will be added to our preferred customer mailing list. Thank you.

6145

Name Kimberle Laslett

Address 234 Ferndale Ave.

City Glenwood State NM Zip 88039

 35¢ OFF

Please clearly print your name and address below before redeeming coupon. By providing this information you will be added to our preferred customer mailing list. Thank you.

6145

Name Walter Maenpaa

Address 8581 Carnelian Lane

City St. Joseph State MO Zip 64502

 35¢ OFF

Please clearly print your name and address below before redeeming coupon. By providing this information you will be added to our preferred customer mailing list. Thank you.

6145

Name Bailey Newville

Address 2719 Balmoral Parkway

City Hoboken State NJ Zip 07030

 35¢ OFF

Please clearly print your name and address below before redeeming coupon. By providing this information you will be added to our preferred customer mailing list. Thank you.

6145

Name Andre Prescott

Address 4701 Mark Terrace

City Woodville State MS Zip 39669

 35¢ OFF

Please clearly print your name and address below before redeeming coupon. By providing this information you will be added to our preferred customer mailing list. Thank you.

6145

Name Victoria Blasiak

Address 6202 Boarshead Rd.

City Wrenshall State MN Zip 55797

 35¢ OFF

Please clearly print your name and address below before redeeming coupon. By providing this information you will be added to our preferred customer mailing list. Thank you.

6145

Name Wallace Chalmers

Address 4399 Diamond Eight Terr.

City Soldier State KY Zip 41173

 30¢ OFF

Please clearly print your name and address below before redeeming coupon. By providing this information you will be added to our preferred customer mailing list. Thank you.

6145

Name John Yehouda

Address 2946 Emerson St. W.

City Salem State OR Zip 91715

 30¢ OFF

Please clearly print your name and address below before redeeming coupon. By providing this information you will be added to our preferred customer mailing list. Thank you.

6145

Name Kathleen Zieghan

Address 640 N E Quernoy

City Blaine State MN Zip 55410

COUPONS

 35¢ OFF

Please clearly print your name and address below before redeeming coupon. By providing this information you will be added to our preferred customer mailing list. Thank you.

6145

Name Crystal Gatzow

Address 4939 Oliver Place

City Windsor State MA Zip 01270

5 70002 12022 3

 35¢ OFF

Please clearly print your name and address below before redeeming coupon. By providing this information you will be added to our preferred customer mailing list. Thank you.

6145

Name LJ Haddorff

Address 3943 Deerwood Drive

City Newhall State IA Zip 52315

5 70002 12022 3

 35¢ OFF

Please clearly print your name and address below before redeeming coupon. By providing this information you will be added to our preferred customer mailing list. Thank you.

6145

Name William Sacarella

Address 2232 Devonshire Curve

City Northwood State MD Zip 21239

5 70002 12022 3

 35¢ OFF

Please clearly print your name and address below before redeeming coupon. By providing this information you will be added to our preferred customer mailing list. Thank you.

6145

Name Frances Joncas

Address 6007 Arkwood Place

City Warren State IN Zip 46792

5 70002 12022 3

 35¢ OFF

Please clearly print your name and address below before redeeming coupon. By providing this information you will be added to our preferred customer mailing list. Thank you.

6145

Name Lyle Kroonblaud

Address 2901 Cutters Grove

City York Harbor State ME Zip 03911

5 70002 12022 3

 35¢ OFF

Please clearly print your name and address below before redeeming coupon. By providing this information you will be added to our preferred customer mailing list. Thank you.

6145

Name Gilbert Loken

Address 3624 Cedar Blvd

City Woodlawn State IL Zip 62898

5 70002 12022 3

 35¢ OFF

Please clearly print your name and address below before redeeming coupon. By providing this information you will be added to our preferred customer mailing list. Thank you.

6145

Name Judith Nevarez

Address 1641 Whiterock Road

City Pierre Port State LA Zip 70339

5 70002 12022 3

 35¢ OFF

Please clearly print your name and address below before redeeming coupon. By providing this information you will be added to our preferred customer mailing list. Thank you.

6145

Name Kim Reever

Address 2907 Pontiac Lane

City Boise State ID Zip 53707

5 70002 12022 3

DATA ENTRY JOB 22:
DRIVER'S LICENSE REGISTRATION

PURPOSES

1. To practice entering personal data from source documents
2. To provide additional experience in entering data of a personal nature

PREPARATION

1. In Job 22, prepare to enter 30 Driver's License Registration forms in alphabetic order according to the driver's last name.
2. Every field must contain data. Check to see that every field is complete.

PROCEDURE

Data Entry Screen

Job #22:   DRIVER'S LICENSE APPLICATION

LAST NAME   FIRST NAME   MI

STREET ADDRESS   CITY   STATE ZIP CODE

BIRTHDATE/EXPIRATION DATE   HEIGHT   WEIGHT

EYE COLOR   GLASSES   SEX

ORGAN DONOR   RESTRICTIONS (Y/N)

General Entry

1. Enter Last Name—cursor return.
2. Enter First Name—cursor return.
3. Enter MI—auto advance.
4. Enter Address—cursor return.
5. Enter City—cursor return.
6. Enter State—auto advance.
7. Enter Zip—auto advance.
8. Enter Birth/Exp (place zeros before single digit numbers)—cursor return.
9. Enter Height (place a zero before a single digit number for inches)—cursor return.
10. Enter Weight—cursor return.
11. Enter Eye Color using Shift key for first letter—cursor return.
12. Enter **Y** or **N** for Glasses—cursor return.
13. Enter **F** or **M** for Sex—cursor return.
14. Enter **Y** or **N** for Organ Donor—cursor return.
15. Enter **Y** or **N** for Restrictions—cursor return.

Keying Aids

1. Automatic generation of Record Number
2. Automatic cursor advance from MI, STATE, and ZIP

DRIVER'S LICENSE APPLICATION

LAST NAME _Ahrendt_ FIRST NAME _Cynthia_ MI _D._

STREET ADDRESS _1414 West Broadway_

CITY _San Diego_ STATE _CA_ ZIP CODE _32175_

BIRTHDATE/
EXPIRATION DATE _1 -9 -61_ HEIGHT _5'2"_ WEIGHT _130_

EYE COLOR _Green_ GLASSES _No_ SEX _Female_

ORGAN DONOR _No_ RESTRICTIONS (Y/Ⓝ) _No_

DRIVER'S LICENSE APPLICATION

LAST NAME **Ballard** FIRST NAME **Nigel** MI **T.**

STREET ADDRESS **16616 Colefax Avenue**

CITY **Shorewood** STATE **NY** ZIP CODE **54670**

BIRTHDATE/
EXPIRATION DATE **11 -17 -59** HEIGHT **5'11"** WEIGHT **190**

EYE COLOR **Brown** GLASSES **No** SEX **Male**

ORGAN DONOR **No** RESTRICTIONS (Y/Ⓝ) **No**

DRIVER'S LICENSE APPLICATION

LAST NAME _Chamberlain_ FIRST NAME _Donald_ MI _G._

STREET ADDRESS _7004 Bristol Blvd._

CITY _Centerville_ STATE _IL_ ZIP CODE _65401_

BIRTHDATE/
EXPIRATION DATE _5 -6 -75_ HEIGHT _6'1"_ WEIGHT _205_

EYE COLOR _Hazel_ GLASSES _Yes_ SEX _Male_

ORGAN DONOR _No_ RESTRICTIONS (Ⓨ/N) _Yes_

DRIVER'S LICENSE APPLICATION

LAST NAME _Hannah_   FIRST NAME _Stewart_   MI _N._

STREET ADDRESS _2822 NE Fillmore St._

CITY _Fridley_   STATE _NM_ ZIP CODE _10023_

BIRTHDATE/
EXPIRATION DATE _4_ – _28_ – _78_   HEIGHT _5'11_   WEIGHT _180_

EYE COLOR _Green_   GLASSES _No_   SEX _Male_

ORGAN DONOR _No_   RESTRICTIONS (Y/N) _No_

DRIVER'S LICENSE APPLICATION

LAST NAME _Jenson_   FIRST NAME _Darlene_   MI _A._

STREET ADDRESS _6800 Canterbury Lane_

CITY _New Market_   STATE _NH_ ZIP CODE _35714_

BIRTHDATE/
EXPIRATION DATE _2_ – _16_ – _77_ HEIGHT _5'1"_   WEIGHT _105_

EYE COLOR _Blue_   GLASSES _No_ SEX _Female_

ORGAN DONOR _No_   RESTRICTIONS (Y/N) _No_

DRIVER'S LICENSE APPLICATION

LAST NAME _King_   FIRST NAME _Gladys_   MI _M._

STREET ADDRESS _410 Groveland Ave._

CITY _Centerville_   STATE _AR_ ZIP CODE _60021_

BIRTHDATE/
EXPIRATION DATE _3_ – _9_ – _78_ HEIGHT _5'9"_   WEIGHT _135_

EYE COLOR _brown_   GLASSES _yes_   SEX _Female_

ORGAN DONOR _yes_   RESTRICTIONS (Y/N) _yes_

DRIVER'S LICENSE APPLICATION

LAST NAME _Sandquist_   FIRST NAME _Janice_   MI _I._

STREET ADDRESS _7601 Viewcrest Lane_

CITY _Tyler_   STATE _WA_ ZIP CODE _87831_

BIRTHDATE/
EXPIRATION DATE _3-14-77_ HEIGHT _5'10_   WEIGHT _145_

EYE COLOR _green_   GLASSES _no_   SEX _Female_

ORGAN DONOR _no_   RESTRICTIONS (Y/N) _no_

DRIVER'S LICENSE APPLICATION

LAST NAME _Schmidt_   FIRST NAME _Peter_   MI _K._

STREET ADDRESS _9568 Jackson St._

CITY _Des Moines_   STATE _IA_ ZIP CODE _92775_

BIRTHDATE/
EXPIRATION DATE _8-27-77_ HEIGHT _5'7"_   WEIGHT _175_

EYE COLOR _hazel_   GLASSES _no_   SEX _male_

ORGAN DONOR _no_   RESTRICTIONS (Y/N) _no_

DRIVER'S LICENSE APPLICATION

LAST NAME _Smith_   FIRST NAME _Anthony_   MI _J._

STREET ADDRESS _900 Washington Ave. SE_

CITY _Pueblo_   STATE _CO_ ZIP CODE _31056_

BIRTHDATE/
EXPIRATION DATE _4-16-76_ HEIGHT _6'0"_   WEIGHT _210_

EYE COLOR _blue_   GLASSES _no_   SEX _male_

ORGAN DONOR _no_   RESTRICTIONS (Y/N) _no_

DRIVER'S LICENSE APPLICATION

LAST NAME _Metcalfe_   FIRST NAME _David_   MI _C._

STREET ADDRESS _8635 Emerson Avenue_

CITY _Michigan City_   STATE _IN_   ZIP CODE _62011_

BIRTHDATE/
EXPIRATION DATE _1_ - _3_ - _78_   HEIGHT _6'2_   WEIGHT _235_

EYE COLOR _blue_   GLASSES _yes_   SEX _male_

ORGAN DONOR _yes_   RESTRICTIONS (Y/N) _yes_

DRIVER'S LICENSE APPLICATION

LAST NAME _Moriarty_   FIRST NAME _Joseph_   MI _A._

STREET ADDRESS _6651 67th Avenue North_

CITY _Buffalo_   STATE _NY_ ZIP CODE _63800_

BIRTHDATE/
EXPIRATION DATE _12_ - _14_ - _68_   HEIGHT _5'9"_   WEIGHT _175_

EYE COLOR _hazel_   GLASSES _yes_   SEX _male_

ORGAN DONOR _no_   RESTRICTIONS (Y/N) _no_

DRIVER'S LICENSE APPLICATION

LAST NAME _Neumann_   FIRST NAME _Pamela_   MI _C._

STREET ADDRESS _104 Wooddale Avenue_

CITY _San Antonio_   STATE _TX_   ZIP CODE _32922_

BIRTHDATE/
EXPIRATION DATE _1_ - _27_ - _77_   HEIGHT _5'6"_   WEIGHT _170_

EYE COLOR _brown_   GLASSES _no_   SEX _Female_

ORGAN DONOR _no_   RESTRICTIONS (Y/N) _no_

DRIVER'S LICENSE APPLICATION

LAST NAME _Doherty_   FIRST NAME _Kay_   MI _M._

STREET ADDRESS _5561 NE Oberlin Circle_

CITY _Andover_   STATE _NC_ ZIP CODE _92032_

BIRTHDATE/
EXPIRATION DATE _3_ -_15_- _72_ HEIGHT _5'8"_   WEIGHT _140_

EYE COLOR _blue_   GLASSES _Yes_   SEX _Female_

ORGAN DONOR _No_   RESTRICTIONS (Y/N) _Yes_

DRIVER'S LICENSE APPLICATION

LAST NAME _Duffy_   FIRST NAME _Todd_   MI _R._

STREET ADDRESS _97462 Dorset Lane_

CITY _Woodland_   STATE _VA_ ZIP CODE _43915_

BIRTHDATE/
EXPIRATION DATE _7_ -_6_ - _75_ HEIGHT _6'_   WEIGHT _195_

EYE COLOR _Brown_   GLASSES _No_   SEX _Male_

ORGAN DONOR _Yes_   RESTRICTIONS (Y/N) _No_

DRIVER'S LICENSE APPLICATION

LAST NAME _Gabriel_   FIRST NAME _Linda_   MI _T._

STREET ADDRESS _425 NW Main St._

CITY _Lexington_   STATE _KY_ ZIP CODE _67215_

BIRTHDATE/
EXPIRATION DATE _6_ -_22_- _77_ HEIGHT _5'5"_   WEIGHT _125_

EYE COLOR _Brown_   GLASSES _No_   SEX _Female_

ORGAN DONOR _Yes_   RESTRICTIONS (Y/N) _No_

DRIVER'S LICENSE APPLICATION

LAST NAME **Lawrence**   FIRST NAME **Charles**   MI **M.**

STREET ADDRESS **16109 Valley View Rd**

CITY **Bloomington**   STATE **IN** ZIP CODE **73329**

BIRTHDATE/
EXPIRATION DATE **4 -2 - 64** HEIGHT **6'4"** WEIGHT **250**

EYE COLOR **brown**   GLASSES **no**   SEX **male**

ORGAN DONOR **no**   RESTRICTIONS (Y/N) **no**

DRIVER'S LICENSE APPLICATION

LAST NAME *Linderman*   FIRST NAME *Theodore*   MI *R.*

STREET ADDRESS *6566 France Avenue*

CITY *St. Louis*   STATE *MO* ZIP CODE *35417*

BIRTHDATE/
EXPIRATION DATE *7 -1 - 75* HEIGHT *5'10* WEIGHT *190*

EYE COLOR *brown*   GLASSES *no*   SEX *male*

ORGAN DONOR *no*   RESTRICTIONS (Y/N) *no*

DRIVER'S LICENSE APPLICATION

LAST NAME *Martel*   FIRST NAME *Patricia*   MI *A.*

STREET ADDRESS *8007 Washburn Circle*

CITY *Bakersfield*   STATE *AZ* ZIP CODE *90147*

BIRTHDATE/
EXPIRATION DATE *11 - 10 - 77* HEIGHT *6'0"* WEIGHT *155*

EYE COLOR *blue*   GLASSES *no*   SEX *Female*

ORGAN DONOR *no*   RESTRICTIONS (Y/N) *no*

DRIVER'S LICENSE APPLICATION

LAST NAME _Prudhomme_ FIRST NAME _Kathleen_ MI _H._

STREET ADDRESS _11889 NW Dogwood St._

CITY _North Bay_ STATE _ME_ ZIP CODE _76788_

BIRTHDATE/
EXPIRATION DATE _6_ -_12_-_77_ HEIGHT _5'10"_ WEIGHT _145_

EYE COLOR _brown_ GLASSES _yes_ SEX _Female_

ORGAN DONOR _yes_ RESTRICTIONS (Y/N) _yes_

DRIVER'S LICENSE APPLICATION

LAST NAME _Ranzinger_ FIRST NAME _Larry_ MI _T._

STREET ADDRESS _6890 Meadowbrook Blvd._

CITY _Jackson_ STATE _WY_ ZIP CODE _80565_

BIRTHDATE/
EXPIRATION DATE _7_ -_21_-_78_ HEIGHT _5'10"_ WEIGHT _160_

EYE COLOR _brown_ GLASSES _yes_ SEX _male_

ORGAN DONOR _no_ RESTRICTIONS (Y/N) _yes_

DRIVER'S LICENSE APPLICATION

LAST NAME _Robinson_ FIRST NAME _Dianah_ MI _C._

STREET ADDRESS _655 York Avenue_

CITY _Newport_ STATE _RI_ ZIP CODE _31036_

BIRTHDATE/
EXPIRATION DATE _2_ -_12_-_77_ HEIGHT _5'4"_ WEIGHT _110_

EYE COLOR _brown_ GLASSES _no_ SEX _female_

ORGAN DONOR _no_ RESTRICTIONS (Y/N) _no_

DRIVER'S LICENSE APPLICATION

LAST NAME **Thayer**   FIRST NAME **Richard**   MI **G.**

STREET ADDRESS **12941 Garrett Blvd.**

CITY **Ramsey**   STATE **NE** ZIP CODE **10320**

BIRTHDATE/
EXPIRATION DATE **3-9-78** HEIGHT **5'6"**   WEIGHT **145**

EYE COLOR **brown**   GLASSES **no**   SEX **male**

ORGAN DONOR **no**   RESTRICTIONS (Y/N) **no**

DRIVER'S LICENSE APPLICATION

LAST NAME **Thompson**   FIRST NAME **Patricia**   MI **A.**

STREET ADDRESS **331 Main St.**

CITY **Hamelwood**   STATE **AR** ZIP CODE **43185**

BIRTHDATE/
EXPIRATION DATE **8-10-78** HEIGHT **5'3"**   WEIGHT **120**

EYE COLOR **brown**   GLASSES **yes**   SEX **female**

ORGAN DONOR **no**   RESTRICTIONS (Y/N) **yes**

DRIVER'S LICENSE APPLICATION

LAST NAME **Ullmann**   FIRST NAME **Louise**   MI **J.**

STREET ADDRESS **5220 Lincoln Dr.**

CITY **Bethel**   STATE **IN** ZIP CODE **79313**

BIRTHDATE/
EXPIRATION DATE **5-6-77** HEIGHT **6'1**   WEIGHT **170**

EYE COLOR **brown**   GLASSES **no**   SEX **Female**

ORGAN DONOR **yes**   RESTRICTIONS (Y/N) **no**

DRIVER'S LICENSE APPLICATION

LAST NAME Osborne   FIRST NAME Christine   MI C.

STREET ADDRESS 1349 Pennsylvania Ave.

CITY Fresno   STATE KS ZIP CODE 41148

BIRTHDATE/
EXPIRATION DATE 1 -31 - 78 HEIGHT 5'8 WEIGHT 150

EYE COLOR brown   GLASSES no   SEX Female

ORGAN DONOR yes   RESTRICTIONS (Y/N) no

DRIVER'S LICENSE APPLICATION

LAST NAME Paciotti   FIRST NAME Mark   MI W.

STREET ADDRESS 15126 Spruce Place

CITY Tampa   STATE Fl ZIP CODE 92685

BIRTHDATE/
EXPIRATION DATE 12 - 30 - 61 HEIGHT 5'7" WEIGHT 200

EYE COLOR blue   GLASSES no   SEX male

ORGAN DONOR yes   RESTRICTIONS (Y/N) no

DRIVER'S LICENSE APPLICATION

LAST NAME Parker   FIRST NAME Jeff   MI T.

STREET ADDRESS 1532 Knobb Hill

CITY Charlotte   STATE NC ZIP CODE 84639

BIRTHDATE/
EXPIRATION DATE 9 - 17 - 75 HEIGHT 6'1" WEIGHT 220

EYE COLOR green   GLASSES no   SEX male

ORGAN DONOR yes   RESTRICTIONS (Y/N) no

DRIVER'S LICENSE APPLICATION

LAST NAME _Vickers_   FIRST NAME _Elizabeth_   MI _M._

STREET ADDRESS _102 W. Diamond Lake Rd_

CITY _Hanover_   STATE _MD_ ZIP CODE _54440_

BIRTHDATE/
EXPIRATION DATE _9 - 10 - 77_ HEIGHT _5'2"_   WEIGHT _100_

EYE COLOR _blue_   GLASSES _no_   SEX _Female_

ORGAN DONOR _no_   RESTRICTIONS (Y/N) _no_

DRIVER'S LICENSE APPLICATION

LAST NAME _Williams_   FIRST NAME _Bruce_   MI _K._

STREET ADDRESS _21701 Maple Avenue_

CITY _Farmington_   STATE _MO_ ZIP CODE _48345_

BIRTHDATE/
EXPIRATION DATE _10 - 9 - 75_ HEIGHT _5'11"_   WEIGHT _200_

EYE COLOR _brown_   GLASSES _no_   SEX _male_

ORGAN DONOR _yes_   RESTRICTIONS (Y/N) _no_

DRIVER'S LICENSE APPLICATION

LAST NAME _Wilson_   FIRST NAME _Scott_   MI _D._

STREET ADDRESS _3630 Phillips Pkwy._

CITY _Kansas City_   STATE _KS_ ZIP CODE _50905_

BIRTHDATE/
EXPIRATION DATE _11 - 17 - 63_ HEIGHT _5'9_   WEIGHT _175_

EYE COLOR _green_   GLASSES _yes_   SEX _Male_

ORGAN DONOR _yes_   RESTRICTIONS (Y/N) _yes_

DATA ENTRY JOB 23:
AUTOMOBILE REGISTRATION

PURPOSES

1. To provide additional practice in entering data from handwritten material
2. To provide experience in keying in data from handwritten material to more than one screen

PREPARATION

1. Enter the data onto two different screens.
2. Do not sort data but enter in the order as found in the book.

PROCEDURE

Data Entry Screen One

Job #23: Auto Registration

LAST NAME	FIRST NAME	MI
STREET ADDRESS		
CITY	STATE	ZIP

Data Entry Screen Two

VEHICLE SERIAL#	MAKE	MODEL
YEAR	LIEN	ODOMETER
GVN	EXPIRATION DATE	ASSESSED VALUE

General Entry

1. Enter Last Name—cursor return.
2. Enter First Name—cursor return.
3. Enter MI—auto advance.
4. Enter Street Address—cursor return.
5. Enter City—cursor return.
6. Enter State—auto advance.
7. Enter Zip—cursor return.
8. Enter Vehicle Serial #—auto advance.
9. Enter Make—cursor return.
10. Enter Model—cursor return.
11. Enter Year—auto advance.
12. Enter Lien—cursor return.
13. Enter Odometer—cursor return.
14. Enter GVN—auto advance.
15. Enter Expiration Date—cursor return.
16. Enter Assessed Value—cursor return.

Keying Aids

1. Program generates Record Number.
2. Cursor automatically advances from MI, State, Vehicle Serial#, Year and GVN.

AUTOMOBILE REGISTRATION

(SCREEN 1)

LAST NAME Siegel   FIRST NAME Gary   MI B

STREET ADDRESS 1939 Marshall Ave.

CITY Norfolk   STATE VA ZIP CODE 80473

. . . .

(SCREEN 2)

VEHICLE SERIAL # 14202-1 MAKE Volkswagon MODEL Cabriolet

YEAR 1990 LIEN Union State Bank ODOMETER 171,026

GVN 2012 EXPIRATION DATE 3-1-95 ASSESSED VALUE _____

AUTOMOBILE REGISTRATION

(SCREEN 1)

LAST NAME Ulrich   FIRST NAME Steven   MI G.

STREET ADDRESS 3924 Beau D'Rue Dr.

CITY New Orleans   STATE LA ZIP CODE 65402

. . . .

(SCREEN 2)

VEHICLE SERIAL # 65201-8 MAKE Fiat   MODEL Spyder

YEAR 1974 LIEN N/A   ODOMETER 426

GVN 4035 EXPIRATION DATE 7-4-96 ASSESSED VALUE $1,500

AUTOMOBILE REGISTRATION

(SCREEN 1)

LAST NAME Hughes   FIRST NAME Mark   MI D

STREET ADDRESS 1862 Orange Ave. E.

CITY Lake Charles   STATE JA ZIP CODE 30689

. . . .

(SCREEN 2)

VEHICLE SERIAL # 41152-7 MAKE Pontiac   MODEL Sunbird

YEAR 1988   LIEN Midstate Savings ODOMETER 66,729

GVN 4016 EXPIRATION DATE 6-12-98 ASSESSED VALUE $4,545

AUTOMOBILE REGISTRATION

(SCREEN 1)

LAST NAME Pieper   FIRST NAME Dennis   MI M.

STREET ADDRESS 18 Arlington Ave.

CITY Rochester   STATE MN ZIP CODE 507.25

. . . .

(SCREEN 2)

VEHICLE SERIAL # 26147-3 MAKE GMC   MODEL Suburban

YEAR 1991   LIEN GMAC Finance ODOMETER 88,431

GVN 2912 EXPIRATION DATE 8-9-97 ASSESSED VALUE $10,465

AUTOMOBILE REGISTRATION

(SCREEN 1)

LAST NAME **Harbaugh**   FIRST NAME **Amy**   MI **S.**

STREET ADDRESS **1404 Meadowlark Dr.**

CITY **Wilkes-Barre**   STATE **PA**   ZIP CODE **71725**

. . . .

(SCREEN 2)

VEHICLE SERIAL # **42366-6**   MAKE **GMC**   MODEL **Cadillac**

YEAR **1992**   LIEN **GMAC Finance**   ODOMETER **27,118**

GVN **3463** EXPIRATION DATE **10-1-95** ASSESSED VALUE **$35,000**

AUTOMOBILE REGISTRATION

(SCREEN 1)

LAST NAME *Ecker*   FIRST NAME *Larry*   MI *R.*

STREET ADDRESS *944 Maple Dr.*

CITY *Youngstown*   STATE *OH* ZIP CODE *21649*

. . . .

(SCREEN 2)

VEHICLE SERIAL # *11120-4* MAKE *Mitsubishi* MODEL *Eclipse*

YEAR *1994*   LIEN _____   ODOMETER *111*

GVN *2219* EXPIRATION DATE *7-15-99* ASSESSED VALUE *$13,000*

AUTOMOBILE REGISTRATION

(SCREEN 1)

LAST NAME Bastin   FIRST NAME Glen   MI T.

STREET ADDRESS 1900 Victoria St.

CITY Albany   STATE NY   ZIP CODE 51826

. . . .

(SCREEN 2)

VEHICLE SERIAL # 84926-5   MAKE Pontiac   MODEL Grand Prix

YEAR 1987   LIEN 1st National   ODOMETER 79,875

GVN 4314   EXPIRATION DATE 8-12-94 ASSESSED VALUE $2,500

AUTOMOBILE REGISTRATION

(SCREEN 1)

LAST NAME Mitchell   FIRST NAME Annette   MI A

STREET ADDRESS 18782 Southpointe Terrace

CITY Tyler   STATE TX ZIP CODE 21487

. . . .

(SCREEN 2)

VEHICLE SERIAL # 08892-0 MAKE Dodge   MODEL Charger

YEAR 1989   LIEN City Bank Corp.   ODOMETER 52,322

GVN 1031   EXPIRATION DATE 12-1-94 ASSESSED VALUE $1,750

AUTOMOBILE REGISTRATION

(SCREEN 1)

LAST NAME Woelm   FIRST NAME Camille   MI A

STREET ADDRESS 8789 Ironwood Ave.

CITY Yakima   STATE WA   ZIP CODE 50926

. . . .

(SCREEN 2)

VEHICLE SERIAL # 77935-9 MAKE Mercedes Benz MODEL Mercedes

YEAR 1994   LIEN   ODOMETER 762

GVN 2461 EXPIRATION DATE 8-1-99 ASSESSED VALUE $46,500

AUTOMOBILE REGISTRATION

(SCREEN 1)

LAST NAME Swenson   FIRST NAME Betty   MI T.

STREET ADDRESS 18 Randolph Dr.

CITY Wausau   STATE WI   ZIP CODE 71507

. . . .

(SCREEN 2)

VEHICLE SERIAL # 22208-7 MAKE Chevrolet   MODEL Impala

YEAR 1977   LIEN Western Life   ODOMETER 189,272

GVN 4036 EXPIRATION DATE 9-12-94 ASSESSED VALUE $925

AUTOMOBILE REGISTRATION

(SCREEN 1)

LAST NAME _Pearson_   FIRST NAME Richard   MI _D_

STREET ADDRESS 11620 Lockridge Ave.

CITY _Shreveport_   STATE _NE_ ZIP CODE _97612_

. . . .

(SCREEN 2)

VEHICLE SERIAL # _01159-9_ MAKE Toyota   MODEL _Tercel_

YEAR _1989_   LIEN _Federal Credit_   ODOMETER _50,000_

GVN _3721_ EXPIRATION DATE _6-15-94_ ASSESSED VALUE _$5,225_

AUTOMOBILE REGISTRATION

(SCREEN 1)

LAST NAME _Wilkins_   FIRST NAME _Tammy_   MI _C._

STREET ADDRESS _2339 Pueblo Dr._

CITY _Alberta_   STATE _NM_ ZIP CODE _51,237_

. . . .

(SCREEN 2)

VEHICLE SERIAL # _21089-1_ MAKE _Honda_   MODEL _Prelude_

YEAR _1993_   LIEN _____   ODOMETER _22,731_

GVN _41.29_ EXPIRATION DATE _1-5-98_ ASSESSED VALUE _$10,450_

AUTOMOBILE REGISTRATION

(SCREEN 1)

LAST NAME __Rhodes__   FIRST NAME __Camron__   MI __E__

STREET ADDRESS __667 Cherokee Ave.__

CITY __Beaumont__   STATE __MS__ ZIP CODE __31510__

- -

(SCREEN 2)

VEHICLE SERIAL # __56162-8__ MAKE __Chevrolet__ MODEL __Vega__

YEAR __1975__   LIEN __First State Bank__   ODOMETER __106,731__

GVN __2952__ EXPIRATION DATE __6-9-94__ ASSESSED VALUE __$500__

AUTOMOBILE REGISTRATION

(SCREEN 1)

LAST NAME __Nelson__   FIRST NAME __Brenda__   MI __M.__

STREET ADDRESS __1325 Grand Ave.__

CITY __St. Paul__   STATE __MN__ ZIP CODE __55105__

- -

(SCREEN 2)

VEHICLE SERIAL # __22089-2__ MAKE __AMC__ MODEL __Pacer__

YEAR __1982__   LIEN __American Saving__   ODOMETER __124,326__

GVN __1736__ EXPIRATION DATE __10-1-94__ ASSESSED VALUE __$200__

AUTOMOBILE REGISTRATION

(SCREEN 1)

LAST NAME _Juarez_   FIRST NAME _Alex_   MI _J._

STREET ADDRESS _10332 Bridge St._

CITY _Troy_   STATE _MO_   ZIP CODE _23145_

. . . .

(SCREEN 2)

VEHICLE SERIAL # _56118-7_   MAKE _Chevrolet_   MODEL _Camaro_

YEAR _1985_   LIEN _____   ODOMETER _75,626_

GVN _5212_   EXPIRATION DATE _11-17-94_ ASSESSED VALUE _$2,750_

AUTOMOBILE REGISTRATION

(SCREEN 1)

LAST NAME _Horsch_   FIRST NAME _Gerhard_   MI _W._

STREET ADDRESS _1520 Alameda Blvd._

CITY _Athens_   STATE _GA_   ZIP CODE _51048_

. . . .

(SCREEN 2)

VEHICLE SERIAL # _72089-3_   MAKE _Mercury_   MODEL _Tracer_

YEAR _1985_   LIEN _____   ODOMETER _89,325_

GVN _4095_   EXPIRATION DATE _12-28-94_ ASSESSED VALUE _$1,045_

AUTOMOBILE REGISTRATION

(SCREEN 1)

LAST NAME <u>Gibbons</u>   FIRST NAME <u>Arthur</u>   MI <u>B.</u>

STREET ADDRESS <u>1807 Belmont Ct.</u>

CITY <u>Tuscany</u>   STATE <u>WV</u>   ZIP CODE <u>30498</u>

. . . .

(SCREEN 2)

VEHICLE SERIAL # <u>51596-9</u> MAKE <u>Plymouth</u>   MODEL <u>Voyager</u>

YEAR <u>1994</u>   LIEN <u> </u>   ODOMETER <u>951</u>

GVN <u>2871</u> EXPIRATION DATE <u>9-14-99</u> ASSESSED VALUE <u>$12,500</u>

AUTOMOBILE REGISTRATION

(SCREEN 1)

LAST NAME <u>Jones</u>   FIRST NAME <u>Julie</u>   MI <u>M.</u>

STREET ADDRESS <u>43530 Northbrook Blvd</u>

CITY <u>Rome</u>   STATE <u>IN</u>   ZIP CODE <u>20855</u>

. . . .

(SCREEN 2)

VEHICLE SERIAL # <u>81590-1</u>   MAKE <u>Ford</u>   MODEL <u>Festiva</u>

YEAR <u>1986</u>   LIEN <u>Lincoln Savings</u>   ODOMETER <u>100,267</u>

GVN <u>3344</u> EXPIRATION DATE <u>7-11-94</u> ASSESSED VALUE <u>$450</u>

AUTOMOBILE REGISTRATION

LAST NAME La Valle   FIRST NAME Jamie   MI S.

STREET ADDRESS 2400 Farrington Circle

CITY   Durango   STATE CO ZIP CODE 30379

. . . .

VEHICLE SERIAL # 49511-8 MAKE Saturn   MODEL SC1

YEAR 1993   LIEN American Finance   ODOMETER 4,073

GVN 2766 EXPIRATION DATE 4-15-98 ASSESSED VALUE $10,750

AUTOMOBILE REGISTRATION

LAST NAME Weismann   FIRST NAME Lois   MI G.

STREET ADDRESS 401 Sibley St.

CITY Savannah   STATE GA ZIP CODE 40412

. . . .

VEHICLE SERIAL # 31099-2 MAKE Mazda   MODEL RX-7

YEAR 1991   LIEN 1st Bank   ODOMETER 45,021

GVN 1861 EXPIRATION DATE 3-1-95 ASSESSED VALUE $3,075

AUTOMOBILE REGISTRATION

(SCREEN 1)

LAST NAME **Baxter** FIRST NAME **Sandi** MI **C.**

STREET ADDRESS **111 E. Kellogg Blvd.**

CITY **New Bedford** STATE **MA** ZIP CODE **50845**

. . . .

(SCREEN 2)

VEHICLE SERIAL # **10023-5** MAKE **Chrysler** MODEL **LeBaron**

YEAR **1994** LIEN **Federal Savings** ODOMETER **562**

GVN **1435** EXPIRATION DATE **4-16-99** ASSESSED VALUE **$15,500**

AUTOMOBILE REGISTRATION

(SCREEN 1)

LAST NAME *Arehart* FIRST NAME *John* MI *H.*

STREET ADDRESS *6229 Hyacinth Ave. E.*

CITY *Hagerstown* STATE *MD* ZIP CODE *301.25*

. . . .

(SCREEN 2)

VEHICLE SERIAL # *30194-6* MAKE *Plymouth* MODEL *Duster*

YEAR *1985* LIEN _____ ODOMETER *66,727*

GVN *3401* EXPIRATION DATE *2-26-94* ASSESSED VALUE *$995*

AUTOMOBILE REGISTRATION

(SCREEN 1)

LAST NAME _Dodd_ FIRST NAME _Jeanene_ MI _B._

STREET ADDRESS _2030 Charlton Ridge_

CITY _Kalamazoo_ STATE _MI_ ZIP CODE _75310_

. . . .

(SCREEN 2)

VEHICLE SERIAL # _31160-6_ MAKE _Pontiac_ MODEL _LeMans_

YEAR _1991_ LIEN _1st Savings_ ODOMETER _34,022_

GVN _2436_ EXPIRATION DATE _1-14-96_ ASSESSED VALUE _$2,005_

AUTOMOBILE REGISTRATION

(SCREEN 1)

LAST NAME _Ruberto_ FIRST NAME _Maria_ MI _B._

STREET ADDRESS _27248 McKnight Rd._

CITY _Jenson City_ STATE _Fl_ ZIP CODE _80844_

. . . .

(SCREEN 2)

VEHICLE SERIAL # _12699-4_ MAKE _Chevrolet_ MODEL _Blazer_

YEAR _1993_ LIEN _Western Life_ ODOMETER _10,062_

GVN _3651_ EXPIRATION DATE _4-1-98_ ASSESSED VALUE _$21,326_

AUTOMOBILE REGISTRATION

(SCREEN 1)

LAST NAME _Spaulding_   FIRST NAME _Paul_   MI _C_

STREET ADDRESS _49 W. Hoyt Ave._

CITY _Malibu_   STATE _CA_   ZIP CODE _65432_

. . . .

(SCREEN 2)

VEHICLE SERIAL # _02113-5_   MAKE _Ford_   MODEL _Mustang_

YEAR _1969_   LIEN _____   ODOMETER _100,324_

GVN _2237_   EXPIRATION DATE _4-30-94_ ASSESSED VALUE _$4,755_

AUTOMOBILE REGISTRATION

(SCREEN 1)

LAST NAME _Van Patten_   FIRST NAME _Kenneth_   MI _T._

STREET ADDRESS _1286 Hazelwood St._

CITY _Elmira_   STATE _NY_   ZIP CODE _10025_

. . . .

(SCREEN 2)

VEHICLE SERIAL # _31160-1_ MAKE _Chevrolet_ MODEL _Chevette_

YEAR _1985_ LIEN _____   ODOMETER _95,726_

GVN _5755_ EXPIRATION DATE _2-12-94_ ASSESSED VALUE _$1,275_

AUTOMOBILE REGISTRATION

(SCREEN 1)

LAST NAME _Goldschmidt_   FIRST NAME _Louann_   MI _S._

STREET ADDRESS _2260 Cypress Dr._

CITY _Harrisburg_   STATE _OR_   ZIP CODE _21605_

· ·

(SCREEN 2)

VEHICLE SERIAL # _28142-7_   MAKE _Geo_   MODEL _Storm_

YEAR _1991_   LIEN _____   ODOMETER _31,004_

GVN _2066_   EXPIRATION DATE _12-6-95_   ASSESSED VALUE _$5,525_

AUTOMOBILE REGISTRATION

(SCREEN 1)

LAST NAME **Cohen**   FIRST NAME **Lisa**   MI **T.**

STREET ADDRESS **326 Woodbury St.**

CITY **Fayetteville**   STATE **NC**   ZIP CODE **91900**

· ·

(SCREEN 2)

VEHICLE SERIAL # **46137-4**   MAKE **Ford**   MODEL **Ranger**

YEAR **1994**   LIEN **First State Bank**   ODOMETER **125**

GVN **4222**   EXPIRATION DATE **3-21-99**   ASSESSED VALUE **$14,500**

AUTOMOBILE REGISTRATION

(SCREEN 1)

LAST NAME McIntyre   FIRST NAME Joseph   MI C.

STREET ADDRESS 2029 Kenwood Dr.

CITY Paducah   STATE KY   ZIP CODE 65325

. . . .

(SCREEN 2)

VEHICLE SERIAL # 46167-8 MAKE Toyota   MODEL Camry

YEAR 1984   LIEN _____   ODOMETER 91,067

GVN 2472 EXPIRATION DATE 6-16-94 ASSESSED VALUE $2,525

AUTOMOBILE REGISTRATION

(SCREEN 1)

LAST NAME Kendall   FIRST NAME Bridgette   MI L.

STREET ADDRESS 4835 Sheffield Lane

CITY Salina   STATE KS   ZIP CODE 50441

. . . .

(SCREEN 2)

VEHICLE SERIAL # 61143-3 MAKE Honda   MODEL CRX

YEAR 1989   LIEN City Bank Corp.   ODOMETER 49,521

GVN 3299 EXPIRATION DATE 8-9-94 ASSESSED VALUE $4,620

DATA ENTRY JOB 24:
CENSUS SURVEY

PURPOSES

1. To practice entering data from a document that has handwritten material and bubbles
2. To provide additional experience in entering data that has mixed fields and some fields that are missing

PREPARATION

1. In Job 24, examine the twenty forms for completeness of data.
2. Sort the cards according to ZIP Code information with the smallest number first.
3. For Head of Household marital status, press the Tab key to advance to the appropriate status. Press cursor return to enter the X. Press the Tab key to advance to the next field.

Data Entry Screen

CENSUS REGISTRATION FORM

ZIP CODE   HEAD OF HOUSEHOLD   MARRIED   O

SINGLE   O

DIVORCED   O

HEAD OF HOUSEHOLD	SEX M F	RACE	BIRTH DATE	EDUC. LEVEL	BIRTH PLACE	OCCUP.	ANNUAL INCOME
SPOUSE	O O						
DEPENDENT 1	O O						
DEPENDENT 2	O O						
DEPENDENT 3	O O						
DEPENDENT 4	O O						
DEPENDENT 5	O O						

General Entry

1. Enter Zip Code—auto advance.
2. Enter Head of Household marital status (X)—auto advance.
3. Enter Sex—cursor return.
4. Enter Race—cursor return.
5. Enter Birthdate—auto advance.
6. Enter Educational Level—cursor return.
7. Enter Birthplace—auto advance.
8. Enter Occupation—cursor return.
9. Enter Annual Income—cursor return.

Data

For Spouse and Dependent

1. Zip Code remains the same—cursor return.
2. Head of Household marital status remains the same—cursor return.
3. Program automatically generates position in household.
4. Repeat steps 3–9 from above.

Keying Aids

1. Program generates Record Number.
2. Cursor automatically advances on Birth Date and Birth Place.
3. Pres Alt + A to move cursor to Zip Code in current record.

CENSUS REGISTRATION FORM

ZIP CODE 10023 HEAD OF HOUSEHOLD (Married) ●
(Single) ○
(Divorced) ○

	SEX M F	RACE	BIRTH DATE	EDUC. LEVEL	BIRTH PLACE	OCCUP.	ANNUAL INCOME
HEAD OF HOUSEHOLD	○ ●	A	6/20/55	16	IL	Admin	$29,500
SPOUSE	● ○	A	9/6/54	12	IN	Lab	$25,000
DEPENDENT 1	○ ○						
DEPENDENT 2	○ ○						
DEPENDENT 3	○ ○						
DEPENDENT 4	○ ○						

CENSUS REGISTRATION FORM

ZIP CODE 35714 HEAD OF HOUSEHOLD (Married) ○
(Single) ○
(Divorced) ●

	SEX M F	RACE	BIRTH DATE	EDUC. LEVEL	BIRTH PLACE	OCCUP.	ANNUAL INCOME
HEAD OF HOUSEHOLD	● ○	C	10/27/61	16	CA	Prof	$35,000
SPOUSE	○ ○						
DEPENDENT 1	○ ○						
DEPENDENT 2	○ ○						
DEPENDENT 3	○ ○						
DEPENDENT 4	○ ○						

CENSUS REGISTRATION FORM

ZIP CODE 35417   HEAD OF HOUSEHOLD (Married) ○
                                       (Single)   ●
                                       (Divorced) ○

	SEX M F	RACE	BIRTH DATE	EDUC. LEVEL	BIRTH PLACE	OCCUP.	ANNUAL INCOME
HEAD OF HOUSEHOLD	○ ●	N	8/9/57	15	PA	Prof	$39,000
SPOUSE	○ ○						
DEPENDENT 1	○ ○						
DEPENDENT 2	○ ○						
DEPENDENT 3	○ ○						
DEPENDENT 4	○ ○						

CENSUS REGISTRATION FORM

ZIP CODE 90147   HEAD OF HOUSEHOLD (Married) ○
                                       (Single)   ○
                                       (Divorced) ●

	SEX M F	RACE	BIRTH DATE	EDUC. LEVEL	BIRTH PLACE	OCCUP.	ANNUAL INCOME
HEAD OF HOUSEHOLD	○ ●	C	7/11/50	12		Prof	$27,500
SPOUSE	○ ○						
DEPENDENT 1	○ ○						
DEPENDENT 2	○ ○						
DEPENDENT 3	○ ○						
DEPENDENT 4	○ ○						

CENSUS REGISTRATION FORM

ZIP CODE <u>43915</u> HEAD OF HOUSEHOLD (Married) ●
(Single) ○
(Divorced) ○

	SEX M F	RACE	BIRTH DATE	EDUC. LEVEL	BIRTH PLACE	OCCUP.	ANNUAL INCOME
HEAD OF HOUSEHOLD	● ○	N	1/6/59	16	MO	Admin	$33,500
SPOUSE	○ ●	C	4/22/60	16	MO	Prof	$28,000
DEPENDENT 1	○ ●	N	8/6/85		MO		
DEPENDENT 2	○ ●	N	2/15/87		MO		
DEPENDENT 3	○ ○						
DEPENDENT 4	○ ○						

CENSUS REGISTRATION FORM

ZIP CODE <u>67215</u> HEAD OF HOUSEHOLD (Married) ●
(Single) ○
(Divorced) ○

	SEX M F	RACE	BIRTH DATE	EDUC. LEVEL	BIRTH PLACE	OCCUP.	ANNUAL INCOME
HEAD OF HOUSEHOLD	● ○	A	5/6/65	12	MA	Lab	$26,000
SPOUSE	○ ●	A	3/10/65	12	CT	Prof	$18,000
DEPENDENT 1	○ ○						
DEPENDENT 2	○ ○						
DEPENDENT 3	○ ○						
DEPENDENT 4	○ ○						

CENSUS REGISTRATION FORM

ZIP CODE _62011_ HEAD OF HOUSEHOLD (Married) ●
(Single) ○
(Divorced) ○

	SEX M F	RACE	BIRTH DATE	EDUC. LEVEL	BIRTH PLACE	OCCUP.	ANNUAL INCOME
HEAD OF HOUSEHOLD	○ ●	H	6/19/35	12	NE	Prof	$32,000
SPOUSE	● ○	H	2/12/32	14	NE	Ret	$20,000
DEPENDENT 1	○ ○						
DEPENDENT 2	○ ○						
DEPENDENT 3	○ ○						
DEPENDENT 4	○ ○						

CENSUS REGISTRATION FORM

ZIP CODE _63800_ HEAD OF HOUSEHOLD (Married) ○
(Single) ○
(Divorced) ●

	SEX M F	RACE	BIRTH DATE	EDUC. LEVEL	BIRTH PLACE	OCCUP.	ANNUAL INCOME
HEAD OF HOUSEHOLD	● ○	J	5/22/60	16	NY	Admin	$44,000
SPOUSE	○ ○						
DEPENDENT 1	● ○	J	7/7/84	4	NY		
DEPENDENT 2	○ ○						
DEPENDENT 3	○ ○						
DEPENDENT 4	○ ○						

CENSUS REGISTRATION FORM

ZIP CODE _60021_   HEAD OF HOUSEHOLD (Married)   ○
                                          (Single)   ○
                                          (Divorced) ●

	SEX M F	RACE	BIRTH DATE	EDUC. LEVEL	BIRTH PLACE	OCCUP.	ANNUAL INCOME
HEAD OF HOUSEHOLD	● ○	C	12/1/53	12	TX	Lab	$37,000
SPOUSE	○ ○						
DEPENDENT 1	● ○	C	9/7/73	12	TX	Lab	$11,500
DEPENDENT 2	○ ●	C	6/15/75	12	TX	Stu	
DEPENDENT 3	○ ○						
DEPENDENT 4	○ ○						

CENSUS REGISTRATION FORM

ZIP CODE _73329_   HEAD OF HOUSEHOLD (Married)   ○
                                          (Single)   ○
                                          (Divorced) ●

	SEX M F	RACE	BIRTH DATE	EDUC. LEVEL	BIRTH PLACE	OCCUP.	ANNUAL INCOME
HEAD OF HOUSEHOLD	○ ●	C	6/10/68	14	OH	Prof	$23,000
SPOUSE	○ ○						
DEPENDENT 1	○ ○						
DEPENDENT 2	○ ○						
DEPENDENT 3	○ ○						
DEPENDENT 4	○ ○						

CENSUS REGISTRATION FORM

ZIP CODE _65401_   HEAD OF HOUSEHOLD (Married) ○
(Single) ○
(Divorced) ●

	SEX M	SEX F	RACE	BIRTH DATE	EDUC. LEVEL	BIRTH PLACE	OCCUP.	ANNUAL INCOME
HEAD OF HOUSEHOLD	○	●	C	11/17/64	16	A3	Prof	$35,000
SPOUSE	○	○						
DEPENDENT 1	●	○	C	7/14/82	6	A3		
DEPENDENT 2	○	●	C	3/20/87	2	A3		
DEPENDENT 3	○	○						
DEPENDENT 4	○	○						

CENSUS REGISTRATION FORM

ZIP CODE _92032_   HEAD OF HOUSEHOLD (Married) ○
(Single) ●
(Divorced) ○

	SEX M	SEX F	RACE	BIRTH DATE	EDUC. LEVEL	BIRTH PLACE	OCCUP.	ANNUAL INCOME
HEAD OF HOUSEHOLD	●	○	H	10/1/58	12	CO	Lab	$42,000
SPOUSE	○	○						
DEPENDENT 1	○	○						
DEPENDENT 2	○	○						
DEPENDENT 3	○	○						
DEPENDENT 4	○	○						

CENSUS REGISTRATION FORM

ZIP CODE _31036_   HEAD OF HOUSEHOLD (Married) O
                                        (Single) O
                                        (Divorced) ●

	SEX M F	RACE	BIRTH DATE	EDUC. LEVEL	BIRTH PLACE	OCCUP.	ANNUAL INCOME
HEAD OF HOUSEHOLD	O ●	n	11/14/48	16	CA	Prof	$44,000
SPOUSE	O O						
DEPENDENT 1	● O	n	9/1/74	14	CA		
DEPENDENT 2	O ●	n	4/18/77	11	CA		
DEPENDENT 3	O O						
DEPENDENT 4	O O						

CENSUS REGISTRATION FORM

ZIP CODE _87831_   HEAD OF HOUSEHOLD (Married) O
                                        (Single) O
                                        (Divorced) ●

	SEX M F	RACE	BIRTH DATE	EDUC. LEVEL	BIRTH PLACE	OCCUP.	ANNUAL INCOME
HEAD OF HOUSEHOLD	● O	A	2/1/59	18	ME	Admin	$50,000
SPOUSE	O O						
DEPENDENT 1	O O						
DEPENDENT 2	O O						
DEPENDENT 3	O O						
DEPENDENT 4	O O						

CENSUS REGISTRATION FORM

ZIP CODE ___76788___ HEAD OF HOUSEHOLD (Married) ○
(Single) ●
(Divorced) ○

	SEX M F	RACE	BIRTH DATE	EDUC. LEVEL	BIRTH PLACE	OCCUP.	ANNUAL INCOME
HEAD OF HOUSEHOLD	● ○	C	4/9/54	11	NH	Lab	$55,000
SPOUSE	○ ○						
DEPENDENT 1	○ ○						
DEPENDENT 2	○ ○						
DEPENDENT 3	○ ○						
DEPENDENT 4	○ ○						

CENSUS REGISTRATION FORM

ZIP CODE ___80565___ HEAD OF HOUSEHOLD (Married) ○
(Single) ●
(Divorced) ○

	SEX M F	RACE	BIRTH DATE	EDUC. LEVEL	BIRTH PLACE	OCCUP.	ANNUAL INCOME
HEAD OF HOUSEHOLD	○ ●	C	12/2/70	17	AL	Prof	$34,500
SPOUSE	○ ○						
DEPENDENT 1	○ ○						
DEPENDENT 2	○ ○						
DEPENDENT 3	○ ○						
DEPENDENT 4	○ ○						

CENSUS REGISTRATION FORM

ZIP CODE 92685   HEAD OF HOUSEHOLD (Married) ●
                                     (Single) ○
                                     (Divorced) ○

	SEX M F	RACE	BIRTH DATE	EDUC. LEVEL	BIRTH PLACE	OCCUP.	ANNUAL INCOME
HEAD OF HOUSEHOLD	○ ●	N	10/17/64	14	VT	Prof	$30,000
SPOUSE	● ○	N	12/24/63	12	FL	Lab	$21,500
DEPENDENT 1	○ ○						
DEPENDENT 2	○ ○						
DEPENDENT 3	○ ○						
DEPENDENT 4	○ ○						

CENSUS REGISTRATION FORM

ZIP CODE 84639   HEAD OF HOUSEHOLD (Married) ○
                                     (Single) ●
                                     (Divorced) ○

	SEX M F	RACE	BIRTH DATE	EDUC. LEVEL	BIRTH PLACE	OCCUP.	ANNUAL INCOME
HEAD OF HOUSEHOLD	● ○	C	10/1/58	10	MN	Lab	$29,700
SPOUSE	○ ○						
DEPENDENT 1	○ ○						
DEPENDENT 2	○ ○						
DEPENDENT 3	○ ○						
DEPENDENT 4	○ ○						

CENSUS REGISTRATION FORM

ZIP CODE 32922   HEAD OF HOUSEHOLD (Married) ○
                                        (Single) ○
                                        (Divorced) ●

	SEX M F	RACE	BIRTH DATE	EDUC. LEVEL	BIRTH PLACE	OCCUP.	ANNUAL INCOME
HEAD OF HOUSEHOLD	● ○	A	2/22/46	16	AK	Admin	$79,500
SPOUSE	○ ○						
DEPENDENT 1	○ ●	A	3/16/75	12	AK	Stu	
DEPENDENT 2	● ○	A	11/17/77	10	AK		
DEPENDENT 3	○ ●	A	8/10/79	8	AK		
DEPENDENT 4	○ ○						

CENSUS REGISTRATION FORM

ZIP CODE 41148   HEAD OF HOUSEHOLD (Married) ○
                                        (Single) ○
                                        (Divorced) ●

	SEX M F	RACE	BIRTH DATE	EDUC. LEVEL	BIRTH PLACE	OCCUP.	ANNUAL INCOME
HEAD OF HOUSEHOLD	○ ●	N	3/9/67	15	GA	Prof	$25,700
SPOUSE	○ ○						
DEPENDENT 1	○ ○						
DEPENDENT 2	○ ○						
DEPENDENT 3	○ ○						
DEPENDENT 4	○ ○						

DATA ENTRY JOB 25:

RESTAURANT FOOD COUNT SURVEY

PURPOSES

1. To practice entering data from survey cards
2. To provide additional experience entering data from handwritten material

PREPARATION

1. Each field will automatically advance the operator to the next field.

PROCEDURE

Data Entry Screen

Job #25 RESTAURANT FOOD COUNT SURVEY

NO. _____

Sex: M _____ F _____ Age _____   ZIP Code _____

Preferred Food at Wendell's: (CHECK ONE)

_____ RIBS

_____ CHICKEN

_____ STEAK

_____ HAMBURGER

_____ SHRIMP

_____ HOT DOGS

_____ LIVER

PREFERRED TIME TO DINE _____

SMOKING _____ NON-SMOKING _____

NUMBER OF TIMES YOU DINE OUT AT WENDELL'S PER MONTH _____

NUMBER OF TIMES YOU DINE OUT PER MONTH _____

General Entry

1. Enter Number—auto advance.
2. Enter Sex—auto advance.
3. Enter Age—auto advance.
4. Enter Zip Code—auto advance.
5. Enter Food Preference (X)—auto advance.

6. Enter Preferred Time to Dine—cursor return.
7. Enter "S" for Smoking; "N" for non-smoking—auto advance.
8. Enter Number of times customer dines at Wendel's—auto advance.
9. Enter Number of times customer dines out—auto advance.

```
WENDELL FOODS SURVEY                    NO. ____013____
Sex: M __✓__ F _____ Age __32__ Zip Code __65401__
Preferred Food at Wendell's: (CHECK ONE)
_____✓_____        RIBS
_____        CHICKEN
_____        STEAK
_____        HAMBURGER
_____        SHRIMP
_____        HOT DOGS
_____        LIVER
PREFERRED TIME TO DINE __Evening_____
SMOKING _____ NON-SMOKING ____X_____
NUMBER OF TIMES YOU DINE OUT AT WENDELL'S PER MONTH 5
NUMBER OF TIMES YOU DINE OUT PER MONTH __10__
```

```
WENDELL FOODS SURVEY                    NO. ____014____
Sex: M __✓__ F _____ Age __18__ Zip Code __53211__
Preferred Food at Wendell's: (CHECK ONE)
_____        RIBS
_____        CHICKEN
_____✓_____        STEAK
_____        HAMBURGER
_____        SHRIMP
_____        HOT DOGS
_____        LIVER
PREFERRED TIME TO DINE __Lunch_____
SMOKING _____X_____ NON-SMOKING _____
NUMBER OF TIMES YOU DINE OUT AT WENDELL'S PER MONTH 15
NUMBER OF TIMES YOU DINE OUT PER MONTH __20__
```

WENDELL FOODS SURVEY   NO. _____016_____

Sex: M __✓__ F _____ Age __35__ Zip Code __20125__

Preferred Food at Wendell's: (CHECK ONE)

_____	RIBS
_____✓_____	CHICKEN
_____	STEAK
_____	HAMBURGER
_____	SHRIMP
_____	HOT DOGS
_____	LIVER

PREFERRED TIME TO DINE __Lunch_____

SMOKING _____ NON-SMOKING ___✓_____

NUMBER OF TIMES YOU DINE OUT AT WENDELL'S PER MONTH _5_

NUMBER OF TIMES YOU DINE OUT PER MONTH _25_

WENDELL FOODS SURVEY   NO. _____017_____

Sex: M _____ F __✓__ Age __29__ Zip Code __36472__

Preferred Food at Wendell's: (CHECK ONE)

_____	RIBS
_____✓_____	CHICKEN
_____	STEAK
_____	HAMBURGER
_____	SHRIMP
_____	HOT DOGS
_____	LIVER

PREFERRED TIME TO DINE __Dinner_____

SMOKING _____✓_____ NON-SMOKING _____

NUMBER OF TIMES YOU DINE OUT AT WENDELL'S PER MONTH _10_

NUMBER OF TIMES YOU DINE OUT PER MONTH _15_

```
WENDELL FOODS SURVEY                    NO. _____019_____

Sex: M _____  F ___✓___  Age __42__  Zip Code __76435_____

Preferred Food at Wendell's: (CHECK ONE)

_____        RIBS

_____        CHICKEN

_____        STEAK

_____        HAMBURGER

_____✓_____        SHRIMP

_____        HOT DOGS

_____        LIVER

PREFERRED TIME TO DINE __Dinner_____

SMOKING _____  NON-SMOKING ____✓_____

NUMBER OF TIMES YOU DINE OUT AT WENDELL'S PER MONTH 10

NUMBER OF TIMES YOU DINE OUT PER MONTH __25__
```

```
WENDELL FOODS SURVEY                    NO. _____020_____

Sex: M ___✓___  F _____  Age __55__  Zip Code __73100_____

Preferred Food at Wendell's: (CHECK ONE)

_____✓_____        RIBS

_____        CHICKEN

_____        STEAK

_____        HAMBURGER

_____        SHRIMP

_____        HOT DOGS

_____        LIVER

PREFERRED TIME TO DINE __Lunch_____

SMOKING _____✓_____  NON-SMOKING _____

NUMBER OF TIMES YOU DINE OUT AT WENDELL'S PER MONTH 15

NUMBER OF TIMES YOU DINE OUT PER MONTH __20__
```

```
WENDELL FOODS SURVEY                    NO. ____021____

Sex: M _____  F __✓__  Age __19__  Zip Code __91901__

Preferred Food at Wendell's: (CHECK ONE)

_____     RIBS
_____✓_____     CHICKEN
_____     STEAK
_____     HAMBURGER
_____     SHRIMP
_____     HOT DOGS
_____     LIVER

PREFERRED TIME TO DINE ___Lunch_____

SMOKING _____✓_____  NON-SMOKING _____

NUMBER OF TIMES YOU DINE OUT AT WENDELL'S PER MONTH 5

NUMBER OF TIMES YOU DINE OUT PER MONTH __10__
```

```
WENDELL FOODS SURVEY                    NO. ____022____

Sex: M _____  F __✓__  Age __25__  Zip Code __43190__

Preferred Food at Wendell's: (CHECK ONE)

_____     RIBS
_____✓_____     CHICKEN
_____     STEAK
_____     HAMBURGER
_____     SHRIMP
_____     HOT DOGS
_____     LIVER

PREFERRED TIME TO DINE ___Lunch_____

SMOKING _____  NON-SMOKING ____✓____

NUMBER OF TIMES YOU DINE OUT AT WENDELL'S PER MONTH 10

NUMBER OF TIMES YOU DINE OUT PER MONTH __20__
```

```
WENDELL FOODS SURVEY                    NO. _____025_____

Sex: M ___✓___ F _____ Age __37__ Zip Code __10023__

Preferred Food at Wendell's: (CHECK ONE)

_____        RIBS

_____        CHICKEN

_____        STEAK

_____✓_____        HAMBURGER

_____        SHRIMP

_____        HOT DOGS

_____        LIVER

PREFERRED TIME TO DINE ___Dinner_____

SMOKING _____    NON-SMOKING ____✓_____

NUMBER OF TIMES YOU DINE OUT AT WENDELL'S PER MONTH _2_

NUMBER OF TIMES YOU DINE OUT PER MONTH __5__
```

```
WENDELL FOODS SURVEY                    NO. _____028_____

Sex: M _____ F ___✓___ Age __35__ Zip Code __20015__

Preferred Food at Wendell's: (CHECK ONE)

_____        RIBS

_____        CHICKEN

_____        STEAK

_____        HAMBURGER

_____✓_____        SHRIMP

_____        HOT DOGS

_____        LIVER

PREFERRED TIME TO DINE ___Lunch_____

SMOKING _____    NON-SMOKING ____✓_____

NUMBER OF TIMES YOU DINE OUT AT WENDELL'S PER MONTH _7_

NUMBER OF TIMES YOU DINE OUT PER MONTH __10__
```

```
WENDELL FOODS SURVEY                    NO. _____030_____
Sex: M __✓__ F _____ Age _49_ Zip Code _51361_____
Preferred Food at Wendell's: (CHECK ONE)
_____     RIBS
_____     CHICKEN
_____✓_____     STEAK
_____     HAMBURGER
_____     SHRIMP
_____     HOT DOGS
_____     LIVER
PREFERRED TIME TO DINE _Lunch_____
SMOKING _____ NON-SMOKING ____✓_____
NUMBER OF TIMES YOU DINE OUT AT WENDELL'S PER MONTH _8_
NUMBER OF TIMES YOU DINE OUT PER MONTH _15_
```

```
WENDELL FOODS SURVEY                    NO. _____031_____
Sex: M __✓__ F _____ Age _42_ Zip Code _63125_____
Preferred Food at Wendell's: (CHECK ONE)
_____     RIBS
_____✓_____     CHICKEN
_____     STEAK
_____     HAMBURGER
_____     SHRIMP
_____     HOT DOGS
_____     LIVER
PREFERRED TIME TO DINE _Dinner_____
SMOKING _____✓_____ NON-SMOKING _____
NUMBER OF TIMES YOU DINE OUT AT WENDELL'S PER MONTH _4_
NUMBER OF TIMES YOU DINE OUT PER MONTH _10_
```

```
WENDELL FOODS SURVEY              NO.    034

Sex: M    ✓    F _____   Age  40   Zip Code  60152
Preferred Food at Wendell's: (CHECK ONE)
_____        RIBS
_____        CHICKEN
_____        STEAK
_____✓_____        HAMBURGER
_____        SHRIMP
_____        HOT DOGS
_____        LIVER
PREFERRED TIME TO DINE   Lunch
SMOKING _____   NON-SMOKING    ✓
NUMBER OF TIMES YOU DINE OUT AT WENDELL'S PER MONTH  8
NUMBER OF TIMES YOU DINE OUT PER MONTH   15
```

```
WENDELL FOODS SURVEY                  NO.    035

Sex: M    ✓    F _____   Age  31   Zip Code  40019
Preferred Food at Wendell's: (CHECK ONE)
_____        RIBS
_____        CHICKEN
_____✓_____        STEAK
_____        HAMBURGER
_____        SHRIMP
_____        HOT DOGS
_____        LIVER
PREFERRED TIME TO DINE   Lunch
SMOKING _____   NON-SMOKING       ✓
NUMBER OF TIMES YOU DINE OUT AT WENDELL'S PER MONTH  12
NUMBER OF TIMES YOU DINE OUT PER MONTH   15
```

```
WENDELL FOODS SURVEY                    NO.    040

Sex: M _____ F  ✓  Age  37   Zip Code  60123

Preferred Food at Wendell's: (CHECK ONE)

_____     RIBS

_____✓_____    CHICKEN

_____     STEAK

_____     HAMBURGER

_____     SHRIMP

_____     HOT DOGS

_____     LIVER

PREFERRED TIME TO DINE   Lunch _____

SMOKING _____✓_____ NON-SMOKING _____

NUMBER OF TIMES YOU DINE OUT AT WENDELL'S PER MONTH 10

NUMBER OF TIMES YOU DINE OUT PER MONTH  15
```

```
WENDELL FOODS SURVEY                    NO.    044

Sex: M _____ F  ✓  Age  51   Zip Code  20303

Preferred Food at Wendell's: (CHECK ONE)

_____     RIBS

_____✓_____    CHICKEN

_____     STEAK

_____     HAMBURGER

_____     SHRIMP

_____     HOT DOGS

_____     LIVER

PREFERRED TIME TO DINE   Dinner _____

SMOKING _____✓_____ NON-SMOKING _____

NUMBER OF TIMES YOU DINE OUT AT WENDELL'S PER MONTH 15

NUMBER OF TIMES YOU DINE OUT PER MONTH  25
```

```
WENDELL FOODS SURVEY                      NO.    045

Sex: M _____  F    ✓    Age   27   Zip Code   50015

Preferred Food at Wendell's: (CHECK ONE)

_____      RIBS

_____✓_____      CHICKEN

_____      STEAK

_____      HAMBURGER

_____      SHRIMP

_____      HOT DOGS

_____      LIVER

PREFERRED TIME TO DINE    Dinner _____

SMOKING _____✓_____      NON-SMOKING _____

NUMBER OF TIMES YOU DINE OUT AT WENDELL'S PER MONTH 5

NUMBER OF TIMES YOU DINE OUT PER MONTH    5
```

```
WENDELL FOODS SURVEY                      NO.    046

Sex: M    ✓    F _____ Age   63   Zip Code   39175

Preferred Food at Wendell's: (CHECK ONE)

_____      RIBS

_____      CHICKEN

_____      STEAK

_____✓_____      HAMBURGER

_____      SHRIMP

_____      HOT DOGS

_____      LIVER

PREFERRED TIME TO DINE    Lunch _____

SMOKING _____    NON-SMOKING    ✓    _____

NUMBER OF TIMES YOU DINE OUT AT WENDELL'S PER MONTH 15

NUMBER OF TIMES YOU DINE OUT PER MONTH   20
```

```
WENDELL FOODS SURVEY                    NO.    048

Sex: M   ✓   F _____   Age  24   Zip Code  51902

Preferred Food at Wendell's: (CHECK ONE)

_____   RIBS

_____   CHICKEN

_____   STEAK

_____   HAMBURGER

_____   SHRIMP

_____   HOT DOGS

_____✓_____   LIVER

PREFERRED TIME TO DINE   Lunch

SMOKING _____   NON-SMOKING   ✓

NUMBER OF TIMES YOU DINE OUT AT WENDELL'S PER MONTH  9

NUMBER OF TIMES YOU DINE OUT PER MONTH   15
```

```
WENDELL FOODS SURVEY                    NO.    051

Sex: M _____   F   ✓   Age  32   Zip Code  93015

Preferred Food at Wendell's: (CHECK ONE)

_____✓_____   RIBS

_____   CHICKEN

_____   STEAK

_____   HAMBURGER

_____   SHRIMP

_____   HOT DOGS

_____   LIVER

PREFERRED TIME TO DINE   Lunch

SMOKING _____   NON-SMOKING   ✓

NUMBER OF TIMES YOU DINE OUT AT WENDELL'S PER MONTH  3

NUMBER OF TIMES YOU DINE OUT PER MONTH   5
```

Chapter 5

SPREADSHEET SOFTWARE FOR MICROCOMPUTERS

The machines built in the early days of the computer industry were far from standard. Thus a person or organization who wanted a program to provide instructions for a computer usually had to write it or have it written.

Today, however, computers are much more compatible and have similar circuitry, so a program can be written that will run on a wide range of compatible computers. Today we can purchase software packages, which consist of a program or series of programs together with the documentation on how they are to be used. Many software packages are now available for purposes that vary from playing Star Trek to playing the stock market. Most organizations and individuals who use microcomputers have at least one package from each of the three most popular categories of software: (1) spreadsheets, (2) databases, and (3) word processors. People who work as data entry operators are frequently asked to use one or more of these packages either to perform traditional data entry functions or to enter less traditional material, such as business letters and documents.

This chapter presents a brief introduction to spreadsheet software. Coverage includes a discussion of the purpose of a spreadsheet followed by exercises to be done using a popular spreadsheet software package—Lotus 1-2-3. Whether or not you have the software, study the first part of this chapter for general information about what that spreadsheet software will do. Then, if you have the package, proceed to the laboratory Jobs that give you experience using Lotus 1-2-3.

If you have used the data entry software, you will find that Lotus provides similar assistance to the user. It presents menus (lists of functions from which you can choose) and display prompts (short messages detailing what action or actions to take).

You will remember that the data entry software first presents a master menu that lists the names of all entry and validation jobs and includes prompts, or instructions, on how to select the Job you wish to do. When the Job has been selected, a second-level menu for that Job appears and presents the options of creating the file, adding records to the file, or returning to the master menu. Lotus also uses multiple levels of menus to guide you. The layouts of the menus and the wordings of the prompts are different, but they work in much the same way.

The material you will read and the Jobs you will perform in this chapter are designed to familiarize you with the general terminology and functions of the spreadsheet software—particularly Lotus 1-2-3—rather than to train you in detailed operations.

Lotus is a powerful and sophisticated collection of programs with many options. If you wish to become a proficient user, plan to take a full-length course or to devote hours of your own time to studying Lotus in detail—or both.

This chapter should give you the vocabulary and the familiarity with the general functions of Lotus to prepare you to study on your own or to take an in-depth course devoted to spreadsheets.

▨ GENERAL FUNCTIONAL CHARACTERISTICS

When we jot data down on paper in order to examine it or to process it in other ways, we usually organize the data into rows and columns so that we can compare similar values in an orderly fashion. Electronic spreadsheet programs give us an electronic array of rows and columns in which to store data items. They also manipulate the data for us.

The sizes of the spreadsheets, or worksheets, can be quite large. Popular packages allow hundreds of columns and thousands of rows. On the spreadsheet, the columns are identified with letters, and the rows are identified with numbers. Each location, or cell, is identified by the combination of its row number and its column number. Each location's row number combined with its column number identifies its cell address. For example, the rent for September in the budget spreadsheet in Figure 5-1 is in Cell B7 because it is in Column B of Row 7. The rent for October is in Cell C7, and the food for November is in D9.

You can change the size of the cells in a column, adjusting them to hold longer or shorter items. A cell may hold any type of data, and the user must be careful to use individual items in appropriate ways. For example, the user must not try to perform mathematics with alphabetic data.

A cell also may contain instruction, or formulas. If you wanted to find the cash remaining after you have paid all the expenses for September, you can put the formula +B5-B18 at cell B20. This instructs the spreadsheet package to take the data at B5 (the monthly income) and subtract from it the data at B18 (the total expenses from the month). The result will display at B20, where you placed the formula.

Some mathematical procedures are used in the great majority of spreadsheets. For example, users often want to find the sum of a group of figures. Spreadsheet packages have formulas already written for the frequently used procedures. The prewritten formulas are called **functions**.

Each cell may contain either a value, a label, a formula, or a function. A **value** is a number to be used in calculations. All of the numbers on the budget worksheet are values. The column headings (SEPTEMBER, OCTOBER, NOVEMBER and QUARTERLY TOTALS) and the words in column A are labels. **Labels** give information about the data, as SEPTEMBER labels column B as being the data for the month of SEPTEMBER and RENT labels row 7 as being the row for RENT. We have seen examples of **formulas** and **functions** in the general discussion of spreadsheets.

When you load Lotus 1-2-3 for Windows the screen will display a worksheet window. The top bar is the title bar which will be the name of your spreadsheet once you have named it. This bar will also show a minus in the upper left corner and icons that are used to show how to minimize, maximize, and restore your worksheet in the upper right corner. Under this bar is the menu bar, which has the following selections: File, Edit, View, Style, Tools, Range, Window, and Help. These choices are similar to the choices given in other software applications for Windows, like WordPerfect. Under this menu bar is the bar that indicates that Lotus is ready to operate. The next area below the menu bar includes the selection indicator and the edit line. The selection indicator is on the far left and indicates the current cell address. The edit line contains the contents of the current cell and is used to display and edit data. Below the edit line is the SmartIcon palette. SmartIcons are buttons in the 1-2-3 window that let mouse users choose commonly used commands and macros. To use one of the SmartIcons, click it and then follow the instructions (if any are needed) in the title bar. At the very bottom of the spreadsheet window is the Status Bar. It displays information about the current selection, the current file, and the current status and mode of 1-2-3.

```
E3:   [W11] ^TOTALS                                          READY
```

	A	B	C	D	E	F
1						
2					QUARTERLY	
3		SEPTEMBER	OCTOBER	NOVEMBER	TOTALS	
4						
5	MONTHLY INCOME:	480.00	280.00	280.00	1040.00	
6						
7	RENT	75.00	75.00	75.00	225.00	
8	UTILITIES	30.00	30.00	30.00	90.00	
9	FOOD	60.00	60.00	60.00	180.00	
10	CLOTHING	20.00	20.00	20.00	60.00	
11	GASOLINE	15.00	15.00	35.00	65.00	
12	SUPPLIES	20.00	5.00	5.00	30.00	
13	BOOKS	125.00	10.00	10.00	145.00	
14	ENTERTAINMENT	20.00	20.00	10.00	50.00	
15	SAVINGS	20.00	20.00	20.00	60.00	
16	MISC.	7.00	15.00	15.00	37.00	
17						
18	TOTAL EXPENSES	392.00	270.00	280.00	942.00	
19						
20	REMAINING CASH	88.00	10.00	0.00	98.00	

Figure 5-1. Completed budget spreadsheet with cursor at Cell E3.

If you want to find the total of all expenses for October and display it under the OCTOBER column, you can put a function instead of a data item in Cell C18 (the location in the TOTAL EXPENSES line under the column heading OCTOBER). The formula =@SUM(C7..C16) will tell the spreadsheet program to sum the numbers in all cells from C7 to C16, specifying the column for OCTOBER and identifying the first and last rows of the area in which the entries to be added are stored. To sum all of the RENT expenses for the quarter, the instruction =@SUM(B7..D7) is placed in Cell E7.

The calculations done by the spreadsheet are dynamic: When new values are entered in any of the cells identified in the instruction, or when an old value is changed, the number displayed in the TOTAL EXPENSES line also changes. The change is immediate. A change in the value at Cell B16 (MISC for SEPTEMBER) will cause changes in five other cells: (1) the QUARTERLY TOTAL figure at E16, (2) the TOTAL EXPENSES figure at B18, (3) the REMAINING CASH figure at B20, (4) the TOTAL EXPENSES figure in the QUARTERLY TOTALS column (E18), and (5) the REMAINING CASH figure in the QUARTERLY TOTALS column (E20). All five will change automatically when the value at B16 is changed. Compare Figures 5-2 and 5-3 for an example of such a change.

B16: (F2) [W11] 7
15.00
VALUE

	A	B	C	D	E	F
1						
2					QUARTERLY	
3		SEPTEMBER	OCTOBER	NOVEMBER	TOTALS	
4						
5	MONTHLY INCOME:	480.00	280.00	280.00	1040.00	
6						
7	RENT	75.00	75.00	75.00	225.00	
8	UTILITIES	30.00	30.00	30.00	90.00	
9	FOOD	60.00	60.00	60.00	180.00	
10	CLOTHING	20.00	20.00	20.00	60.00	
11	GASOLINE	15.00	15.00	35.00	65.00	
12	SUPPLIES	20.00	5.00	5.00	30.00	
13	BOOKS	125.00	10.00	10.00	145.00	
14	ENTERTAINMENT	20.00	20.00	10.00	50.00	
15	SAVINGS	20.00	20.00	20.00	60.00	
16	MISC.	7.00	15.00	15.00	37.00	
17						
18	TOTAL EXPENSES	392.00	270.00	280.00	942.00	
19						
20	REMAINING CASH	88.00	10.00	0.00	98.00	

Figure 5-2. Changing the data in Cell B16.

	A	B	C	D	E	F
1						
2					QUARTERLY	
3		SEPTEMBER	OCTOBER	NOVEMBER	TOTALS	
4						
5	MONTHLY INCOME:	480.00	280.00	280.00	1040.00	
6						
7	RENT	75.00	75.00	75.00	225.00	
8	UTILITIES	30.00	30.00	30.00	90.00	
9	FOOD	60.00	60.00	60.00	180.00	
10	CLOTHING	20.00	20.00	20.00	60.00	
11	GASOLINE	15.00	15.00	35.00	65.00	
12	SUPPLIES	20.00	5.00	5.00	30.00	
13	BOOKS	125.00	10.00	10.00	145.00	
14	ENTERTAINMENT	20.00	20.00	10.00	50.00	
15	SAVINGS	20.00	20.00	20.00	60.00	
16	MISC.	15.00	15.00	15.00	45.00	
17						
18	TOTAL EXPENSES	400.00	270.00	280.00	950.00	
19						
20	REMAINING CASH	80.00	10.00	0.00	90.00	

Figure 5-3. Result of changing entry in Cell B16.

In addition to SUM, many other functions are recognized by the spreadsheet program. These allow you to perform functions such as finding an average, finding a standard deviation, or calculating the payment on a mortgage.

Spreadsheets are especially useful because of their dynamic nature. With the budget spreadsheet, you can see immediately the effect of any change in any item on the overall budget. You may also create and store numerous worksheet formats along with the data they contain. You can store the budget spreadsheet and then ask for a second copy of it to use in answering those "what if" questions: "What if the amount for entertainment increases by $50.00?" "What if the tuition increases by $100.00?" The spreadsheet answers such questions immediately.

Spreadsheet packages also allow you to sort the data into ascending or descending order based on the contents of some column on the sheet. In the budget spreadsheet you might wish to sort the area of the sheet that contains the expenses (lines 7 through 16) into order based on the figures in column E (the quarterly totals). When such a sort is done, the highest expense will be placed in the first line on the sheet, the second highest on the second line, and so on. In the budget sheet RENT would remain on line 7, but FOOD would move to line 8, BOOKS would move to line 9, and so on.

Some spreadsheet packages allow you to produce a graph of the data in the worksheet by simply entering a graph command and identifying the data to be used in the graph. The spreadsheet program asks you whether you want a line graph, bar graph, or pie graph, and what data on the sheet is to be graphed. The program then designs and displays the graph.

Many spreadsheet software packages are available with various options, but all perform the basic calculation operations we have examined.

STUDY QUESTIONS

1 How is a cell on a spreadsheet identified?
2 Is it possible to store both numeric and non-numeric data in a spreadsheet?
3 How can you have Lotus put the results of a mathematical calculation in a cell?
4 When the contents of a cell that is referenced in a mathematical calculation are changed, what happens to the result of that calculation?
5 Other than creating a worksheet, what options do spreadsheet packages offer?

INTRODUCTION TO LOTUS 1-2-3

The spreadsheet illustrated in the previous discussion is one of the most popular packages, Lotus 1-2-3. The following exercises will allow you to use some of the basic operations of Lotus.

Examine the general layout of the screen in Figure 5-4. The area set aside to hold data is clearly marked with a contrasting border that contains the column letters across the top and the line numbers down the left margin. The screen displays only the top left corner of the data area, which can contain up to hundreds of columns and thousands of rows.

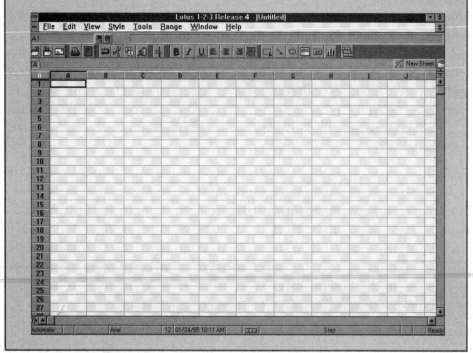

Figure 5-4. Lotus 1-2-3.

In Figure 5-3, the first command line says that the cursor is at Cell B16 and that the cell currently contains 15.00. Cell B16 is highlighted with the cursor.

Some versions of Lotus also use the last line of the screen to display information for the user. On these versions, the date and time appear on the left of the last line. On the right, a keyboard status message—such as CAPS to indicate when CapsLock is engaged or NUM to indicate when NumLock is engaged—displays.

As we communicate with Lotus, we often wish to indicate an area of the worksheet larger than a single cell. Suppose we wish to tell Lotus to sum all of the expenses listed under the month of October. These are located in the cells beginning with C7 and continuing through C16. These cells make up the **range** C7..C16. The cells containing the RENT expenses are at B7, C7, and D7. This range would be indicated by giving the address of the first and last cells: B7..D7. A range, then, is a square or rectangular area of cells on the worksheet. Occasionally you may wish to indicate all the cells in one column and half of the cells in another column as a range. This cannot be done because the cells do not form a rectangle. You must find another way to perform the action you wish.

Lotus is a menu-driven package; the menus display on the control panel of the DOS version. The number of menu options is so great that they cannot all display at once, so they are arranged in groups. The name of each group of menus is listed in the master menu. Because there are so many choices, this grouping of menus is repeated several times. Figure 5-5 shows the Lotus master menu. The cursor is positioned at the Worksheet selection on the master menu, and the options of the submenu group that can be reached through this selection appear on the second line. In Figure 5-6, the cursor is at master menu selection File, and that selection's submenu options are displayed. We will use these menus in selecting the functions we need.

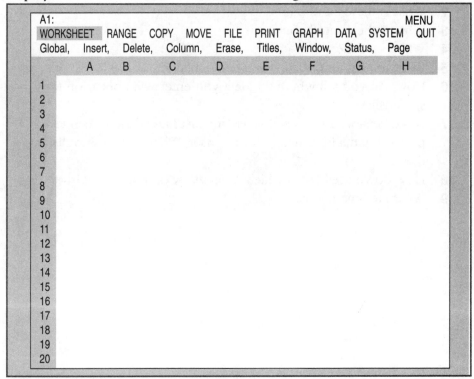

Figure 5-5. Lotus Master Menu: Worksheet option.

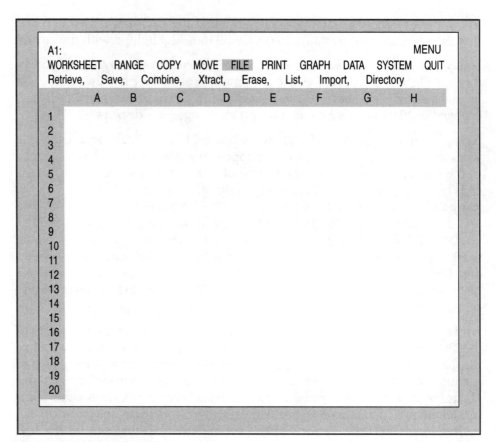

Figure 5-6. Lotus Master Menu: File option.

STUDY QUESTIONS

1 What are the control lines?
2 What is the control panel?
3 What is the control panel for?
4 What is a cell?
5 What four types of data can a cell contain?
6 How can you tell where the data you enter will appear on the spreadsheet?
7 Some versions of Lotus also use the last line of the screen to provide status information for the user. What information displays there?
8 How do you tell Lotus which of its many options you wish to use?
9 What are SmartIcons?

PURPOSES

1. To create a spreadsheet
2. To store the spreadsheet on disk so that it can be used in the future

REQUIRED EQUIPMENT

1. Access to Lotus
2. Formatted data disk

PREPARATION

The Physical Education Department has formed a Run for Your Life Club to promote student and faculty health. Members want to keep a record of the miles they have run during the week. Create the spreadsheet illustrated below to hold the data.

NAME	DAY ONE	DAY TWO	DAY THREE	DAY FOUR	DAY FIVE
SUSAN	3	3	2	2	1
MAXWELL	4	5	4	5	3
JAMES	2	4	2	3	2
DON	4	5	4	5	3
RICHARD	5	7	6	6	5
JONES	10	10	10	9	6
PATRICK	7	8	7	5	1

In creating a spreadsheet, begin by deciding what results you want. In this, as in most spreadsheets, two types of entries are needed: (1) labels, such as column headings and the names of the members, and (2) data, such as the miles run. Visualize the appearance of the completed spreadsheet by inserting column letters and line numbers. After we have a clear picture of the sheet we plan to create, we will (1) create labels, (2) enter the data into the spreadsheet, and (3) save the sheet on disk so that it can be retrieved for later use. When you store the sheet, Lotus will ask for a name for it; choose the name RUN1.

As you begin to work with any software package, one of the first things to learn is how to move around within it. For example, when using menus you may make the wrong menu selection and want to return to the previous menu to choose another, or perhaps to escape from all the menus back to the worksheet. You can return to the previous menu by pressing the ESC key. When you have arrived at the Main Menu, pressing again will take you back to the worksheet.

To move from the worksheet to the main menu, press the / key. Notice that this is the standard slash character, not the backslash. The two are not interchangeable.

Lotus also allows you to move from Lotus into DOS and return without rebooting the Lotus package. To go to DOS, take the SYSTEM option from the main menu. When you have finished with DOS, key in the word EXIT and you will return to Lotus. WARNING, do not attempt to reboot by keying in a boot command such as LOTUS or 123 in this situation. This will result in a message that you do not have enough memory to load Lotus—because Lotus is already in memory and you probably do not have enough memory to hold two copies! Be sure to use the EXIT command to avoid this complication.

PROCEDURE

1. Prepare the package to run, or boot the package.
   The exact procedure for booting the Lotus package will depend on your system configuration and the way Lotus has been installed. Consult your instructor or the system documentation for the proper procedure.
2. In the Windows version, you will open Lotus by double clicking on the Lotus Application group icon shown in the Program Manager Screen. When the Lotus Application window appears, click on the 1 2 3 for Windows icon.
3. A copyright screen will display briefly while instructions are being read from the disk. Then the display will disappear, and the worksheet window will appear. An hourglass will appear for a moment until the system is ready to operate.
   Note: Before entering a software package, be sure to learn how to get out of it! Click on FILE and EXIT to terminate the Lotus program.
4. Create the spreadsheet.
   A. Place column heading labels on the worksheet.
      We want the headings for the name column and the headings for the daily columns to appear across the top of the worksheet. We want the names of the club members to appear down the left side. As you key the data, you will notice that the message LABEL appears on the right of Control Line 1.
      (1) The cursor is positioned at A1. Press the CapsLock key for upper shift and key in the word NAME. The word will appear on the second control line but not on the worksheet. If you make keying errors, simply put the cursor back at the first letter and retype. When the entry is correct, press cursor return. NAME will appear at A1.

(2) Move the cursor to B1 and enter the word DAY. This time, do not press cursor return; press the right arrow instead. This will (1) record DAY at B1 and (2) move the cursor to C1.

(3) Complete the first line of headings by entering ONE at Cell B2, TWO at Cell C2, and so on. You may use either the Enter key or the right arrow to record an item and move the cursor.

B. Enter the data.

(1) Enter the names in Cells A4 through A10.

Use the small arrows to position the cursor at the cells in which you want the labels you enter to appear and follow the same procedure as above.

(2) Enter the miles run.

Position the cursor at B4 and enter the miles run by Susan during Day One: 3. Enter 4 for Maxwell at B5, and so on until the sheet is complete.

Note: The number will not align under the heading previously entered. Do not be confused about this. We will correct it in Lotus Job 2.

5. Print a copy of the spreadsheet.

A. Move the mouse arrow to the SmartIcon for PRINT.

B. Click on the left mouse button while the mouse arrow is on PRINT icon.

C. When the screen displays the Print dialog box, there are a number of options. The PRINT options are as follows;

• Current worksheet
• All worksheets
• Selected range

D. Choose CURRENT WORKSHEET by clicking on the round circle to the left of the option. The circle will then darken, showing your selection of this option.

E. Be sure that your printer is online and the paper is correctly positioned in your printer.

F. Click on OK to send the PRINT command to the printer.

6. Save the spreadsheet on disk.

A. Click on the SmartIcon for saving a document (arrow pointing into a folder).

B. When the Save dialog box appears type in the name of your file, RUN1, in the space provided below File Name.

C. Click on OK to accept this transaction.

7. Terminate the session.

A. Click on FILE on the Menu Bar at the top of the screen. Select EXIT.

B. Remove your disk.

C. Turn the computer off.

LOTUS JOB 2:
TAILORING THE SPREADSHEET

PURPOSES

1. To provide experience in opening a spreadsheet from disk
2. To provide experience in aligning labels
3. To provide experience in summing numeric data
4. To provide experience in repeating a character across a cell

REQUIRED EQUIPMENT

1. Lotus system disk
2. Data disk containing the RUN1 worksheet

PREPARATION

The spreadsheet RUN1 created in Lotus Job 1 above allows us to store data, but the column headings are not aligned very well. When a label is entered, Lotus assumes that it should be aligned with the left margin of the cell, or **left justified**. It assumes that values, functions, and formulas should be **right justified**. We can, however, change the alignment of labels if we wish to do so. Never change alignment of values, formulas or functions. To Lotus, any cell contents that are left aligned or centered are labels. Lotus allows us to specify whether heading labels are to be aligned with the left margin of the cell, aligned with the right margin of the cell, or centered in the cell by entering a control character at the beginning of the heading. The cursor is positioned at A1 when the worksheet is retrieved, and the control panel displays the contents of that cell as 'NAME. The ' specifies alignment with the left margin. The alignment characters are as follows:

*   ' (align with left margin)
*   " (align with right margin)
*   ^ (center)

Caution: Align ONLY labels.

In this exercise, we will improve the alignment. We will also add some arithmetic commands to provide more information. For example, the Physical Education Department wants a total of miles run by all participants for each day and week so that it can estimate how much the track is being used each day. Individual runners also want a total for each week of the contest. With the proper instructions, Lotus will calculate these totals for us. Examine the spreadsheet below. Notice that the total miles during Day One will be the sum of the values stored in Cells B4, B5, B6, B7, B8, B9, and B10 (or the range B4.1.B10). The total for Day Two will be the sum of the values in C4, C5, C6, C7, C8, C9, and C10 (or the range C4.1.C10), and the totals of other days will follow the same pattern.

Looking at the total for Susan in Cell G4, you see that it is the sum of the weekly cells that hold Susan's data—B4, C4, D4, E4, and F4 (range B4.|.F4), whereas the total for Maxwell is found by adding the same cells on Line 5. Remember these patterns as we work with the spreadsheet.

Lotus has several powerful commands called functions to perform tasks that are frequently required, such as summing the contents of a number of cells or finding the average of the data the cells contain. To calculate the sum of a range of cells, such as the total for Susan in B4.|.F4, we can use the SUM function, which is written =@SUM(B4.|.F4). We simply place it on the worksheet at the location where we want the sum to display. To average the entries for Susann for all weeks, the AVERAGE function would be used: =@AVG(B4.|.F4). Other functions are also available; consult your Lotus reference manual for others.

	A	B	C	D	E	F	G	H
		DAY	DAY	DAY	DAY	DAY	INDIV	INDIV
1	NAME	ONE	TWO	THREE	FOUR	FIVE	TOTAL	AVERAGE
2								
3								
4	SUSAN	3	3	2	2	1	11	2.2
5	MAXWELL	4	5	4	5	3	21	4.2
6	JAMES	2	4	2	3	2	13	2.6
7	DON	4	5	4	5	3	21	4.2
8	RICHARD	5	7	6	6	5	29	5.8
9	JONES	10	10	10	9	6	45	9.0
10	PATRICK	7	8	7	5	1	28	5.6
11								
12	WEEKLY	35	42	35	35	21		
13	TOTAL							
14								

In this exercise, we want to calculate weekly totals for all runners, individual totals for each runner, and individual averages for each runner. Before you continue this exercise, examine Cells G4 through G10 and decide which cells should be summed to give the total for each. Then examine H4 through H10 and decide which cells should be averaged for each. Do the same for Cells B12 through F12. Write out the entries you plan to put in each of these cells before you continue; check them against the entries specified for the cells as you follow the instructions below.

PROCEDURE

1. Insert any necessary disk and boot the system.
2. Open the worksheet.
    A. When the empty worksheet form appears, use the mouse to open the worksheet by clicking on FILE from the Menu Bar.

3. Click on OPEN on the File menu.
4. When the Open dialog box is displayed, double click on the file RUN1.WKS.
5. Align the heading labels.

    The NAME label is aligned to the left, but the DAY labels and the labels indicating day numbers are far offset. Align them with the left margin.

    A. Place the mouse pointer at the location of the label. Click and drag the mouse pointer to select the entire column.

    B. Move the mouse pointer to the SmartIcon that aligns text on the right. Click on the RIGHT ALIGN SmartIcon.

6. Create new labels.

    Add labels to head Columns G and H, aligning them with the right margin. Add labels in Positions A12 and A13, aligning them with the left margin. Note that we cannot spell out the word INDIVIDUAL for the headings in Columns G and H because it is too long to fit in the space allowed. We will learn to enlarge the size of cells in Lotus Job 3.

7. Provide for the runners' weekly totals.

    In Cell G4, we want the sum for Susan. Enter =@SUM(B4..F4). Put =@SUM(B5..F5) in G5 to calculate and display the sum for Maxwell and so on until sums display for all runners.

8. Provide for the totals for all runners for each week.

    In Cell B12, enter =@SUM(B4..B10); in C12, enter =@SUM(C4..C10). Continue this process until all weekly totals display.

9. Provide for weekly averages for each runner.

    Enter =@AVG(B4..F4) in Cell H4, =@AVG(B5..F5) in H5, and so on.

10. Examine the interactive nature of the worksheet.

    Change the entry in B4 from 3 to 30 and note the resulting changes in G4, H4, and B12. Restore it to 3 and note changes again.

11. Create lines to make the sheet more readable.

    Place a double line below the labels in rows 1 and 2.

    A. Place the mouse pointer in A3 and select the remaining cells in Row 3 and Row 4.

    B. Once these cells are selected, position the mouse pointer on the word STYLE on the Menu Bar. Click on STYLE.

    C. At the Style Menu, select LINES & COLOR.

    The cell will be filled with equal signs, forming a double line.

    D. At the Lines & Color dialog box, go to the Borders section and select BOTTOM; then go to the Line Style box and select Double Line by clicking and holding the arrow on Line Style until the DOUBLE LINE selection appears.

    E. Click on OK.

    Place a single line below the last row of data—row 10.

F. Place the mouse pointer in All and select the remainder cells in Row 11.

G. Follow the directions above except click on SINGLE LINE in the Line Style box.

12. Print a copy of the spreadsheet.

A. Move the mouse arrow to the SmartIcon for PRINT.

B. Click on the left mouse button while the mouse arrow is on the PRINT icon.

C. When the screen displays the Print dialog box, there are a number of options. The Print options are as follows:
   - Current worksheet
   - All worksheets
   - Selected range

D. Choose CURRENT WORKSHEET by clicking on the round circle to the left of the option. The circle will then darken, showing your selection of this option.

E. Be sure that your printer is online and the paper is correctly positioned in your printer.

F. Click on OK to send the print command to the printer.

13. Save the spreadsheet on disk.

A. Click on the SmartIcon for saving a document (arrow pointing into a folder).

B. When the Save dialog box appears, type in the name of your file, RUN1, in the space provided below File Name.

C. Click on OK to accept this transaction.

14. Terminate the session.

A. Click on FILE on the Menu Bar at the top of the screen. Select EXIT.

B. Remove your disk.

C. Turn the computer off.

LOTUS JOB 3:

CREATING A NEW SPREADSHEET

PURPOSES

1. To introduce procedures for adjusting column size
2. To introduce the use of mathematical statements

REQUIRED EQUIPMENT

1. Lotus system disk
2. Data disk

PREPARATION

A retail store dealing in sportswear wants a record of the stock it has purchased, including (1) the item number, (2) the description of the item, (3) the price paid to the wholesaler for the item, (4) the amount by which it is to be marked up for retail, (5) the resulting retail price, (6) the projected profit for each item, and (7) the projected profit for the total stock in each category. A proposed worksheet for the category SWEATERS is shown below.

```
^^^^^^^^^A^^^^^^^^^B^^^^^^^^^^^^^C^^^^^^D^^^^^^E^^^^^^^F^^^^^^^G
^1^^^PRICING^REPORT
^2
^3^^^^^^^^^CATEGORY:^^SWEATERS
^4
^5^^^^^ITEM^^^^DESCRIPTION^^^^^^^^^NO^^^ITEM^^MARKUP^^RETAIL^^^ITEM
^6^^^^^^NO^^^^^^^^^^^^^^^^^^^^^^^^BOUGHT^PRICE^AMOUNT^^PRICE^^^PROFIT
^7
^8^^^^^101^CABLE^KNIT^^^^^^^^^^^20^^^15.00^^4.50^^^19.50^^^^90.00
^9^^^^^112^GOLFER^^^^^^^^^^^^^^^^25^^^12.50^^3.75^^^16.25^^^^93.75
^10^^^^116^TURTLENECK^^^^^^^^^^^25^^^14.50^^5.07^^^19.57^^^126.75
^11^^^^125^V^NECK^^^^^^^^^^^^^^^^25^^^13.00^^3.25^^^16.25^^^^81.25
^12^^^^126^CREW^NECK^^^^^^^^^^^^25^^^15.00^^2.25^^^17.25^^^^56.25
^13^^^^128^MOCK^TURTLENECK^^^^^^25^^^15.00^^3.00^^^18.00^^^^75.00
^14^^^^131^CARDIGAN^^BUTTON^^^^25^^^20.00^^7.00^^^27.00^^^175.00
^15^^^^133^CARDIGAN^-^ZIP^^^^^^^30^^^20.00^^7.00^^^27.00^^^210.00
^16
^17
^18^^^^^^^^PROJECTED^PROFIT:^^^^^^^^$908.00
```

For this project, some columns (for the DESCRIPTION) must be wider than the standard 9-position width that Lotus automatically assigns. Others (the ITEM NUMBER, NUMBER BOUGHT, etc.) can be shorter. We will adjust the column sizes with the SetWidth option from the menu.

The data to be input for each item consists of the item number, the description, the number purchased, the wholesale price paid, and the amount by which the item is to be marked up. Other values will be calculated and inserted.

Some numbers contain decimals. One number, the projected profit, contains decimals and begins with a dollar sign. We will include decimals, commas, and dollar signs, using the Format option from the menu.

After the physical size of the worksheet has been adjusted and the format of the data to be displayed in each cell has been specified, we will arrange for Lotus to calculate the sum of retail prices and the sum of wholesale prices. This can be done with the =@SUM command. However, we cannot calculate the markup amount and the retail price with Lotus functions. To calculate markup amount and retail price, we must use arithmetic statements.

FORMULAS IN LOTUS. Arithmetic statements in Lotus are very similar to ordinary math. Compare the following examples of how operations are stated in standard mathematical notation and in Lotus. The data names are, of course, the cell address of the items to be used.

Operation	Standard Math	Lotus
Addition	A1 + B1	+ A1 + B1
Subtraction	A1 - B1	+ A1 - B1
Multiplication	A1 x B1	+ A1 * B1
Division	A1 / B1	+ A1 / B1
Exponentiation	$A1^3$	+ A1^3

When we want the result of a mathematical operation to appear in a cell, we simply put the formula that will calculate it into that cell. For example, we want the RETAIL PRICE for the first item (CABLE KNIT sweaters) to appear in F8. This price is calculated by adding the MARKUP AMOUNT in E8 to the ITEM PRICE in D8, so we will put the formula +D8+E8 at Cell F8. The PROJECTED PROFIT at G8 is calculated by multiplying the NO BOUGHT at C8 by the MARKUP AMOUNT at E8, so we will put the formula +C8*E8 at Cell G8. We will repeat these formulas in the similar location for each item, changing the cell locations they include to those on the line on which they appear. The formulas have a plus sign before the first cell address to indicate that the following characters are a formula rather than a label.

Be cautious when you use formulas: Lotus has a certain order in which it performs the operations within a formula. Lotus performs exponentiation first, multiplication and division second, and addition and subtraction third. For example, consider the following formula:

    +A3+A4+A5+A6/A7

This formula will first divide the contents of Cell A6 by the contents of Cell A7 and then add the contents of Cells A3, A4, and A5 to the result of that division. If this is not what is needed—perhaps you want to add the first four cells and then divide the sum by the contents of A7—you can use parentheses to tell Lotus which operation or operations to perform first. In this case, use the following formula:

    (+A3+A4+A5+A6)/A7

You can use several sets of parentheses if needed, and you can put parentheses within parentheses if the formula requires them.

PROCEDURE

1. Insert any necessary disk and boot Lotus.
2. Build the worksheet.
   A. Enter the labels.
      When the empty worksheet form appears, enter the labels.
      (1) Enter the Report Labels: PRICING REPORT at A1, CATEGORY: SWEATERS at B3, and PROJECTED PROFIT at B18.
      (2) Enter the column labels in Columns A through G, Lines 5 and 6. Center these by using the ∧ as the first character.
   B. Adjust the column sizes.
      In analyzing the data, we have decided that the following sizes will be appropriate for the columns in the areas that hold the data relating to the individual items on the worksheet:

Range	Cell Size
A8-A15	6
B8-B15	18
C8-C15	7
D8-D15	8
E8-E15	7
F8-F15	8
G8-G15	9

      To change the width of the columns for this spreadsheet, follow these steps:
      (1) Place the cursor at A8.
      (2) Select STYLE from the Menu Bar.
      (3) Select Column Width from the Style Menu.
      (4) From the COLUMN WIDTH dialog box change the size to 6.
      (5) Click on OK to make this change.
      (6) Place the mouse pointer at B8 and repeat Steps (1) through (5), selecting 18 when asked for the column width.
      (7) Continue adjusting column sizes by repeating Steps (1) through (5), until C, D, E, F, and G have been adjusted to the sizes chosen earlier.
      Caution: Remember to place the cursor in the column to be adjusted as the first step in the procedure.
3. Enter the first line of data only.
   Key in the data for the first entry, including the decimals in the items that contain them:

   101∧∧∧∧∧∧CABLE∧KNIT∧∧∧∧∧20∧∧∧∧∧∧15.00∧∧∧∧∧4.50

   Normally, you would not enter data until the worksheet is completely set up. We will enter data now, however, in order to observe how formatting cells and the insertion of equations change the appearance of the worksheet.

Do not enter RETAIL PRICE and PROJECTED PROFIT figures; these will be calculated. Next you will format columns and insert formulas. As you do, observe how the displayed data changes.

4. Format the columns.

Notice how the numbers entered as ITEM PRICE and as MARKUP AMOUNT change when the cells that contain them are formatted. Begin by formatting Column D for fixed decimals with two decimal positions.

A. Place the mouse pointer in D8 and select the remaining cells between D8 and D15.

B. Once these cells are selected, position the mouse pointer on the word STYLE on the Menu Bar. Click on STYLE.

C. At the Style Menu, click on NUMBER FORMATTING.

D. At the Number Formatting dialog box, go to the Formatting section and select FIXED. Check that the decimal places defaulted to 2.

E. Position the mouse pointer and click on OK.

F. Format Columns E through G following the steps above.

5. Format the cells for the PROJECTED PROFIT.

A. Place the mouse pointer in D18.

B. Position the mouse pointer on the word STYLE on the Menu Bar. Click on STYLE.

C. At the Style Menu, click on NUMBER FORMATTING.

D. At the Number Formatting dialog box, go to the Formatting section and select FIXED. Check that the decimal places defaulted to 2.

E. Position the mouse pointer and click on OK.

6. Enter the function for TOTAL PROJECTED PROFIT.

A. Place the mouse pointer at D18 and enter the function =@SUM(G8..G15) to calculate the TOTAL PROJECTED PROFIT.

B. Enter the formulas to calculate the RETAIL PRICE.

   (1) At F8, enter the formula for the RETAIL PRICE for Line 8: +D8+E8. Notice that the price for the item is immediately calculated and displayed.

   (2) Copy the formula to other cells in Column F.
   You can key in the formula for each cell individually, adjusting the row numbers appropriately, but Lotus will do this for you with the Copy option.

      a. Place the mouse pointer in F8.

      b. Select the Copy function on the SmartIcon Bar.

      c. Click and drag through the cells where the formula is to appear and select these cells.

      d. Click on the Paste function on the SmartIcon Bar.

      e. Observe that the prices are immediately calculated.

7. Enter the formulas for the ITEM PROFITS.

A. In G8, enter the formula for Row 8: +C8*E8

   (1) Copy the formula to other cells in Column G following the steps outlined in 6B(2) and substituting Column G for Column F. Observe that the values are calculated immediately when the formulas are entered. Most are zero, but they will change when you enter data into the worksheet.

8. Enter the data.

A. For each item, enter amounts for the following into the worksheet:

   (1) ITEM NO

   (2) DESCRIPTION

	(3)	NO BOUGHT
	(4)	ITEM PRICE
	(5)	MARKUP AMOUNT

Notice that in entering data for only 8 sweaters, you are relieved of entering 17 figures by the calculations performed by the functions and formulas you placed on the worksheet. Imagine the saving if you were entering data for 800 sweaters!

9. Create lines to make the sheet more readable.

   Place a double line below the labels in rows 5 and 6.

   A. Place the mouse pointer in A7 and select the remainder cells in Row 5 and Row 6.

   B. Once these cells are selected, position the mouse pointer on the word Style on the Menu Bar. Click on STYLE.

   C. At the Style Menu, click on LINES & COLOR.

   D. At the Lines & Color dialog box, go to the Borders section and select Bottom; then go to the Line Style area and select DOUBLE LINE by clicking and holding the arrow on Line Style until the DOUBLE LINE selection appears.

   E. Position the mouse pointer and click on OK

10. Place a single line below the last row of data—Row 15.

    A. Place the mouse pointer in A16 and select the remaining cells in Row 16.

    B. Follow the directions above except click on SINGLE LINE in the Line Style box.

11. Print a copy of the spreadsheet.

    A. Move the mouse arrow to the SmartIcon for PRINT.

    B. Click on the left mouse button while the mouse arrow is on the PRINT icon.

    C. When the screen displays the Print dialog box, there are a number of options. The Print options are as follows:
    - Current worksheet
    - All worksheets
    - Selected range

    D. Choose CURRENT WORKSHEET by clicking on the round circle to the left of the option. The circle will then darken, showing your selection of this option.

    E. Be sure that your printer is online and the paper is correctly positioned in your printer.

    F. Click on OK to send the print command to the printer.

12. Save the spreadsheet on disk.

    A. Click on the SmartIcon for saving a document (arrow pointing into a folder).

    B. When the Save dialog box appears, type in the name of your file, PROFIT, in the space provided below File Name.

    C. Click on OK to accept this transaction.

13. Terminate the session.

    A. Click on FILE on the Menu Bar at the top of the screen. Select EXIT.

    B. Remove your disk.

    C. Turn the computer off.

LOTUS JOB 4:
SORTING THE DATA AREA

PURPOSE

1. To introduce the sort

REQUIRED EQUIPMENT

1. Lotus system disk
2. Data disk containing the PROFIT worksheet

PREPARATION

To determine which of the sales items on the worksheet PROFIT is the most profitable, the worksheet is to be sorted into order based on the figure in the ITEM PROFIT column. It is not difficult to see the relative profit figures on a small sheet such as the one we have created, but it would be much more difficult on a sheet with fifty lines or so.

In order to sort, Lotus must have three pieces of information:

1. What area of the sheet is to be sorted?
   Of course, headings and marking lines are not sorted. They are to remain where they have been placed in order to identify the various rows and columns on the sheet and to increase readability. The rows containing the data for the sweaters must be sorted. When the profit figure for the CABLE KNIT sweaters, 90.00, moves, we wish the entire line to move with it so that the ITEM NO, DESCRIPTION, NO BOUGHT, MARKUP AMOUNT, and RETAIL PRICE for that item remain associated with its ITEM PROFIT. It is necessary then to include the cells that contain these values along with the cells that contain the ITEM PROFIT in the sort area. The range A8 through G15 contains all the data that we wish to move when the sort is done. This is the **sort range**.
2. What column contains the data on which the sorting is to be based?
   In this case, column G contains the data on which we wish to base the sort.
3. Is the data to be sorted in ascending order (1, 2, 3 or A, B, C) or descending order (3, 2, 1 or C, B, A)?
   To bring the largest figure to the top, sort in descending order.

PROCEDURE

1. Open the worksheet PROFIT.
2. Access the Sort Menu.
   A. Select the cells to be sorted by clicking and dragging A8 through G15.
   B. Select RANGE from the Menu Bar.

C. Select SORT from the Range Menu.

D. At the Sort dialog box, type in the cell that the sort will be based on, which in this case is G8.

E. Click on the descending radio button to make the order of the sort descending.

F. Click on OK.

3. Print a copy of the spreadsheet.

A. Move the mouse arrow to the SmartIcon for PRINT.

B. Click on the left mouse button while the mouse arrow is on the PRINT icon.

C. When the screen displays the Print dialog box, there are a number of options. The Print options are as follows:
- Current worksheet
- All worksheets
- Selected range

D. Choose CURRENT WORKSHEET by clicking on the round circle to the left of the option. The circle will then darken, showing your selection of this option.

E. Be sure that your printer is online and the paper is correctly positioned in your printer.

F. Click on OK to send the print command to the printer.

4. Experiment with other sorts.

A. Sort on MARKUP AMOUNT.

(1) Select the cells to be sorted by clicking and dragging A8 through G15.

(2) Select RANGE from the Menu Bar.

(3) Select SORT from the Range Menu.

(4) At the Sort dialog box, type in the cell that the sort will be based on, which in this case is E8.

(5) Declare that the order of the sort is to be ascending by clicking on the ascending radio button.

(6) Click on OK.

B. Sort on NO BOUGHT.

(1) Select the cells to be sorted by clicking and dragging A8 through G15.

(2) Select Range from the Menu Bar.

(3) Select Sort from the Range Menu.

(4) At the Sort dialog box, type in the cell that the sort will be based on, which in this case is C8.

(5) When asked for ascending or descending order, pick either one by clicking on the ascending or descending radio button.

(6) Click on OK.

5. Terminate the session.

A. Click on FILE on the Menu Bar at the top of the screen. Select EXIT.

B. Remove your disk.

C. Turn the computer off.

PURPOSE

1.   To introduce the graphing capability of Lotus

REQUIRED EQUIPMENT

1.   Lotus system disk
2.   Data disk containing the PROFIT worksheet

PREPARATION

In many circumstances, the meaning of numeric data is understood more easily when it is presented as a picture, or a graph. Lotus allows us to draw several types of these pictorial representations, or graphs. For example, we can see from the PROFIT worksheet that the type of sweater described as CARDIGAN-ZIP had $210.00 in profit, the CARDIGAN-BUTTON had $175.00, and so on, but suppose you wish to know what amount of the total profit is represented by each of the different styles. A pie chart graph will present a clear illustration of the share of each different style.

In order to draw a graph, Lotus must have two pieces of information:

1.   What area of the sheet contains the values that are to be the basis for the graph?
     Graphs are the pictorial representation of numerical data, so we can graph only values, functions or formulas—never labels. For this exercise the data that is to be graphed is the column containing the ITEM PROFIT. This is in the range G8..G15.
2.   What type of graph is to be drawn?
     The graphs that can be drawn with Lotus include the Pie Chart, Line, Bar, Stacked Bar, and XY. We will draw a Pie Chart.
     This information will enable Lotus to draw the graph, allocating larger or smaller pieces of the pie based on the figures in range G8..G15, but it is also desirable to label the pieces of the pie with the descriptions of the sweaters that made the profits in range G8..G15. Notice that these descriptions are in the range B8.|.B15.

PROCEDURE

1.   Open the worksheet PROFIT.
2.   Select the range for the graph: Position the mouse pointer on cell G8 and click and drag through cell G15.
3.   Select the TOOLS option on the Menu Bar.
4.   Select CHART on the Tools Menu.
5.   Click and drag where you want to display the chart on your screen.
6.   Click on the Chart Title box and type Items Profit.

7. Change the chart to a Pie Chart by positioning the mouse pointer on the SmartIcon Bar and clicking on the PIE CHART icon.

8. Print the chart by clicking on the chart on your worksheet.

9. Once the chart is selected, click on the PRINT icon on the SmartIcon Bar.

10. When the Print dialog box appears, make sure that the CHART option is selected and click on OK to print the chart.

11. Terminate the session. There is no need to save the worksheet because it is already on the disk.
   A. Click on FILE on the Menu Bar at the top of the screen. Select EXIT.
   B. Remove your disk.
   C. Turn the computer off.

OPTIONAL LOTUS JOBS

If you wish to have more experience in Lotus, you can set up spreadsheets for the Jobs in Chapter 4 of the text. Jobs 1, 2, 3, 4, 14, 15, 16, 17, and 18 are best for Lotus applications. Below are notes relating to various Jobs. Ask your instructor whether you should enter an entire Job or only part of a Job.

In Job 16, add another column to contain the Gross Pay for each employee. In this column, put a formula to calculate the Gross Pay by adding the Regular Pay and the Overtime Pay to relieve the operator of entering that figure.

In Job 17, add another column to hold the Total Price. In the column, put a formula to calculate the Total Price (Qty times Price). Job 17 contains totals at the end of each sheet. You can insert the Lotus function =@SUM to calculate these, but you must create a spreadsheet for each page if you wish to do so.

In Job 18, include all the data relating to one person in one line.

Chapter 6

DATABASE MANAGEMENT SOFTWARE FOR MICROCOMPUTERS

Among the most powerful software packages available for microcomputers are the database management systems. These sophisticated programs allow a nontechnical user to create large systems of integrated data, to manipulate this data, and to extract information from it—all with simple, English-like commands.

Databases can be thought of as electronic index cards. Let us examine a system of cardboard index cards used by a salesperson who wants to keep information on clients in a form that is easily accessible. He or she writes the information for each client on one card. This might include customer number; name; an address broken down into city, state, and ZIP Code; a phone number with an area code; the date of the customer's last purchase; the specific goods the customer usually orders; and the dollar amount of goods he or she purchased in the last three months.

When the salesperson is going to visit a particular city, the file can be sorted so that all the cards for that city are together and can be examined easily. The salesperson may pull out all the cards for that one city to form a small file easily carried along. In the city, he or she may want the cards sorted by ZIP Code so that sales calls can be planned to visit people located closely together rather than zig-zagging across the city.

At other times, the salesperson wants to telephone the customers who have not purchased anything recently and wants to sort the file into order by the amount of purchase so that people or businesses with low figures in this field appear first in the file.

Perhaps our salesperson has another file in which the cards contain information about the items in the company inventory. On a sales trip to a particular region, he or she may wish to pull out the cards for items in the inventory that are often purchased by the customers in this region and collate them with the records pulled from the customer file, placing the record for an item with the record for the customer who often purchases it, thus merging selected records from two files to create a new file.

Database software packages replace the cardboard cards with electronic media. They can sort the cards at electronic speeds, select cards with low amounts of purchase and create a new file for them, select cards from different files and merge them to create a new file, or sort records into ascending or descending order based on the contents of any field in the record.

One of the most useful capabilities of database packages is their ability to search the file for records that contain certain information. For example, you can ask a database to show you the contents of all records in which the last name of the customer is Johnson and the records of all people named Johnson will appear on the screen of the computer or on a printed report, whichever you specify.

Databases also provide assistance when you wish to set up a new file, enter new records into a file, change the contents of records already in the file, produce printed or displayed reports, and so on.

The English-like words used to give instructions to a database package make up its command language and query language. Commands differ from package to package, but they are all simple English words that are easily related to the function they perform. For example, one package recognizes the word CREATE as the command to set up a new database or file. Another package recognizes DEFINE as commanding the same function.

Some packages use the item- (or field-) record-file terminology of file systems. Others picture the data as a series of lines on a form such as this:

Andrews, John (416) 624-1863
Bishop, Susan (205) 854-1200
Bailes, Dick   (416) 736-3278

These database packages refer to the first group of data relating to John Andrews (the data we would call his record) as a line. The individual items (such as name, area code, and phone number) are called columns. In this terminology, the area code for Susan Bishop is in Line 2 at Column 2.

A primary difference between files and databases is that in files the collections of related facts (records) have the same format and contain the same types of items in the same positions. A database, however, may contain many files, and the records in one file may have entirely different formats and contain different data from those in another file. The records in a file system are related in only one way and cannot be combined to reflect other relationships. But by using a database, we can merge files and put records together in many combinations to represent many relationships, as we combined records from the Customer File with records from the Inventory File to form a new file representing the relationship of the customer to the items he or she purchases.

Figure 6-1 shows the commands entered by a user to create a database. The screen depicted here is the Control Center and is the beginning screen of dBase IV. Note the menu selections that appear at the top of the screen. These are similar to the commands used in other database programs.

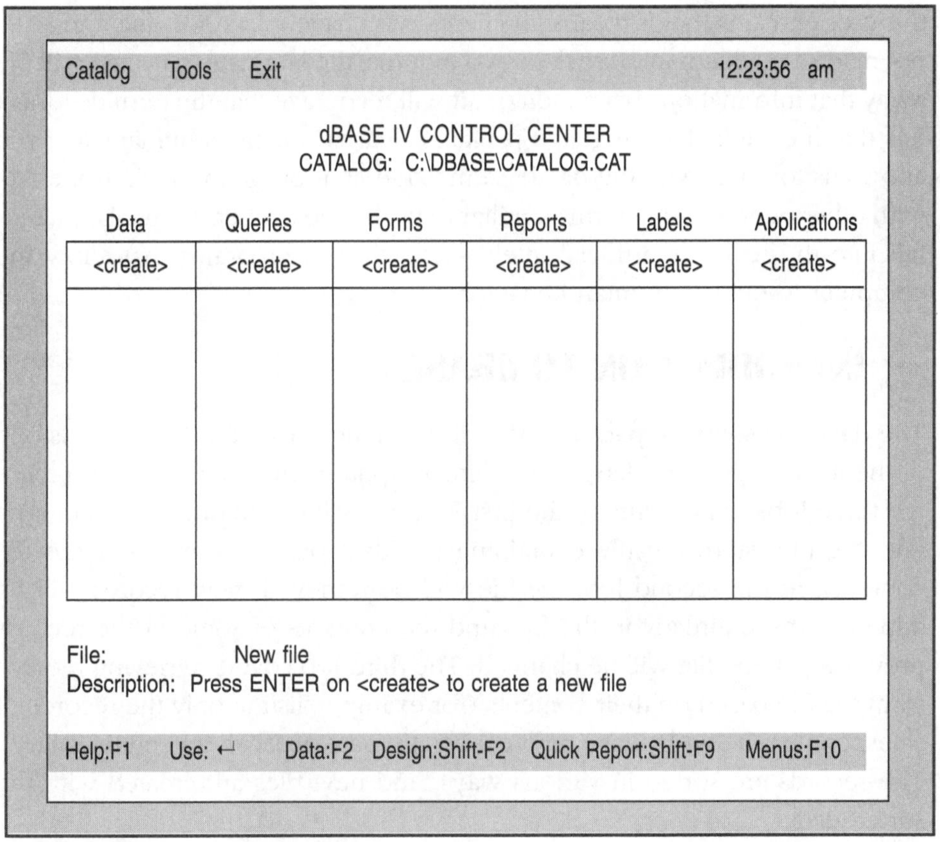

dBASE IV CONTROL CENTER
CATALOG: C:\DBASE\CATALOG.CAT

Data	Queries	Forms	Reports	Labels	Applications
<create>	<create>	<create>	<create>	<create>	<create>

File: New file
Description: Press ENTER on <create> to create a new file

Help:F1   Use: ↵   Data:F2   Design:Shift-F2   Quick Report:Shift-F9   Menus:F10

Figure 6-1. dBase IV Control Center.

After data is loaded into a program, the database package allows the user to manipulate it in many ways. All data from a file can be displayed with the F2 command or by clicking on DATA at the bottom of the Control Center screen. Data can be selected for display based on some characteristic or series of characteristics: QUERIES ZIP=35215 will display only records that contain a ZIP Code of 35215. Records can be sorted into a different order using the SORT command. SORT ON CUSTNAME TO TEMP1 will sort the records into alphabetical order by the customer name and store the sorted records in a file named TEMP1.

It is also possible to join files together so that information can be extracted from both at the same time. The commands to display data extracted from any or all files within the database can be issued. For example, we can retrieve the names of all clients who live in the area of ZIP Code 35215, have a zero balance due and a superior credit rating, and have not had a charge to their accounts in the last six months.

Comprehensive database packages also provide options such as passwords for security and editing capabilities during data entry. A few also have conversational languages. Conversational languages allow the user to enter queries such as SHOW ME ALL THE DEADBEATS. Because deadbeat is not a common term, the conversational language will ask for a definition. When the user explains that it means all clients who have a balance due and have not made a payment in more than two months, the language package will file away that information. From then on, it will recognize that the term deadbeat has that meaning. The language package "learns" much as humans learn. It allows us to "talk" with the database management program much as we talk with other people, using terms familiar to both. The conversational languages fall into the realm of artificial intelligence, that is, programs that allow the computer to emulate human behavior.

INTRODUCTION TO dBASE

The database software package we will examine is called dBase IV. It is one of the most popular packages for microcomputers. In this introduction there are three Jobs to be done. In the first Job, we will create one file, enter data into the file, store the file containing the data on disk, and print the file contents. In the second Job, the file will be retrieved, new records will be added to those already in the file, and the contents of some of the records previously in the file will be changed. The third Job covers retrieving records from the file based on their contents (for example, listing only the records of salespeople who were hired before a certain date or receive a certain salary). The records are sorted in various ways, and new files are created with the sorted data.

Let us note two key combinations that will be used often in dBase. The escape key (ESC) is generally the signal to terminate an activity without saving the work done. Use this only when you wish to wipe out the result of your last activity. To exit from an activity and save the work done, click on EXIT at the top of the Control Center screen. Then click on QUIT to return to DOS. These are not interchangeable; both terminate the activity, but with very different results.

TWO WAYS OF USING dBASE IV

There are two ways to use dBase IV. You are already familair with the Control Center. The second method is through the dot prompt. This method allows you to issue commands directly to the dBase IV interpreter without using menus. You can go to the dot prompt mode from the Control Center by selecting EXIT, then EXIT TO DOT PROMPT. When you do this, the screen clears and you will see a dot (.) at the bottom left of the screen.

Figure 6-2. The dBase IV dot prompt screen.

Why would you want to use dBase IV like this? Very often, when one becomes familiar with a software package, it is quicker for the user to type in commands, rather than move from menu to menu. Nonetheless, in this introduction, we will be using the Control Center.

dBASE JOB 1:

CREATING A DATABASE FILE AND ENTERING DATA INTO THE RECORDS

PURPOSES

1. To provide experience loading dBase
2. To create a file
3. To print a copy of the file contents
4. To store the file for future use

REQUIRED EQUIPMENT

1. dBase system disk
2. Formatted blank disk

PREPARATION

A wholesale firm that supplies goods to many retail stores wants to keep records of its salespeople in a database so that it can retrieve information quickly. First, the database is planned: Decisions are made about what data items are to be stored in each record and what type of data each item represents, such as digits only (numeric), alphabetic or mixed characters (character), dates (date), and so on.

Next, names are chosen to identify the file and the items stored. Eventually, the database will contain multiple files, so each must be given an individual name, such as EMPDATA or EMMASTER, so that we can identify which file is to be retrieved for us by dBase. When reports using the data are run, we may want to list all the data in a record or only part of the data. Therefore, we must give a name to each field so that we can specify which items are to appear on the report. If the name EMNAME is chosen for the Employee Name field and EMSALARY for the field containing the salary, we can instruct dBase to DISPLAY EMNAME FOR EMSALARY = 2000.00, and it will display on the screen only the names of employees whose records contain a salary amount of $2000.00. To begin, then, we must decide (1) which items are to be stored in each record, (2) the type of each item, and (3) the length of each item. Then we must choose a name for the file and a name for each of the items. The actual data is shown in Figure 6-3.

The wholesale firm wants to store an employee number, name, date hired, salary, and bonus percentage in each record. The length of each item (which will determine the width of the field that must be provided for it in the record) also has been determined. We will choose the name EMPDATA for the file.

Item	Name	Type	Width	Dec
Employee Number	NUMBER	Numeric	2	0
First Name	NAME 1	Character	10	
Last Name	NAME 2	Character	15	
Date Hired	DATE	Date	8	
Salary	SALARY	Numeric	7	2
Bonus Percentage	BONUS	Numeric	5	3

Figure 6-3. Records to be entered in the EMPDATA file.

Now that these decisions have been made, the file can be created. The dBase commands needed for this job are as follows:

CREATE   To instruct dBase to set up a new file
DISPLAY To display on the screen or on the printer the records from a file
QUIT   To terminate the session and store the data

Note: Some options in dBase, as in other packages, require the use of the arrow keys, the mouse, and/or the cursor return in order to move through the software.

PROCEDURE

1. Load dBase into the computer.
    The procedure for booting the package will depend on your system configuration and the way dBase has been installed. Consult your instructor or system documentation for the procedure to follow.
2. When the boot is complete:
    A. The screen shown in Figure 6-1 or the screen in Figure 6-2 will appear.
    B. IF you have the display in Figure 6-2,
        (1) Press F2 to display the screen in Figure 6-1.
3. Create the database on the disk in Drive A.
    A. Insert formatted blank disk into drive A.
    B. Position cursor in DATA CREATE.
    C. Press cursor return.
4. The screen in Figure 6-4 will appear. This is where you define the database. Note that we have not yet named the new database. This is done after the structure is defined. The prompts along the bottom tell you the following:
    * How to delete (1) a character from a field name (DEL key), or (2) an entire line (Ctrl—U).
    * How to insert (1) a character into a field name (INS key), or (2) a field before the first field or between two existing fields (Ctrl—N).
    * How to move the cursor to the previous field (up arrow) and the next field (down arrow).
    * How to terminate the creation of the database by either
        (a) saving the information you have keyed in and exiting (EXIT)
             or
        (b) exiting without saving the information (ESC key).

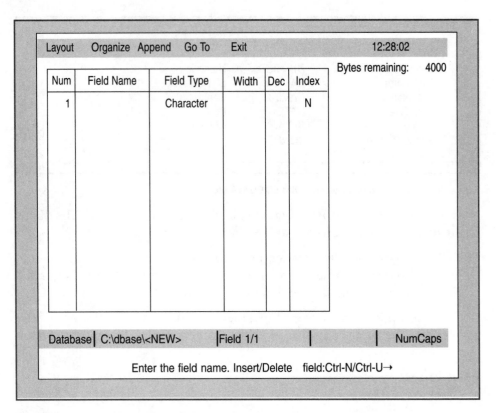

Figure 6-4. The dBase structure screen.

Above this information is the area in which you will enter the description of your record. It prompts you to enter Field Name, Type, Width, and number of decimal places if it is a numeric field (Dec).

Just beneath the command line is another prompting area that provides information about the data you are expected to enter next. When the cursor is in the Field Name area, the prompt says *Enter the field name* and tells you what characters can be used to make up a legal name. As you move from one column to another, defining the Name, the Type, and the Width, this prompt will change and provide you with information about the entry you are to make in the column.

    A. Describe the Employee Number field.
        (1)   Enter the Field Name.
               Refer to your list of Field Names, Types, and Widths (Figure 6-3) and enter the name for the first field, NUMBER. Press cursor return to move to the Type column.
        (2)   Enter the Type.
               The Character type is displayed. It is the default, or the option dBase will take if it is not instructed otherwise. This item is to be a number, so press the space bar to change the Type to Numeric; then press cursor return to move to the Width column.

Note: If you continue to press the space bar, other field types will display. When the last available type has displayed, dBase will display Character and begin the cycle through the available names again.

(3) Enter the Width.

Enter 2 and press cursor return.

(4) Enter the Decimals.

This amount will contain no decimals. Press cursor return. When the description of the Employee Number field is complete, the cursor will move to the next line.

(5) Correct any errors.

You can correct errors by using the cursor positioning keys to return to the error and rekeying it.

B. Describe the First Name field.

(1) Enter the Field Name.

Enter the name NAME1 as previously chosen and press cursor return.

(2) Enter the Type.

Press cursor return to accept the default.

(3) Enter the Width.

Enter 10 and press cursor return.

C. Describe the Last Name field.

(1) Enter the Field Name.

Enter the name NAME2 as previously chosen and press cursor return.

(2) Enter the Type.

Press cursor return to accept the default.

(3) Enter the Width.

Enter 15 and press cursor return.

D. Describe the Hire Date field.

(1) Enter the Field Name DATE and press cursor return.

(2) Enter the Type.

a. Press the space bar twice.

b. The Type Date will display.

c. Press cursor return.

d. The cursor will not stop at Width because a Date field is automatically assigned 8 positions.

E. Describe the Salary field.

(1) Enter the Field Name SALARY and press cursor return.

(2) Enter the Type.

Press the space bar to change the Type to Number and press cursor return.

(3) Enter the Width—7—and press cursor return.

(4) Enter the Decimals—2—and press cursor return.

F. Describe the Bonus field.

(1) Enter the Field Name BONUS and press cursor return.

(2) Enter the Type.

Press the space bar once to change the Type to Number and press cursor return.

(3) Enter the Width—5—and press cursor return.

(4) Enter the Decimals—3—and press cursor return.
5. Name and store the record description.
   A. After the last field has been described, examine the description and make any needed corrections.
      (1) Check your description against the original list (Figure 6-3). If there are errors, follow these steps:
        a. Press the space bar.
        b. Place the cursor at the beginning of the column entry containing the error.
        c. Rekey the entry.
        d. Press cursor return.
   B. When the last field has been described and the cursor is in the Field Name column of the next line,
      (1) Press cursor return. The system will prompt you with *Save as:* for the new database name.
      (2) Type a:\EMPDATA and press cursor return.
   C. The file structure will be written on disk and the prompt line will display

       Input data records now? (Y/N)

   Note: After the structure has been created it can be changed if errors are found—field sizes prove to be too small, the type assigned to a field is incorrect, a field is to be added, a field is to be deleted, and so on. Issue the command MODIFY STRUCTURE and make the necessary changes. Press cursor return to confirm changes.
6. Enter the data.
   A. Select the Input option.
      (1) Enter Y, move arrow to YES, or click on YES with the mouse in response to the *Input data records now?* prompt.
   B. The screen in Figure 6-5 will appear.
The name of each field is displayed, followed by a mask that shows its length. The cursor is positioned at the beginning of the first field.

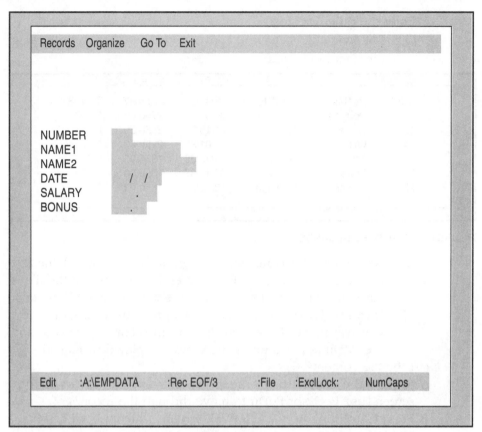

```
  Records   Organize    Go To    Exit



   NUMBER
   NAME1
   NAME2
   DATE              /  /
   SALARY             .
   BONUS              .







  Edit      :A:\EMPDATA        :Rec EOF/3        :File    :ExclLock:    NumCaps
```

Figure 6-5. Data entry screen for EMPDATA.

    C. Enter the first employee record from Figure 6-6.
        (1)   Enter the Employee Number.
            a.   The number will fill the field.
            b.   The system will beep to alert you that the field is full.
            c.   The cursor will move to the Name field.
        (2)   Enter the First Name.
            a.   The name will not fill the field.
            b.   Press cursor return to move to the next field.
        (3)   Enter the Second Name.
            a.   The name will not fill the field.
            b.   Press cursor return to move to the next field.
        (4)   Enter the Hire Date.
            a.   Key in 06 01 79 (dBase will insert slashes).
            b.   The cursor will advance automatically.
        (5)   Enter the Salary.
            a.   Enter 275000 (dBase will insert the decimal).
            b.   The cursor will advance automatically.
        (6)   Enter the Bonus Percent.
            a.   Enter 0100 (dBase will insert the decimal).
            b.   The cursor will advance automatically.
   D. dBase will accept the record.
      The record will disappear from the screen but remain in the memory of the computer. It will be written on disk later. If you wish to examine prior records, the PgUp key moves you back in the file; the PgDn moves you forward.

E. Enter the other records.
   (1) Following the steps in C above, enter the other records using the data in Figure 6-6.

NUMBER	NAME1	NAME2	DATE	SALARY	BONUS
08	Douglas	O'Neil	06/01/79	2750.00	0.100
12	Gloria	Totorice	01/15/80	2550.00	0.075
14	William	Trice	04/01/80	2250.00	0.075
23	James	Lincoln	09/15/85	1975.00	0.060
27	Frank	Dexheimer	06/15/87	1850.00	0.050
28	Jo Ann	Foreman	12/15/87	1850.00	0.050

FIGURE 6-6. EMPLOYEE RECORDS.

   (2) Notice that the command line gives the number of the last record entered: Rec: EOF/4. The end of the data in the file is currently at Record 4 when you are entering Record Number 5.
   (3) If you wish to see the contents of a previous record, the PgUp key will move the screen display up record by record, and the PgDn key will move the screen display down again.
7. List the file contents.
   A. Position the display so that the first record entered appears on the screen (use PgUP or PgDn to move through the records.
   B. Press F2 to bring up the BROWSE screen, which lists all records.
   C. The display in Figure 6-7 will appear.

Records	Organize	Fields	Go To	Exit

NUMBER	NAME1	NAME2	DATE	SALARY	BONUS
08	Douglas	O'Neil	06/01/79	2750.00	0.100
12	Gloria	Totorice	01/15/80	2550.00	0.075
14	William	Trice	04/01/80	2250.00	0.075
23	James	Lincoln	09/15/85	1975.00	0.060
27	Frank	Dexheimer	06/15/87	1850.00	0.050
28	Jo Ann	Foreman	12/15/87	1850.00	0.050

Browse   :A:\EMPDATA   :Rec EOF/6   :File   :ExclLock: Num

Add new records

Figure 6-7. Result of BROWSE for EMPDATA.

8. Make a hard copy of the file.
   A. Ready your printer.
   B. Enter the command SHIFT+F9.
   C. Press cursor return.
9. Terminate the work session.
   Caution: This procedure is very important. Records are accumulated in a holding area in memory until it is full and are only then stored on disk. If the area has not been filled when you finish entering your data, the records will not be written on disk unless you go through the QUIT procedure. Issue the QUIT command *only* when you have completed all dBase tasks to be done in the work session. It is not necessary to QUIT when changing from one dBase job to another.
   A. Select the EXIT command (Alt+E or mouse selection).
   B. The screen will display:

   > EXIT TO DOT PROMPT
   > QUIT TO DOS

   Choose one of these options.
   C. Remove any disks.
   D. Turn the system off.

dBASE JOB 2:
CHANGING DATA IN EXISTING RECORDS, ADDING
NEW RECORDS TO THE FILE, AND DELETING RECORDS

PURPOSES

1. To add new records to the end of the existing file
2. To provide experience changing the data in records presently in the file
3. To print a copy of the revised file contents
4. To store the revised file for future use

REQUIRED EQUIPMENT

1. dBase system disk
2. Data disk with EMPDATA file

PREPARATION

The firm that uses the EMPDATA file has awarded its yearly raises and has hired three new employees. To keep the data in the file current, the salary and bonus figures must be changed in existing records, and records for the two new employees must be added. The file has already been established and the record description described, so these tasks need not be done again. The following new commands are needed for the present activities:

USE To declare which file we are going to work with

APPEND To declare that new records are to be appended or added to the bottom of the file.

EDIT To declare that the contents of an existing record are to be changed.

DELETE To mark a record for deletion.

PACK To remove all marked records from the file.

PROCEDURE

1. Load dBase into the computer:
   The procedure for booting the package depends on your system configuration and the way dBase has been installed. Ask your instructor or consult your system documentation how this should be done.
2. Issue the command to open the file EMPDATA on the disk in Drive A for use:
   A. Select the EMPDATA file with the arrow keys or the mouse (do not press cursor return).
3. Access the Edit screen to add new records.
   A. Press SHIFT+F2 at the Control Center screen.
   B. Select APPEND on the database structure screen. If you are in the table, press F10 to get to the Structure Menu, then select APPEND.
   C. Highlight **Enter records from keyboard** (Figure 6-8), then press cursor return.

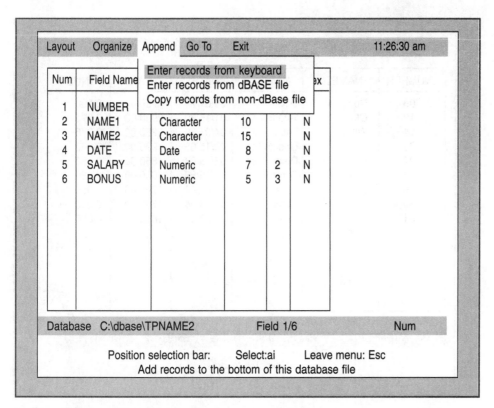

```
┌─────────────────────────────────────────────────────────────────┐
│  Layout   Organize   Append  Go To    Exit              11:26:30 am │
│                      ┌──────────────────────────────────┐         │
│  ┌───────┬───────────│ Enter records from keyboard      │         │
│  │ Num   │ Field Name│ Enter records from dBASE file    │ex       │
│  │       │           │ Copy records from non-dBase file │         │
│  │   1   │ NUMBER    └──────────────────────────────────┘         │
│  │   2   │ NAME1       Character        10           N            │
│  │   3   │ NAME2       Character        15           N            │
│  │   4   │ DATE        Date              8           N            │
│  │   5   │ SALARY      Numeric           7      2    N            │
│  │   6   │ BONUS       Numeric           5      3    N            │
│  │       │                                                        │
│  │       │                                                        │
│  └───────┴─────────────────────────────────────┘                 │
│  Database  C:\dbase\TPNAME2            Field 1/6           Num     │
│                                                                   │
│        Position selection bar:    Select:ai    Leave menu: Esc    │
│              Add records to the bottom of this database file      │
└─────────────────────────────────────────────────────────────────┘
```

Figure 6-8. Add New Records screen.

4. Enter the data.

Enter these records for the three new employees:

NUMBER	NAME1	NAME2	DATE	SALARY	BONUS
29	Bob	Baker	Today's Date	1,700.00	0.050
30	Sharon	Ross	Today's Date	1,700.00	0.050
31	Brenda	Key	Today's Date	1,850.00	0.050

A. Enter the data for Baker as you entered data in Job 1. Use today's date in the 12/15/99 format for the date.

B. When the data for Baker is complete, the empty layout will display again.

C. Enter the data for Ross.

D. Terminate the APPEND activity. When the empty layout displays again, select EXIT (ALT+E or mouse selection).

E. Press cursor return to confirm.

5. Check to see if the records were added (Figure 6-9).

A. Press F2 twice to bring up the Browse screen.

B. Check for the two new records at the end of the file.

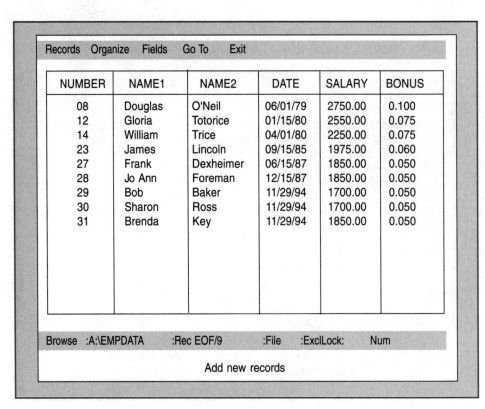

Figure 6-9. Checking to see if new records added.

6. Modify the existing records.

Make the following changes in the records already in the file:

EMPLOYEE	FIELD TO CHANGE	NEW DATA FOR FIELD
O'Neil	Salary	3,000.00
Totorice	Bonus	0.080
Lincoln	Salary	2,550.00
Dexheimer	Bonus	0.060
Jo Ann Foreman	Bonus	0.060

A. Enter the command F2.
   (1) All records will be displayed. Use the arrow keys or the mouse to move the cursor to the desired record to be changed. If not all records are displayed, use PgUp or PgDown to move the cursor to the desired location.

B. Update the top record.
   (1) IF you have the data for Ross,
       Press the arrow keys or use the mouse to move back through the fields until the record for O'Neil is displayed.
   (2) Press cursor return to bypass the Name fields.
   (3) Press cursor return to bypass the Date field.
   (4) Enter the new salary figure in the Salary field.
   (5) Press cursor return to bypass the Bonus field.

C. Update the remaining records.

(1) Use cursor return to move to the field to be modified and to bypass other fields.

D. Check your changes.

(1) Use the PgUp key to return to the records previously modified and recheck the changes.

7. Make a hard copy of the file.

A. Press F2 to bring up the Browse screen.

B. Ready your printer.

C. Press SHIFT+F9 for Quick Report.

D. Press cursor return.

8. Delete an unwanted record.

Brenda Key has left the organization and her record is to be removed from the file.

A. Place cursor on record to delete.

B. Go to Records on the Command Menu and highlight: MARK THE RECORD FOR DELETION. Note status line at bottom of screen, "Del."

C. Press cursor return to confirm.

D. Go to Organize on the Command Menu and highlight: ERASE MARKED RECORDS.

E. Press cursor return to confirm. Notice that the record is no longer included.

9. Make a hard copy of your file (Figure 6-10).

A. Ready your printer.

B. Press SHIFT+F9 for Quick Report.

C. Press cursor return.

10. If you are finished with dBase, terminate the work session.

A. Enter the EXIT command (ALT+E or mouse selection).

B. Press cursor return.

C. Remove any disks.

D. Turn the system off.

NUMBER	NAME1	NAME2	DATE	SALARY	BONUS
08	Douglas	O'Neil	06/01/79	2750.00	0.100
12	Gloria	Totorice	01/15/80	2550.00	0.075
14	William	Trice	04/01/80	2250.00	0.075
23	James	Lincoln	09/15/85	1975.00	0.060
27	Frank	Dexheimer	06/15/87	1850.00	0.050
28	Jo Ann	Foreman	12/15/87	1850.00	0.050
29	Bob	Baker	11/29/94	1700.00	0.050
30	Sharon	Ross	11/29/94	1700.00	0.050
31	Brenda	Key	11/29/94	1850.00	0.050

Figure 6-10. Checking to see new records added.

Selective operations in dBase, such as those in which we select certain records from the file to print, use the symbols of standard mathematical comparisons:

=	Indicates equal to
>	Indicates greater than
<	Indicates less than

To display all records in which the SALARY field contains the number 2500.00, the command would be:

DISPLAY ALL FOR SALARY = 2500.00

And to display those with salaries less than 2500.00, the command is:

DISPLAY ALL FOR SALARY < 2500.00

The symbols used for comparisons can also be combined. To display the records for employees with salaries less than or equal to 2500.00, the command would be:

DISPLAY ALL FOR SALARY <= 2500.00

To display records with salaries greater than or equal to 2500.00, issue the command:

DISPLAY ALL FOR SALARY >= 2500.00

There are three rules to observe when comparing symbols are used to select certain records. First, there must be a blank space before the first and after the last symbol. Second, if two symbols are used, there may not be a blank between the two. Third, when the equal sign is combined with another symbol, the equal sign must be the last symbol used.

PURPOSES:

1. To display selected fields from the records rather than all fields in the records
2. To print a copy of the selected fields
3. To introduce the history buffer

REQUIRED EQUIPMENT

1. dBase system disk
2. Data disk with EMPDATA file

PREPARATION

Often someone using a database file will not require all the information contained in the records, but only one or two fields. Sometimes the user requires the names and salaries of employees, at another time the names and date hired are required, and at yet another time the name and bonus percentage are wanted. Listings of selected fields are done with the DISPLAY statement we have been using, but rather than say DISPLAY ALL, we specify the names of the fields we want to print.

In this and previous Jobs, dBase remembers the commands issued from the time you begin to work until you terminate the session. These are kept in a holding area called the **history buffer**. You can access the history buffer and look back through prior commands by simply pressing the cursor positioning keys that move the cursor up and down. Pressing the up arrow moves to the last command issued, pressing it again moves it to the one before that, and so on. This is convenient when you wish to review commands or to issue the same command again. We will discover another useful application in this Job.

The commands needed for this Job are:

USE	To declare which file we are going to work with
DISPLAY	To display the specified output on the screen or on the printer
QUIT	To terminate the activity

PROCEDURE

1. Load dBase into the computer:
   The procedure for booting the package depends on your system configuration and the way dBase has been installed. Ask your instructor or consult your system documentation how this should be done.
2. Issue the command to open the file EMPDATA on the disk in Drive A for use:

A. Select the EMPDATA file with the arrow keys or the mouse (do not press ENTER).

3. Print the employee number, the first name and the last name of all employees.

   A. From the Control Center, arrow or click on the QUERIES column.

   B. All items of the EMPDATA are selected. To deselect the items you do not want to appear on the report, tab or use your mouse to click in the fields you do not want to show and press the F5 key. As you go to each field to deselect, only the fields that have been left selected will appear at the bottom of the screen.

4. Print the first name, last name, and salary of all employees.

   A. Specify these fields:

   NAME1, NAME2, SALARY

   B. The names and the salary will display.

   C. Press SHIFT+F9 to print.

   D. Press cursor return to confirm your selection.

5. Print the last name, date hired, and salary.

   A. Press F5 to restore all fields.

   B. Specify NAME2, DATE, SALARY.

   C. The last name, date, and salary will display.

   D. Press SHIFT+F9 to print.

   E. Press cursor return to confirm your selection.

6. Terminate the work session.

   A. Enter the EXIT command (ALT+E or mouse selection).

   B. Press cursor return to confirm.

   C. Remove the disks.

   D. Turn the system off.

PURPOSES

1. To display only records that contain certain data or meet certain conditions
2. To print a copy of the selected records

REQUIRED EQUIPMENT

1. dBase system disk
2. Data disk with the EMPDATA file

PREPARATION

In Job 3 you selected certain *fields* to display from all records in the file. Now you will select certain *records* to display from the file. When the personnel director or sales manager has questions about the sales people in the EMPDATA file, he or she usually needs one or two pieces of information rather than a list of all the data in the file. Perhaps the question is "How many salespeople do we have with a monthly salary over $2,500.00?" or "How many people have been with us more than five years?" or "How many people who have been with us more than five years are earning a bonus of less than 5 percent?"

When specific information such as this is required, we can use the DISPLAY statement to produce the desired report. For these applications, conditions such as the following will be added to the DISPLAY statement:

DISPLAY ALL FOR SALARY > 2500.00

Selective operations in dBase, such as those in which we select certain records from the file to print, use the symbols of standard mathematical comparisons:

$=$ Indicates equal to
$>$ Indicates greater than
$<$ Indicates less than

To display all records in which the SALARY field contains the number 2500.00, the command would be:

DISPLAY ALL FOR SALARY = 2500.00

And to display those with salaries less than 2500.00, the command is:

DISPLAY ALL FOR SALARY < 2500.00

The symbols used for comparisons can also be combined. To display the records for employees with salaries less than or equal to 2500.00, the command would be:

DISPLAY ALL FOR SALARY <= 2500.00

To display records with salaries greater than or equal to 2500.00, issue the command:

> DISPLAY ALL FOR SALARY >= 2500.00

There are three rules to observe when comparing symbols are used to select certain records. First, there must be a blank space before the first and after the last symbol. Second, if two symbols are used, there may not be a blank between the two. Third, when the equal sign is combined with another symbol, the equal sign must be the last symbol used.

The new commands for this Job are the following:

USE	To declare which file we are going to work with
DISPLAY	To display the record(s) specified on the screen or printer
CLEAR	To erase the display and clear the screen

PROCEDURE

1. Load dBase into the computer.
2. Open the file for use.
   A. Select with arrows or mouse the file EMPDATA from the Control Center screen.
3. Check the contents of the file.
   A. Press F2 to bring up the Browse screen.
   B. Examine the listing, noting the order of the records.
4. Print a list of people earning more than $2,500.00
   A. Exit to the Control Center screen.
   B. Use the arrow keys or click on the QUERIES column on the Control Center screen.
   C. Type in the Salary Field:
      >2500.00
   D. Press SHIFT+F9 to print.
   E. Press cursor return to confirm.
   F. Only the records of people earning more than $2,500.00 will print.
5. Check the list for correctness.
   A. Compare the list of people earning more than $2,500.00 to the file listing printed in Step 3.
      (1) Did the records of everyone earning more than $2,500.00 print?
      (2) Did any other records print?
6. Print a list of people with a bonus percentage of 0.06 or less.
   A. You should still be in the QUERIES column.
   B. Delete the >2500.00 in the Salary Field.
   C. Type in the Bonus field:
      <=0.06
   D. Press SHIFT+F9 to print and press the cursor return.
   E. Check the printout against the file contents.

7. Print a list of people with a bonus percentage less than 0.070.
   A. You should still be in the QUERIES column.
   B. Delete the <=0.06 in the Bonus Field.
   C. Type in the Bonus field:

      <0.070

   D. Press SHIFT+F9 to print and press the cursor return.
   E. Check the printout against the file contents.
8. Print a list of people who have a salary greater than $1,700.00 and are earning less than a 7 percent bonus.
   A. You should still be in the QUERIES column.
   B. Delete what is in the Bonus Field.
   C. Type in the Salary field:

      >1700.00

   D. Type in the Bonus field:

      <0.070

   E. Press SHIFT+F9 to print and press the cursor return.
   F. Check the printout against the file contents.
9. If you are finished with dBase, terminate the work session.
   A. Enter the EXIT command (ALT+E or mouse selection).
   B. Press cursor return to confirm.
   C. Remove any disks.
   D. Turn the system off.

dBASE JOB 5:
SORTING THE EMPDATA FILE AND CREATING NEW FILES

PURPOSES

1. To sort the records into various orders and place them into new files in those orders
2. To print the contents of the new files

REQUIRED EQUIPMENT

1. dBase system disk
2. Data disk with EMPDATA file

PREPARATION

The records in the EMPDATA file are in order by salesperson number. Because these numbers are assigned when people are hired, the records that are in order by salesperson number are also in order by hire date. This is convenient for many applications. Sometimes, however, it is more convenient for the records to be in alphabetical order by last name or in order by amount of salary. To sort the file, create a new file, and place the records into the new file, the SORT command is used. Its format is:

SORT ON NAME2 TO TPNAME2

This command will do the following:

1. Create a new file named TPNAME2.
2. Sort the records into order by last name (the field named NAME2).
3. Place the records into TPNAME2 in alphabetical order by last name.

The name TPNAME2 was chosen for this file because it is a TemPorary file created to hold the data in order by last name (NAME2). In this Job, three new files will be created:

1. TPNAME2 (records in order by last name)
2. TPSALARY (records in order by amount earned)
3. TPBONUS (records in order by bonus percentage)

The new command for this Job is SORT. Use the SORT command to resequence the records in the order specified and place them into a new file in the new sequence.

PROCEDURE

1. Load dBase into the computer.
2. Open the file EMPDATA.
3. Check the contents of the file.
   A. Press SHIFT+F9 to print and press cursor return.
   B. The contents of EMPDATA will print.
   C. Examine the list, noting the order of the records.

4.	Create the new file with data sorted on employee last name (NAME2). The name of the new file is to be TPNAME2, and it is to be placed on the disk in Drive A.

A. Select with the arrow keys or the mouse the file EMPDATA from the Control Center screen.

B. Press cursor return to have the following selections appear on the top of the Control Center screen:

USE FILE   MODIFY STRUCTURE/ORDER   DISPLAY DATA

C. Use arrow keys or mouse to select MODIFY STRUCTURE/ORDER; then press cursor return.

D. A menu will appear on top of the Structure screen that has the following choices:

> CREATE NEW INDEX
> MODIFY EXISTING INDEX
> > ORDER RECORDS BY INDEX
> > ACTIVATE .NDX INDEX FILE
> > INCLUDE .NDX INDEX FILE
> > REMOVE UNWANTED INDEX TAG
>
> SORT DATABASE ON FIELD LIST
> UNMARK ALL RECORDS
> ERASE MARKED RECORDS

E. Use the arrow keys or the mouse to select: SORT DATABASE ON FIELD LIST; then press cursor return.

F. A Field Order/Type of Sort menu will appear; type in NAME2.

G. Press cursor return twice.

H. A prompt will ask:

ENTER NAME OF SORTED FILE:

I. Type in TPNAME2 and press cursor return twice.

J. Return to the Control Center screen.

K. The sort will be completed and the Control Center screen will appear with two data files in the Data Column. These two files are EMPDATA and TPNAME2.

L. To print a copy of the sorted file TPNAME2, select the file by using the arrow or mouse to highlight the file.

M. Press SHIFT+F9 to print; then press cursor return.

5.	Create the file with data sorted by salary amount.

A. Repeat steps 3A-E from last Job.

B. Type in SALARY and press cursor return twice.

C. Type in the name to save as TPSALARY and press cursor return twice.

D. Return to the Control Center.

E. To print a copy of the sorted file TPSALARY, select the file by using the arrow keys or the mouse to highlight the file.

F. Press SHIFT+F9 to print and press cursor return.

6.	Create the file with data sorted by BONUS amount.

A. Repeat steps 3A-E from the last Job.

B. Type in BONUS and press cursor return twice.

C. Type in the name to save as TPBONUS and press cursor return.

D. Return to the Control Center.

E. To print a copy of the sorted file TPBONUS, select the file by using the arrow or mouse to highlight the file.

F. Press SHIFT+F9 to print and press cursor return.

7. If you have finished with dBase, terminate the work session.

A. Enter the EXIT command (ALT+E or mouse selection).

B. Press cursor return to confirm.

C. Remove any disks.

D. Turn the system off.

If you wish to do additional Jobs in dBase, you can set up files for the Jobs in Chapter 4 of the text. Jobs 1, 2, 3, 4, 14, 15, 16, and 17 are the best for dBase applications. To use Job 18, include all the data relating to one person in one record rather than in two as indicated in the text. Do not use Jobs 19 through 25. Note that (1) you will not need to include the Record Number as input data because dBase numbers the records automatically, and (2) on the Jobs that have page totals (Jobs 16 and 17), the totals should not be entered.

Below are suggestions for SORT and SELECT commands on various Jobs. Ask your instructor if you should enter an entire Job or only part of a Job.

JOB	SORT	SELECT FOR
Job 2	—	Chemistry majors
Job 4	Author	Author
		1. G.W. Allen
		2. I. Asimov
		Books checked out by
		1. Burton, Harold A.
		2. Tyron, Paul J.
Job 14	Item Number	—
Job 15	Institution Name	1. EENG majors
		2. EENG majors who
		a. attended Univ. of Penn.
		b. attended Univ. of Alabama
		3. Major MGT and degree MS
Job 16	Social Security No.	1. All working overtime
		2. All earning more than 3.50 per hour
		3. All earning more than 3.50 per hour who worked overtime
Job 17	Item Number	1. All weighing 5 pounds or more
		2. All sold by Clerk Number 3075

Chapter 7

WORD PROCESSING SOFTWARE FOR MICROCOMPUTERS

Word processors are powerful application programs that enable us to enter text material through a keyboard into the memory of a computer. Once it is stored electronically, the material can be manipulated in many ways. Characters, lines, or whole blocks of text can be changed, deleted, or inserted into the original material. Paragraphs can be moved from one location to another. Margins can be changed and the text can be aligned automatically to the new margins. The text can be searched for specified words or phrases that, when found, can be replaced with others supplied by the user.

When the user is satisfied with the form and content of the material, she or he can store it on disk for future use. Of course, it can also be printed, and the word processor can insert page headings, page numbers, and footnotes.

Word processing is performed using a combination of an ordinary computer and a word processing program that it follows to electronically store, edit, and otherwise manipulate text material. In most cases, the owner of the computer uses it for many other purposes, reading in the word processing program from disk when it is needed. Another type of word processor, a dedicated system, is a computer designed to do nothing but word processing. The program it follows cannot be changed.

Word processors are very useful in business correspondence. Many organizations send identical or very similar letters to many people. These letters can be entered, edited, and stored on disk. When a letter is to be sent to a customer or client, a secretary can read the previously created letter back from disk, enter the name and address of the customer or client, and instruct the printer to print a copy.

Many other features are available. One option provides a "dictionary" of tens of thousands of words and permits the user to add words so that the terminology of a particular business or profession can be included in the list. The program checks the spelling of each word in the text against the dictionary and flags or displays any words not found. The user may elect to change the spelling or leave the word as it is.

Modern word processors also have graphics capabilities. The system disks contain extensive files of various pictures that the user can insert into the text as it is entered to create eye-catching memos, signs, and so on. Many fonts or styles of type are also available, so that a user may choose to print a document in modern block type, Old English letters, italics, or one of many other type styles. The user may change the font by calling up a menu within the word processor and selecting a different type style. Within each style of type, the user also may choose the size of the letters and the darkness with which each will print. Of course, when graphics or various fonts are used, the printer must be capable of graphics output.

The **mail merge** feature takes names and addresses from a file, inserts them into a prewritten letter, and can print hundreds or thousands of individually addressed letters. **Syntax checks** point out trite or overused phrases. Punctuation checkers check spacing before and after punctuation marks, detect incorrectly capitalized words, point out frequently repeated words, and so on.

Although we may think of word processors as electronic typewriters, they are much more than that. They are also electronic erasers, electronic copyeditors, electronic crayons, and electronic cut-and-paste. By eliminating many routine and repetitive tasks, word processors allow people to spend their time on more interesting work.

INTRODUCTION TO WORDPERFECT FOR WINDOWS

Dozens of word processing packages are currently on the market. One of the most widely used is called WordPerfect. As we explore WordPerfect, you will find that it uses menus and prompts to assist you. Also, the instructions in the laboratory exercises will tell you to respond to various circumstances. WordPerfect does not use commands, as does dBase, but many of its functions are requested by pressing a function key or a combination of another key and a function key or using the mouse pointer to click on a word on the Menu Bar or an icon on the Button or Power Bars.

Several icons are frequently used or are generally helpful in WordPerfect. Some that will be helpful in your first few jobs are these:

 Open allows you to go to the file and retrieve a preexisting file.

 Save allows you to save a file on your disk.

 Print allows you to print a file on your screen.

 Close allows you to close a file on your screen.

Exit, found in the File Menu of the Menu Bar, allows you to exit the WordPerfect program.

Page up and Page down allow you to move your cursor either to the top of the page or the bottom of the page.

PURPOSES

1. To enter text into memory and create a document
2. To provide experience with the Print Menu
3. To print a copy of the document
4. To save the document for future use

REQUIRED EQUIPMENT

1. WordPerfect system package
2. Formatted data disk

PREPARATION

In this job, we will create an electronic document in the memory of the computer. When the document is complete, we will save it on the disk and print a copy. Read the instructions for the entire Job very carefully before you start to work.

PROCEDURE

1. Load WordPerfect into the computer.
   The procedure for booting the package will depend upon your system configuration. Consult your instructor or your user's manual to determine the booting procedure.
2. The screen shown in Figure 7-1 will display. This is the clear editing window. Notice the lower right-hand corner of the screen gives information about the current position of the cursor.

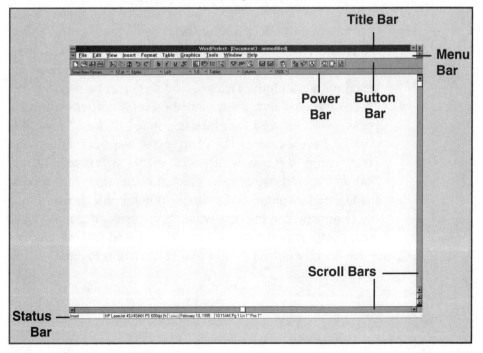

Figure 7-1. Document window

3. Create the document file.

A. Read about these functional characteristics of WordPerfect.

(1) WordPerfect is in Insert mode when you begin to work and remains there unless you specify otherwise. Of course this means that you can insert characters, lines, or paragraphs into existing text by simply placing the cursor where you wish them to appear and entering the text. Sometimes you may wish to type over and replace existing characters rather than inserting material before or after them. In this case press the Insert key. The word *Typeover* will appear at the bottom left of your screen and remain until the Insert key is pressed again to return to the Insert mode.

(2) Remember that WordPerfect, like all word processors, has word wrap. Do not hit the cursor return at the end of each line. WordPerfect will move automatically to the next line when the current line is full. Press the cursor return at the end of each paragraph. Do not forget to do this; several WordPerfect commands look for the paragraph marker that is inserted when the cursor return is pressed, and they will not work properly if it is not present.

(3) As you key, notice that the cursor position displayed in the lower right-hand corner of the screen changes. You also will notice that you cannot move the cursor outside of the area where you have entered data. WordPerfect requires that you "encumber space" by entering characters (yes, a blank is a character) and then allows you to move freely within this encumbered space.

(4) The margins and tab stops are set automatically and we will not change them in this Job. You may use the Tab key to move to the right in steps of five character positions. When you tab, WordPerfect inserts invisible codes into the text at the tab position. If your text begins to move around strangely, you may have inadvertently inserted an extra tab. These can be taken out with the Delete key if they can be seen.

(5) To see the tabs and other control codes Wordperfect inserts, press Alt+F3; or with your mouse pointer, click on View, then click on Reveal Codes. The plain text will appear at the top of your screen; the text with codes visible will display at the bottom. To remove a code, place the cursor on it and press the Delete key or take your mouse pointer and click and drag the command out into the white space area. Press Alt+F3 or click on View and then click on Reveal Codes to deselect it.

B. Create the document by keying the text shown in Figure 7-2.

> This is a sample document that you may use to practice word processing techniques. In Job 1, you will create the document, save it on disk, and print it. In Job 2, you will open and edit it.
>
> Word processors are powerful application programs that let us key in text material through the keyboard and put it into the memory of a computer. Once saved in memory, the material can be manipulated in many ways. You can make changes. Characters, lines, or whole blocks of text can be changed, deleted, or inserted into original material. Paragraphs can be moved. Margins can be changed and the text automatically aligned to the new margins.

Figure 7-2.

4. Save the document.
   When you have completed the material, follow this procedure to save it on disk.
   A. With the mouse pointer, click on File in the Menu Bar or click on the icon that shows a disk and the word Save in the Toolbar.
   B. Click on Save As...; at this point, you will name the document.
   C. Type as follows: A:\essay
   D. You will notice the filename you gave to this document, ESSAY, now appears at the top of the screen.
5. Print the document.
   A. With the mouse pointer, click on File on the Menu Bar or click on the icon that shows the printer and the word Print in the Toolbar.
   B. Click on Print.
   C. The Print dialog box appears and Full document is already designated. Click on Print.

   Note: If you have difficulties in printing, ask your instructor or supervisor to check the printer selection for this document. One error commonly encountered here is "Printer not selected."
   Check with your instructor to see if you need to make a printer selection correction.
6. Check the disk directory to see that the document is saved.
   A. Display the directory.
      (1) With the mouse pointer, click on File on the Menu Bar.
      (2) Click on Open to display the files on your disk.
   B. Find the filename, ESSAY, in the directory. Note that the directory is in alphabetical order.
   C. Cancel the display by clicking on Cancel.
7. Terminate the exercise.
   A. With the mouse pointer, click on File on the Menu Bar.
   B. Click on Exit. We have already saved this document.
   C. Remove the disk.

WORDPERFECT JOB 2:
OPENING AND EDITING A SAVED DOCUMENT

PURPOSE

1. To open a document from disk
2. To edit the document in the following ways:
   A. Inserting and deleting characters
   B. Inserting and deleting words
   C. Undeleting
   D. Realigning lines made uneven by editing
   E. Centering a line
   F. Adding more text
3. To print a copy of the document
4. To save the revised document for future use

REQUIRED EQUIPMENT

1. WordPerfect system package
2. Formatted data disk containing ESSAY file

PREPARATION

In this Job, we will open the document ESSAY we created and saved in Job 1 and edit it. When it reads as we wish, we will save the corrected document on disk and print a copy. Read the instructions for the entire Job before you start to work.

PROCEDURE

1. Load WordPerfect into the computer.
   The procedure for booting the package will depend upon your system configuration. Consult your instructor or your user's manual to determine the booting procedure.
2. The WordPerfect clear editing window will display.
3. Open the document ESSAY from disk.
   A. Insert your floppy disk into the disk drive.
   B. Click on File in the Menu Bar and select Open, or click on the Open icon on the Toolbar (file folder with an open arrow).
   C. Select the ESSAY file by highlighting it and clicking with the mouse pointer on ESSAY. Once it is selected, click on OK.
   D. The document will be open and displayed in the editing window.
4. Edit the document.
   A. Remove unwanted lines.
   We want to take out the entire first paragraph. To do this, use the Select feature in the Edit Menu.
   (1) Place your cursor at the beginning of the first line.
   (2) Place your mouse pointer on Edit and click.
   (3) Click on Select and click on Sentence.

(4)   Back in the document, the line you want to delete has been selected, and you will press the Delete key to delete this line.

(5)   Delete the other three lines in the first paragraph.

B. Remove unwanted words.

Now we want to remove the sentence that says, "You can make many changes." We cannot use Line delete because there is other text on the line that we do not wish deleted.

(1)   With your mouse pointer, click and drag through the words you want to delete.

(2)   After these words have been selected, press the Delete key.

C. Undelete words that have been deleted. When you make a mistake and delete words that you did not intend to delete, you have the Undelete or Undo option.

(1)   With the mouse pointer, click on Edit on the Menu Bar.

(2)   Click on Undo and the last word or words you deleted will appear back in the text.

(3)   Clicking on Undelete will allow you to recall the last three deletes you made.

(4)   The Undo and Undelete features also work for formatting operations such as changing margins, line spacing, etc.

D. Make changes in wording.

(1)   In the first sentence, delete the words "let us key in" and replace them with "enable us to enter."

(2)   In the same sentence, delete "and put it."

(3)   Change the sentence that begins "Once saved in memory" to say "Once electronically saved."

E. Add the following heading and center it over the text:

STANDARD FEATURES OF WORD PROCESSORS

(1)   Place the cursor at the beginning of the first line of the paragraph and press cursor return twice to insert two blank lines before the existing text. Place the cursor at the beginning of the first blank line.

(2)   Hold down the Shift key and press F6 to indicate that you want to center the material you key in next.

(3)   Key in the words STANDARD FEATURES OF WORD PROCESSORS on the first of the two blank lines. WordPerfect will center the title as you type it.

(4)   Press cursor return at the end of the title.

When the user is satisfied with the form and content of the material, he or she can store it on disk, where it is available for future use. Of course, it can also be printed, and the word processor can insert page headings, page numbers and footnotes.

Many added features are available. One option provides a "dictionary" of tens of thousands of words and permits the user to add words, so that the terminology of a particular business or profession can be included in the list. The program checks each word in the text against the dictionary and flags or displays the words not found. The user may elect to change the spelling or to leave the word as it appears.

Figure 7-3.

F. Add more paragraphs. Add the two paragraphs in Figure 7-3 to the document.
   - (1) Place the cursor at the end of the last line in the paragraph.
   - (2) Press cursor return twice. The first return will take the cursor to the beginning of the next line. The second return will take it down another line, leaving a blank line between the old paragraph and the first new paragraph.
   - (3) Key in the text for the first paragraph in Figure 7-3.
   - (4) Press cursor return twice.
   - (5) Key in the text for the second paragraph in Figure 7-3.

5. Save the document.

   When you have finished editing, follow the procedure below to save the document on disk.
   - A. With the mouse pointer, click on File on the Menu Bar.
   - B. Click on Save As...; at this point, you will name the document.
   - C. Type as follows: A:\ESSAY2
   - D. Notice that the filename you gave to this document, ESSAY2, now appears at the top of the screen.

6. Print the document.
   - A. With the mouse pointer, click on File on the Menu Bar.
   - B. Click on Print.
   - C. The Print dialog box appears and Full document is already designated. Click on Print.
     Note: If you have difficulties in printing, ask your instructor or supervisor to check the printer selection for this document. One error commonly encountered here is "Printer not selected." Check with your instructor to see if you need to make a printer selection correction.

7. Check the disk directory to see that the document is saved.
   - A. Display the directory.
     - (1) With the mouse pointer, click on File on the Menu Bar.
     - (2) Click on Open to display the files on your disk.
   - B. Find the filename, ESSAY2, in the directory. Note that the directory is in alphabetical order.
   - C. Cancel the display by clicking on Cancel.

8. Terminate the exercise.
   - A. With the mouse pointer, click on File on the Menu Bar.
   - B. Click on Exit. We have already saved this document.
   - C. Remove the disk.

SETTING MARGINS

PURPOSES

1. To create a new file
2. To provide experience in setting margins
3. To provide experience in setting tabs
4. To print a copy of the document
5. To save the document for future use

REQUIRED EQUIPMENT

1. WordPerfect system package
2. Formatted data disk

PREPARATION

In this Job, we will create a new document. WordPerfect allows us to set margins and tabs and then to change the settings within the document if we wish.

In this document we will use two margins: one for the general text of the letter and a second for quoted material within the body of the letter. We will set one margin and use it until we reach the place in the letter where the quoted material begins. Then we will change the margin settings to those we wish to use for the quoted material. When the quoted material ends, we will change the margins back to the original settings. Two tab settings are also needed: one for paragraph indentation and a second for the closing of the letter.

When tabs and margins are set, WordPerfect embeds codes in the text to indicate these settings. These are not displayed on the entry screen, but can be seen (and deleted if necessary) by using the Reveal Codes option (ALT+F3).

PROCEDURE

1. Load WordPerfect into the computer.
2. The WordPerfect clear editing window screen will display.

March 12, 199-

Mr. M. C. Moorer
MCM Systems Inc.
1000 Restone Parkway
Huntsville, AL 35802

Dear Michael:

While reading this month's crop of magazines, I came across a review of a new personal database that may be of interest to you as you look for a personal database. The author is a contributing editor to several personal computer magazines with a strong background in databases. Here's what he has to say:

A little brother to Microbase's programmable, networkable dBASE 3.1, Personal Mbase comes with a well-organized interface, the best relational skills in the roundup, good data entry validation, and flexible queries and reports. Add an aggressive $200.00 list price, and you get a Best Buy.

Let me know what you decide about the database. My son is going to college in September and wants one to use in his engineering courses.

Best personal regards,

4 lines

Joseph P. Congleton
Acquisitions Editor

Fig 7-4.

3. Set margins for the new document.

WordPerfect has default values (that will be used if you do not instruct otherwise) for many different options. The margins, for example, are usually set so that the document you create always has a one-inch margin on the left and on the right unless you change these settings. Defaults are a good idea. They are set to accommodate most documents and you need only change them when you have something out of the usual pattern to enter.

You will be creating the document shown in Figure 7-4. Notice that this document has two different margins: one for the letter itself and another for the material quoted in the letter. Tab settings will also be needed: one to use for indenting at the beginning of the paragraph and another to be used in indenting the closing of the letter.

First, we will set the margins for the letter itself, and then we will set the tabs we will need. The codes for the margin settings and the tabs will be inserted into our document at the beginning. When we reach the quoted material we will insert other codes for other margins at that point.

The way in which margins are set differs with various versions of WordPerfect. The following are instructions for WordPerfect for Windows.

    A. With your mouse pointer, click on Format on the Menu Bar.

    B. Click on Margins.

    C. At the Margins dialog box, note you can change all four margins (left, right, top, and bottom).

    D. Change the left and right margins to 1.5 inches by clicking on the top arrow of each selection.

    E. When you have made the changes to the side margins, click on OK.

4.   Set tabs for the new document.

Two tab settings are needed for the document: one at 2 inches to be used for paragraph indentation and a second at 4 inches to be used to indent for the date and closing lines. WordPerfect allows several types of tabs; we will use the type called the left tab.

    A. With your mouse pointer, click on Format on the Menu Bar.

    B. Click on Line and then Tab Set.

    C. The Tab Set dialog box will appear.

    D. Set the tabs for Absolute by clicking on the round radio button in the "Position From" box.

    E. Click on the Clear All button.

    F. Type the following tabs at the Position box: 1.5, 2.0, and 4.0. Remember to click on the Set button after every setting you type.

    G. Click on OK to accept this change in tab settings.

5.   Examine the margin and tab codes.

    A. Press Alt+F3 or click on View on the Menu Bar, and then select Reveal Codes.

    B. The plain text will display at the top of your screen; the display of text at the bottom of the screen will show the codes embedded by WordPerfect when you set the margins and tabs.

    C. Cancel the Reveal Codes display by pressing Alt+F3.

6.   Type the date and address shown in Figure 7-4.

Enter the date at the third tab setting (4.0), and press cursor return four times. As you enter the address, press cursor return at the end of each line; press cursor return two times after the last line of the address. Type the salutation and press cursor return twice.

7.   Type the first paragraph.

Use the Tab key to indent the paragraph. After you have keyed the material, press cursor return twice.

8.   Reset the margins for the second paragraph.

The second paragraph consists of material quoted from an article on databases for microcomputers and is indented an additional one-half (.5) inch on either side to indicate that it is a quote. The margins of the first paragraph are at 1.5 inches, so we will set the margins for this paragraph at 2 inches.

Note: Begin by placing the cursor at the position in the document where you want the new margin settings to take effect—after the end of the first paragraph. Placing it within the first paragraph will reset the margins within the paragraph.

A. With your mouse pointer, click on Format on the Menu Bar.

B. Click on Margins.

C. At the Margins dialog box, note you can change all four margins (left, right, top, and bottom).

D. Change the left and right margins to 2.0 inches by clicking on the top arrow of each selection.

E. When you have made the changes to the side margins, click on OK.

9. Type the second paragraph.

If you encounter erratic cursor movement or other unexpected results, use Reveal Codes (Alt+F3) to examine the embedded codes and to delete them if necessary.

After you have keyed the paragraph, press cursor return twice.

10. Reset the margins for the third paragraph.

The third paragraph returns to the margins used in the first paragraph (1.5 and 1.5), so they must be reset.

A. With your mouse pointer, click on Format on the Menu Bar.

B. Click on Margins.

C. At the Margins dialog box, note you can change all four margins (left, right, top, and bottom).

D. Change the left and right margins to 1.5 inches by clicking on the bottom arrow of each selection.

E. When you have made the changes to the side margins, click on OK.

11. Type the third paragraph.

Use the Tab key to indent the paragraph. After you have keyed the paragraph, press cursor return twice.

12. Type the closing.

A. Press the Tab key three times to take the cursor to the third setting (4.0) before you type each line.

B. Press cursor return four times after you type the closing line.

C. Type the name and press cursor return once; then type the person's title.

13. Save the document.

When you have finished keying, follow the procedure below to save the document on disk.

A. With the mouse pointer, click on File on the Menu Bar.

B. Click on Save As...; at this point, you will name the document.

C. Type as follows: A:\ESSAY2

D. You will notice that the filename you gave to this document, ESSAY2, now appears at the top of the screen.

14. Print the document.
    A. With the mouse pointer, click on File on the Menu Bar.
    B. Click on Print.
    C. The Print dialog box appears and Full document is already designated. Click on Print.
    Note: If you have difficulties in printing, ask your instructor or supervisor to check the printer selection for this document. One error commonly encountered here is "Printer not selected." Check with your instructor to see if you need to make a printer selection correction.
15. Check the disk directory to see that the document is saved.
    A. Display the directory.
       (1)   With the mouse pointer, click on File on the Menu Bar.
       (2)   Click on Open to display the files on your disk.
    B. Find the filename, ESSAY2, in the directory. Note that the directory is in alphabetical order.
    C. Cancel the display by clicking on Cancel.
16. Terminate the exercise.
    A. With the mouse pointer, click on File on the Menu Bar.
    B. Click on Exit. We have already saved this document.
    C. Remove the disk.

WORDPERFECT JOB 4:
BOILERPLATING

PURPOSES

1. To create new files by merging existing files
2. To provide experience in indenting for paragraphs
3. To introduce alternate ways to save and open files
4. To print copies of the new files

REQUIRED EQUIPMENT

1. WordPerfect system package
2. Formatted data disk

PREPARATION

When organizations analyze the letters they send to clients and customers, most find that essentially they say the same thing to many people. Those who have word processing packages can save a great deal of keying time by creating a series of stock paragraphs and then simply putting these together to create letters, rather than keying each letter individually. The user calls for the paragraphs or blocks of text that are needed to form the body of the letter and adds individual material, such as names and addresses. This technique is called boilerplating.

In this job, we will first create a series of paragraphs; then we will create letters by merging these paragraphs. We also will move text from one location to another within the body of the letter.

Opening files using "Open" from the File Menu to display a disk directory is an excellent approach when you do not know the name of the file. To save a file, a faster way than to use the File Menu and Save is to position the mouse pointer on Save on the Button Bar.

PROCEDURE

1. Load WordPerfect into the computer.
2. The WordPerfect clear editing window will display.
3. Create the first document.
   A. Set the margins at 1.5 inches as you did in Job 3.
   B. Key the text in Figure 7.5.

> We at Acme Suppliers are happy to welcome you to our list of Preferred Customers. As a Preferred Customer, you will be notified in advance of any special pricing events. You also will have a credit limit 50% above that of regular customers. A customer service representative will be assigned to your account to answer any questions or resolve any problems you may have. He or she will be in touch with you shortly. I think you will soon agree with me that our Preferred Customers are also our most satisfied customers.

Figure 7-5. Document One: NEWCUST

    C. Save the document as NEWCUST (for new customer).
       (1) With the mouse pointer, click on File on the Menu Bar.
       (2) Click on Save As....
       (3) Enter NEWCUST as the filename.
    D. Close the document.
       (1) With the mouse pointer, click on File on the Menu Bar.
       (2) Click on Close to clear your screen.

4.   Create the second document.
    A. Set the margins at 1.5 inches.
    B. Key the text in Figure 7.6.

> We have received your order of "DATE" and regret that all of the merchandise you require is not in stock. The "ITEM" has been back ordered and we expect it at any time.
>
> We are shipping the other items and be assured that the remainder of your order will be sent as soon as the merchandise is received. If this creates a problem for you, please call your customer representative.

Figure 7-6. Document Two: BKORDER

    C. Save the document as BKORDER (for back ordered item).
       (1) With the mouse pointer, click on File on the Menu Bar.
       (2) Click on Save As....
       (3) Enter BKORDER as the filename.
    D. Close the document.
       (1) With the mouse pointer, click on File on the Menu Bar.
       (2) Click on Close to clear your screen.

5.   Create the third document.
    A. Set the margins at 1.5 inches.
    B. Key the text in Figure 7.7.

> Acme Dust received a stock of "ITEMS" from "MANUF", one of the country's leading manufacturers, and will soon be offering these at prices ranging up to 60% off the manufacturer's recommended retail price. As a Preferred Customer, you will soon be receiving a mailout about special pricing on these items, but I wished to take this opportunity to give one of our most valued customers an advance notice. Call your customer representative for more details.

Figure 7-7. Document Three: NEWSTOCK

C. Save the document as NEWSTOCK.
    (1)   With the mouse pointer, click on File on the Menu Bar.
    (2)   Click on Save As....
    (3)   Enter NEWSTOCK as the filename.
D. Close the document.
    (1)   with the mouse pointer, click on File on the Menu Bar.
    (2)   Click on Close to clear your screen.
6.   Create the fourth document.
   A. Set the margins at 1.5 inches.
   B. Key the text in Figure 7.8.

> When one applies for a credit account, one accepts a moral and legal obligation to maintain a reasonable payment schedule, not allowing the person or institution carrying his or her credit to suffer because of his or her neglect. It seems that your account with us is now in arrears.

Figure 7-8. **Document Four: OVERDUE**

C. Save the document as OVERDUE (for overdue payment).
    (1)   With the mouse pointer, click on File on the Menu Bar.
    (2)   Click on Save As....
    (3)   Enter OVERDUE as the filename.
D. Close the document.
    (1)   With the mouse pointer, click on File on the Menu Bar.
    (2)   Click on Close to clear your screen.
7.   Create the fifth document.
   A. Set the margins at 1.5 inches.
   B. Key the text in Figure 7.9.

> It has now been four months since we have received a payment on your account, and regrettably, we cannot wait longer to take action on the matter. It always saddens us to come into conflict with one of our customers but you must demonstrate your good faith by arranging to clear your account, or we must take action to clear it by other means. To avoid damage to your credit rating, you should call our credit department immediately and talk with them about arranging a schedule of payment.

Figure 7-9 **Document Five: NOTICE**

C. Save the document as NOTICE (for notice that the firm will take action).
    (1)   With the mouse pointer, click on File on the Menu Bar.
    (2)   Click on Save As ....
    (3)   Enter NOTICE as the filename.
D. Close the document.
    (1)   With the mouse pointer, click on File on the Menu Bar.
    (2)   Click on Close to clear your screen.

8. Create the sixth document.
   A. Set the margins at 1.5 inches.
   B. Key the text in Figure 7.10.

> I regret to inform you that we must submit your name to an agency for the collection of delinquent accounts. This is the last notice you will receive. Unless you have talked with our credit department within ten days, you will be included among those who do not honor their obligations, and your credit rating will suffer irreparable damage. Act now.

Figure 7-10. Document Six: COLLECT

   C. Save the document as COLLECT (for calling in a collection agency).
      (1) With the mouse pointer, click on File on the Menu Bar.
      (2) Click on Save As....
      (3) Enter COLLECT as the filename.
   D. Close the document.
      (1) With the mouse pointer, click on File on the Menu Bar.
      (2) Click on Close to clear your screen.
9. Create the seventh document.
   A. Set the margins at 1.5 inches.
   B. Key the text in Figure 7.11.

> Your last payment was received more than three months ago. At this point, we require some action on your part to reassure us that you plan to pay for your purchase as understood when we accepted you as a credit customer. I remind you that this is not only a moral obligation, it is a legal one, also. Please communicate with our credit department and make arrangements to clear your balance.

Figure 7-11. Document Seven: REMINDER

   C. Save the document as REMINDER (for gentle reminder).
      (1) With the mouse pointer, click on File on the Menu Bar.
      (2) Click on Save As....
      (3) Enter REMINDER as the filename.
   D. Close the document.
      (1) With the mouse pointer, click on File on the Menu Bar.
      (2) Click on Close to clear your screen.
10. Create the eighth document.
   A. Set the margins at 1.5 inches.
   B. Set a tab at 3 inches for the closing indentation.
   C. Key the text in Figure 7.12.

> Give us a call about any of your personal or professional needs. We are glad to hear from you anytime.
>
>   Warmest personal regards,
>
> *4 lines*
>
>   P. T. Barnum
>   Sales Manager

Figure 7-12 Document Eight: SMEND

     D. Save the document as SMEND (for sales manager ending)
       (l)   With the mouse pointer, click on File on the Menu Bar.
       (2)   Click on Save As....
       (3)   Enter SMEND as the filename.
     E. Close the document.
       (1)   With the mouse pointer, click on File in the Menu Bar.
       (2)   Click on Close to clear your screen.

11.   Create the ninth document.
     A. Set the margins at 1.5 inches.
     B. Set a Tab at 3 inches for the closing indentation.
     C. Key the text in Figure 7.13.

> We regret this situation and hope that you will work with us to resolve it speedily.
>
>   Sincerely,
>
>
>   E.B. Scrooge

Figure 7-13 Document Nine: CMEND

     D. Save the document as CMEND (for credit manager ending).
       (1)   With the mouse pointer, click on File on the Menu Bar.
       (2)   Click on Save As....
       (3)   Enter CMEND as the filename.
     E. Close the document.
       (1)   With the mouse pointer, click on File on the Menu Bar.
       (2)   Click on Close to clear your screen.

12.   Create the letters.
     From the paragraphs you have created and saved on disk, you can now create letters. You will create five different letters in a very short time because the majority of the keying already has been done. As you work, consider the amount of time that could be saved by an organization that used these techniques to create letters to clients or customers.
     A. Create the first letter.
       (1)   Set the margins at 1.5 inches.
       (2)   Key in this address and salutation:

> Mr. J. K. LaMarsh
> 2730 Maple Drive
> Homewood, KS 56011
>
> Dear Mr. LaMarsh:

(3) Build the letter from saved paragraphs:

You will use the paragraphs saved as NEWCUST, NEWSTOCK, and SMEND to build the letter. After bringing these paragraphs in from disk, you will perform some editing.

    a.   Place the cursor at the left margin two lines below the greeting.

    b.   With the mouse pointer, click on Insert on the Menu Bar.

    c.   Click on File...

    d.   When the Insert File dialog box appears, click on the filename NEWCUST, then click on OK.

    e.   The paragraph will appear beginning at the point where the cursor was placed.

    f.   Repeat the series of actions above for the paragraphs NEWSTOCK and SMEND.

(4) Edit the letter.

    a.   In the NEWSTOCK paragraph, replace the "ITEM" entry with storm coats and replace the "MANUF" entry with Storm King.

(5) Print the letter.

(6) Save the letter as LETTER.1 and close the document.

B. Create the second letter.

(1) Set your margins at 1.5 inches.

(2) Key in this address and salutation:

> Ms. E. L. ZaBeth General Manager
> Cherchez La Femme
> Phoenix, AZ 85034
>
> Dear Ms. ZaBeth:

(3) Build the letter from saved paragraphs:

You will use the paragraphs saved as BKORDRR, NEWSTOCK, and SMEND to build the letter. After bringing these paragraphs in from disk, you will perform some editing.

    a.   Place the cursor at the left margin two lines below the greeting.

    b.   With the mouse pointer, click on Insert on the Menu Bar.

    c.   Click on File...

    d.   When the Insert File dialog box appears, click on the filename BKORDER, then click on OK.

    e.   The paragraph will appear beginning at the point where the cursor was placed.

       f.   Repeat the series of actions above for the paragraphs NEWSTOCK and SMEND.

    (4)   Edit the letter.

        a.   In the NEWSTOCK paragraph, replace the "ITEM" entry with storm coats and replace the "MANUF" entry with Storm King.

        b.   In the BKORDER paragraph, replace "DATE" with August 10 and replace "ITEM" with half-inch lace.

    (5)   Print the letter.

    (6)   Save the letter as LETTER.2 and close the document.

C. Create a series of letters to send to:

> Mr. S. L. Pay
> 999 South 99th Street
> Dadeville, NY 10023

    (1)   For the first letter,

        (a)   Use paragraphs OVERDUE, REMINDER, and CMEND.

        (b)   Print the letter.

        (c)   Save the document as LETTER.3 and close the document.

    (2)   For the second letter,

        (a)   Use paragraphs OVERDUE, NOTICE, and CMEND.

        (b)   Print the letter.

        (c)   Save the document as LETTER.4 and close the document.

    (3)   For the third letter,

        (a)   Use paragraphs OVERDUE, COLLECT, and CMEND.

        (b)   Print the letter.

        (c)   Save the document as LETTER.5 and close the document.

13.   Terminate the exercise.

A. With the mouse pointer, click on File on the Menu Bar.

B. Click on Exit. We have already saved this document.

C. Remove the disk.

INDEX

Cursor return, 62

Cut, in Windows, 54

D Data, 4-5

Data addressing, 69-70

Databases, 22, 273-76. *See also* dBase IV

Data capture or collection, 13

Data control, 30-37

Data cycle. *See* Data flow

Data entry area, 4-5

Data entry devices, 2, 6-9

Data entry jobs, 9-11

Data entry job skills, 11-12, 19

Data entry operators, 2, 4-5, 10

Data entry procedures, documentation, 37-45

Data entry scanners, 8-9

Data flow, 13-19

Data items longer than field provided, 88

Data keys, 61

Data organization, 21-23

Data processing department, 2-5

Data set, 21

Data storage, 23

Data validation, 13-14, 25-29, 76

dBase IV, 276-77

    calculations, 252-53

    changing column widths, 266

    commands, 279, 286

    creating databases, 279-82

    creating spreadsheets, 257, 258-59

    dot prompt, 276-77

    editing records, 288-89

INDEX